DATE DUE

EASTWARD!

ADONIRAM JUDSON

EASTWARD!

The Story of Adoniram Judson

By

STACY R. WARBURTON

Fit for the loftiest or the lowliest lot,
Self-poised, imperial, yet of simplest ways;
At home alike in castle or in cot,
True to his aim, let others blame or praise.

OLIVER WENDELL HOLMES.

ROUND TABLE PRESS, INC.

NEW YORK   1937

TO MY WIFE

*Loyal companion
and constant helper
through many years
in East and West*

PREFACE

THE chief significance of Adoniram Judson is his leadership in the initiation of the American foreign mission enterprise. He was not the only leader, but he was easily foremost. The actual beginning of American foreign missions was due to him more than to any other man. Judson's relation to his own denomination has caused his significance for other denominations—for all churches—to be largely overlooked, but he belongs to all. Out of what he began to do, all American foreign mission organizations and their work have developed.

No serious study of Judson's life has appeared since Edward Judson published his *Life of Adoniram Judson* more than fifty years ago. That and Wayland's original *Memoir* are out of print. A number of brief biographies have appeared, but have been incomplete, popular in form, and quite uncritical in treatment. Mrs. Morrow's fascinating *Splendor of God* is valuable, but of course is a biographical novel, not a biography, and deals with only a limited portion of Judson's life. A new biography is greatly needed.

The main sources for Judson's life story are few but important. Wayland's two-volume *Memoir* stands first, both because of the liberal quotation from Judson's letters and journal, the originals of which are now mostly lost, and because of Wayland's interpretation of Judson, whom he knew and understood so well. Next comes the *Memoir* of Ann Judson by Knowles, quoting largely from Ann herself, and her own *Particular Relation of the American Baptist Mission to the Burman Empire.* Kendrick's *Life and Letters of Emily C. Judson* is valuable for the later years, and the correspondence from Judson and others in the *Baptist Missionary Magazine* fill in where other chief sources are lacking. Gouger's *Personal Narrative* is invaluable as to the prison experiences. A multitude of details not found in any of these appear in other items listed in the bibliography.

I regret that I could not visit Burma; but all the Burma missionaries have been most cordial and helpful. Effort has been made to consult directly or indirectly every source of information known to exist. On the advice of Burma missionaries the spelling of names of persons and places has been changed from that given by Judson to the modern form, as supplied by missionaries to the Burmans.

It is impossible to list all who have helped with information or advice. Only a few can be mentioned. First of all I acknowledge my debt to Rev. A. C. Hanna, grandson of Judson, who like his grandfather is a missionary to the Burmans. He has cooperated most cordially in every possible way, reading the entire manuscript, answering many questions, and giving most valuable suggestions. The chapter on the Burman Bible has been read (some parts more than once) by Rev. John McGuire, D.D., of Burma, chairman of the Bible revision committee, and he has given, freely and heartily, help which no one else could give. My long-time friend Rev. Enoch F. Bell, D.D., Editorial Secretary of the American Board, has read the sections dealing with Judson's relations with that board, and has offered helpful criticisms and advice.

Others who have generously aided include Rev. H. I. Marshall, D.D., Rev. C. L. Klein and Miss Ruth W. Ranney, all of Burma; Rev. T. C. Richards, biographer of Samuel J. Mills; fellow members of my own faculty in the Berkeley Baptist Divinity School, President C. M. Hill, LL.D., Professor J. W. Bailey, Ph.D., and Professor Sandford Fleming, Ph.D.; Secretary R. L. Howard, D.D., of the American Baptist Foreign Mission Society, a former President of Judson College in Rangoon; and Rev. William A. Hill, D.D., Secretary of the Department of Missionary Education of the Baptist Board of Education, without whose urgent encouragement and advice I am confident that this work would not have been undertaken. Officers and staff of both the American Baptist Foreign Mission Society and the American Board have given most generous help, as have librarians of the many historical collections consulted.

Revisions have been made several times since the manuscript was read by those mentioned, and mistakes may have crept in. But every sentence has been checked and re-checked many times, and every statement has been carefully weighed, in the effort to be perfectly accurate and fair. However, I am fully conscious that the ideal has not been attained, and further help will be welcomed in the study of this great life, so significant in the story of expanding Christianity.

THE AUTHOR.

Berkeley, California,
May 1, 1937.

CONTENTS

CHAPTER I

PUZZLES AND AMBITIONS

EIGHTEEN HUNDRED AND TWELVE! Europe was engrossed in a life and death struggle with Napoleon. Captains of freedom had arisen in South America. British and Dutch and Danish East India Companies were pressing trade and political claims in Asia. The United States was about to go to war with England. New leaders had appeared in Washington. The young nation was eager to let the world know of its new life and strength. Fulton's epoch-making *Clermont* had made its triumphant voyage up the Hudson. The Lewis and Clark Expedition had turned American attention to the far-stretching western lands. American ships were sailing from Philadelphia to Calcutta, from Providence to Canton, from Salem to Zanzibar. Great names were being enrolled for the story of American literature. Revivals had stirred the churches and largely increased their membership. Religious life was expanding in missions to the Indians and the frontier settlements beyond the mountains. William Carey's bold undertaking in India had awakened dreams in America of greater ventures of faith. The days of 1812 were great days—full of achievement, full of daring, full of imagination, full of high purpose. The time was ripe for a challenging enterprise.

It was in this year 1812 that Adoniram Judson and his seven companions began America's foreign mission adventure.

In the making of Adoniram Judson his New England heritage had noteworthy importance: New England itself, with its tales of seafaring, its eagerness for education, its strong moral character; the New England minister's home in which he was reared, with culture, true religion, warm fellowship, stimulus to high achievement. In the light of this heritage the significance of incidents recounted of his childhood can be understood. One story will suffice here.

Young Adoniram was fond of puzzles. The harder they were the more eager he was to tackle them. One day he found one in a newspaper with an intimation from the editor that it could not be solved. That was just the challenge needed to put Adoniram on his mettle. He scarcely ate or slept while he worked on the puzzle. But at last he had the answer. He wrote it out carefully, and with boyish assurance carried the letter to the post-office. But the postmaster suspected that the minister's son was playing a trick on him, so he took the letter to the parsonage and officiously delivered it to Adoniram's father.

The latter said nothing about it until after supper, then produced it—to the boy's astonishment and confusion.

"Is this yours, Adoniram?" asked his father.

"Yes, sir," confessed Adoniram.

"Read it," commanded his father, rather severely.

Adoniram broke the seal and opened the letter, mumbled through it, then handed it to his father. The latter read it, asked for the newspaper in which the puzzle had appeared, spread out paper and letter on the table, and read and re-read them again and again, while young Adoniram sat watching in apprehension.

But nothing happened. His father sat for a long time gazing into the fire, saying nothing. Finally conversation was resumed. The next morning, however, his father handed Adoniram a book, saying that he had bought a book of riddles for him, rather a common one to be sure, but that after he had solved all the puzzles in that one he would get him another. Adoniram seized it eagerly, but imagine his disappointment— it was just a book of arithmetic! However, he quickly recovered from his chagrin when he discovered that it was the book used by the older boys in school. He was bound not to let any one get ahead of him—he wanted to be the leader—so he set himself to master the puzzles and problems in his new book.

At that time the Judsons were living in Wenham, Massachusetts, about twenty miles northeast of Boston. Adoniram had been born on Saturday, August 9, 1788, in Malden, in the same state, where his father, after whom he was named, was pastor of the Congregational Church. Adoniram, Sr., was born in 1750 in Woodbury, Conecticut, the state in which the Judson family had lived since the first settler by that name came from England in 1634. He was a graduate of Yale, in the class of 1775, afterward studying for the ministry with the noted Dr. Joseph Bellamy, and preaching in various churches in Massachusetts until called to Malden in 1786. On account of his vigorous Hopkinsian views, three councils in succession refused to ordain him. But with a persistence and independence that his son inherited, he met still a fourth, which voted approval.

That same year he married Abigail Brown of Tiverton, Rhode Island. At least three churches had called him as pastor before this time (Scituate, Hardwick and Wrentham, Massachusetts), but in each he had declined because the call was not unanimous. Malden proved no better, however. Animosities appeared which he could not reconcile, and in 1791, when Adoniram, Jr., was three years of age, he resigned. The next year he became pastor in Wenham, at a salary of ninety-five pounds (then about $315) and parish lands. Here Adoniram spent his boyhood, with his sister Abigail, born in Malden shortly before they moved to Wenham, and his brother Elnathan, born in Wenham in 1794. Another sister, Mary, was born there in 1796, but died the same year. Quite naturally, the father of this family found ninety-five pounds an insufficient salary, and he resigned in 1799. Braintree, ten miles south of Boston, became the family home for three years, then in 1802 the father was called to the new Third Church in Plymouth, organized because the old First Church had become too liberal. Plymouth was henceforth home to them all. Here Adoniram could look out across the harbor toward the great bay, catch the whiff of the salt breezes in summer and hear the howl of the northeast storms in winter; here he could climb the hill to the historic Pilgrim burial ground, listen on Sundays to his father's sermons in the church near his home, and study in the town grammar school to prepare himself for college; and here his father and mother and sister made their home as long as they lived. In 1817 Mr. Judson accepted his son's Baptist views and resigned his pastorate, to spend the remaining years,

till his death in 1826, preaching in Baptist pulpits in Plymouth
and elsewhere.

Adoniram had a great love for his sister Abigail, who was
only a year and a half younger than he. They were very
chummy, and throughout his life they kept up this close intimacy. With his father it was impossible to be chummy. He
was grave and quiet, stern in bearing and strict in family discipline. Yet he was a man highly respected, and one of his
associates[1] described him as "meek and pious in demeanor,
catholic and candid." Adoniram owed much to him, his stately
courtesy, his dignity of literary style, perhaps his theology, certainly his burning ambition.

Adoniram's mother was apparently a quiet woman, devout,
and deeply interested in her children. She early recognized
Adoniram's precocity, and when he was only three years old
she surprised her husband on his return from a journey by having the lad read a chapter of the Bible which she had taught
him during his father's absence. At least he was able to repeat
the chapter to his father with the book open before him! Adoniram had a deep love for his mother, and when he announced
his infidel views after college days, it was her entreaties and
tears that he carried in his memory, rather than his father's
severe reprimands.

Adoniram was full of spirit, lively and self-confident, and
was a leader among the boys. But he threw more energy into
study than into play. Before he was ten years old he had ac-
quired a reputation for scholarship, especially in arithmetic.
Perhaps the "book of puzzles" that his father had given him
turned his enthusiasm in this direction. At any rate, his interest and ability in figuring were widely known. A man over
in the neighboring town of Beverly heard about him, and sent
him a stiff problem with the offer of a dollar as a prize if he
could work out the answer. The dollar looked big. More than
that, his reputation for scholarship was at stake. But most of
all there was the pull of the unsolved riddle.

So now he shut himself up in his room and went to work
on the problem. It was a tough one, and when the next day

---

[1] Dr. Thacher of Scituate, Mass., where Mr. Judson had his last pastorate.

came he had not discovered the answer. His small brother Elnathan was sick, and he was called from his figuring to amuse him by building a corn-cob house. He worked on the house so closely and carefully that you might have supposed it was absorbing all his thoughts. But all the while he was thinking of the problem and trying to work it out. Suddenly he let out a whoop—"I've got it!" And sending the corn-cobs flying he dashed off to his room to write down the answer. The dollar was his, and his reputation was safe.

At ten he was studying navigation, and soon Greek and Latin. "Old Virgil Dug Up" was the name the boys gave him. He liked to study and he liked to read—anything he could get his hands on. And his father provided him with as many books as he could read.

At sixteen Adoniram entered Brown University, as did Elnathan six years later. One wonders why their father, a Congregational minister, sent them to Brown, a Baptist college. In part, perhaps, it was because Yale, his own alma mater, seemed too far away, while Brown was conveniently located. Harvard, the college nearest at hand, had espoused Unitarian views. Brown was popular with Congregationalists, even though a Baptist institution. Up to the time when Adoniram Judson entered, one hundred and three Brown graduates had become ministers, and of these at least sixty-six were Congregationalists. Only twenty-two were Baptists. Moreover, Brown's catholic spirit attracted many Congregationalists. While the control rested with Baptists, the charter provided that Congregationalists, Episcopalians and Friends should have places among the Trustees; and a third of the Fellows could be of any denomination. Before Judson's time, the first vice-president and several of the faculty had been Congregationalists, as was one of the two professors when Judson entered. All of this doubtless made Brown attractive to Congregationalists. And indeed, the latter had had a considerable share in the founding of the college, almost as much as Baptists.

Judson arrived in Providence on Friday, August 17, 1804, and climbed College Hill to the campus. College Street had earlier been known as Presbyterian Lane. It was still only a lane, unfinished, with possibly one house on it above Benefit

Street. The campus was just a rough field, only eight acres, with here and there a few shade trees. Across the front was a wooden fence, and around the other sides ran a stone wall, which President Manning had probably helped to build with his own hands. The campus was but three hundred feet wide, and extended only a little distance north and south of the present University Hall. There were two buildings, the "college edifice," now University Hall, and the president's house, a plain two-story-and-a-half building a short distance to the northwest, toward the corner where the Carrie Tower now stands. The "college edifice," modeled after Nassau Hall at Princeton, was one hundred and fifty feet long and four stories high, and had excited the ridicule of critics because of its size. It was certainly ample for all needs when Judson came. Within its walls were the recitation rooms, students' rooms, administration offices, the chapel (now room five), the library (either the room on the second floor over room six—the floor had not then been removed and the gallery installed—or the northeast corner room), and the commons or dining room under the library. The college still bore the name Rhode Island College, but the next month after Judson arrived the corporation changed the name to Brown University, in recognition of the first of the many munificient gifts of Nicholas Brown.

In comparison with the marvelously rich curricula of present-day colleges and universities, the Brown curriculum of Judson's time seems terribly meager. But it was as good as any American college offered: Latin, Greek, mathematics, rhetoric, oratory, geography, logic, moral philosophy, astronomy, with special attention the senior year to Locke's *Essay on the Human Understanding* and Bolingbroke's writings on history. Latin and Greek were strongly emphasized. Until a few years before Judson entered, nothing but Latin could be spoken during the hours of study. It was still freely used as a spoken language on the campus, and at Commencement there were Latin and Greek orations. Physical science received scant attention. In 1784 the apparatus had consisted of a telescope, an air-pump, globes and a thermometer! Later a few other instruments were added. Two class sessions were held each day, devoted mostly to recitation on assigned work in textbooks. All studies were prescribed; there were no electives.

But if curriculum and teaching were limited, there was ample opportunity for supplementing these by wide reading, and the best students took advantage of this privilege. Quite likely Judson did so. But the library needed only one small room, and was open only once a week. Probably it contained not more than 3,500 volumes. Study hours were rigidly prescribed: one hour before breakfast, nine to twelve, two to sunset, and seven to nine—"and none shall be out of his chamber after nine o'clock in the evening." All the students ate in commons, and the usual complaints were made about the meals. Tuition was only sixteen dollars a year, room rent four dollars, library fee four dollars. Meals varied in cost, but were less than two dollars a week. Discipline was often needed, and fines from three cents to a dollar and a half were imposed! There was some drinking, though this was not general. But students were frequently suspended, rusticated or expelled. On the other hand, a Praying Society held meetings twice a week, and carried on correspondence with similar societies in other colleges.

In Judson's time the Brown faculty consisted of the president, Asa Messer, who had been on the faculty since his graduation in 1790 and had become president the year Judson entered; David Howell, professor of jurisprudence; Calvin Park, professor of learned languages; two tutors (one was also librarian); and the steward and "register." President Messer was forward-looking, liberal in theology, and very independent, and Brown expanded considerably under his leadership. He took a great personal interest in the students, and was early impressed by the ability and promise of Judson. Towards the end of the latter's first year he wrote to Mr. Judson commending his son's "uniform propriety of conduct," his "intense application to study," and the "charming prospect . . . exhibited in this very amiable and promising son," and expressed his hope that "the Father of mercies may make him now, while a youth, a son in his spiritual family."

Young Judson has profited so well by his training in the schools of Wenham and Plymouth, with his home study and

ravenous reading, that he was able to enter Brown in the sophomore class. He came to college with eagerness for all the life
he should find there, social as well as intellectual, and he was
ambitious to take his full part in it all. Looking back, in later
years, on his college days, he described himself as "remarkable
for active restlessness of mind and extreme gayety of disposi-
tion, a high relish for social life and fashionable amusements,
all combined with an ardor of purpose and energy of pursuit
that never tired." [2] The keen intellectual interest of his preparatory school days was carried over into his college course.
He stuck closely to his books, and one of his classmates said he
could not remember Judson's "ever failing, or even hesitating,
in recitation." He thoroughly enjoyed a good time, but he
was too much interested in study to join in the revelry of some
of his fellow students, even if he had cared for that type of
enjoyment, of which there is no indication.

On the other hand he had no interest in the Praying Society
and its activities. In fact he was not a little drawn to the
French infidelity common then at Brown as at other colleges.
Perhaps this sympathy was due to his independent spirit and
intellectual eagerness. Possibly President Messer's liberal theological attitude unconsciously affected him. But he was influenced chiefly by an intimate friend in the class above him, a
very talented, witty and attractive fellow, who is referred to as
"E——," but is easily identified from the Brown General Cata-
logue. He was the one most responsible for Judson's adopting
infidel views.

Judson's roommate for two years was Willard Preston, of
the class above him, later a distinguished Presbyterian minister
in Savannah, Georgia. In his senior year he roomed alone.
Preston was a fine student, an excellent musician, and a man of
high character. But he did not profess conversion until after
his graduation from Brown, and apparently had no marked
influence upon Judson. The latter's religious attitude and independence of thought appear significantly in the subject of his
Commencement oration: "An oration on free inquiry."

---

[2] Quoted by E. H. Fletcher, *Burmah's Great Missionary*, p. 14, from *Sketch of
Judson* by A. D. Gillette.

Several things besides those mentioned give evidence of the keenness as well as the direction of Judson's intellectual interest. He was a member of the Philermenian Society, which met every two weeks, with debates, speeches, essays and poems, and had a public meeting at Commencement, with an oration and a poem by the best speakers who could be secured. To belong to the Philermenian Society was a considerable honor, as its membership was limited to forty-five. A library was early established, which grew to 3,000 volumes by the time Judson came back to address his old society in 1845. In view of significant features of his later life it is illuminating that the first question debated by him, in the negative, was "Can a person be justified in arguing to support a proposition in which he does not believe?" and that the first question for debate proposed by himself was "Is the study of the dead languages advantageous?" Judson taking the affirmative. President Robinson later said that "in direct education for the work of life" nothing in his college days at Brown equaled the society to which he belonged. Doubtless the Philermenian Society meant something of that to Judson.

But the best evidence we have of Judson's scholarly habits and standing is the fact that at his Commencement in 1807, besides his English oration, he received the appointment of valedictorian, standing first in his class. He had keen competition, especially from his friend John Bailey, later member of Congress from Masschusetts.[3] His class produced two other Congressmen, besides several lawyers and teachers. But he outranked them all. His laconic message to his father, announcing his success in gaining the coveted honor, conceals with difficulty his eager excitement:

> "Dear Father,
>   "I have got it.
>   "Your affectionate son,
>   A. J."

---

[3] Judson and Bailey kept up their intimate friendship, though the current of their lives ran so far apart, and twenty-five years later they were corresponding with each other, Judson asking about their classmates and Bailey telling of them all; reminding Judson also how closely they were related, through Elnathan Judson's wife, "yours and my sister-in-law."

The story goes that his heart beat so loud as he carried the letter to the post-office that he went by a roundabout route, so that he might be somewhat calm when he met his fellow students, especially his friend Bailey.

Judson's gay social spirit, and his close contacts in the Philermenian Society, make it pretty sure that he had many warm friends. A number of outstanding men were in college with him, and probably he was intimate with many of them. One was Theron Metcalf, later justice of the Massachusetts supreme court, a senior when Judson was a sophomore. Another was David Benedict, well-known Baptist historian and a Trustee of Brown for fifty-six years, a member of the class of 1806. Oliver Angell, teacher and author of textbooks, was in his own class of 1807. John B. Francis, governor of Rhode Island and United States senator, was in the class of 1808. Jonathan Going, two classes below him, became the first secretary of the American Baptist Home Mission Society and president of Granville College, now Denison University. David Reed, for forty years editor of the *Christian Register* and leader in the anti-slavery movement, was a freshman when Judson was a senior. And William M. Marcy, New York supreme court justice and governor, United States senator, secretary of war and secretary of state, was a member of the class below him. Most of these were members of Philermenian.

Two years after his graduation Judson's eminent scholarship won him an appointment as tutor, at that time a very important honor. Perhaps if the appointment had come earlier he might have accepted it and become distinguished as a teacher and author. But by 1809 he had heard the call to a wider ministry and was in the midst of his studies at Andover. His scholastic record in college received further recognition a quarter of a century later, when on the institution of a chapter of Phi Beta Kappa in 1830 he was one of the alumni members elected.

During Judson's senior year he was absent six weeks, teaching school in Plymouth. Or perhaps it was the long midwinter vacation that he spent in that work. Evidently he made a success of it, for two weeks after he received his degree of Bachelor of Arts he opened a private school of his own in Plymouth.

But the venture lasted only a year. How many pupils he had we do not know. He certainly kept busy, for during the year, in addition to his teaching, he prepared and published two books, *Elements of English Grammar,* put out in February of 1808, and *The Young Lady's Arithmetic,* which came out in July. The preparation of these two textbooks in less than one year is proof of prodigious application and noteworthy ability.

The ninth of August, 1808, was Adoniram Judson's twentieth birthday. On that day he closed his school, and started on a tour to the west and south. He may have had some thought of settling in the south, where several of his Philermenian brothers had their homes. And perhaps he planned to travel with his college roommate, Willard Preston, just then beginning a southern tour.

Judson's father gave him a horse for his journey and he set out on his adventure. Across Massachusetts he rode toward the west, until he reached Sheffield, where his uncle Ephraim was pastor. Then, leaving his horse, he went on by some other conveyance to Albany. He was eager to see Fulton's great invention, the steamboat *Clermont,* which not long before had revolutionized travel by its record-breaking trip from New York to Albany. Luckily the *Clermont* was in Albany when he arrived, and he took passage on it to New York. Here was an adventure indeed. Most travel along the Hudson had been by land, and comparatively few had looked upon the wonderful highlands from the river itself. The scenery made a tremendous impression on his sensitive and ardent spirit, and more than forty years later he was able to describe it vividly to his wife Emily.

The attractions of the metropolis thrilled him. In some way he became acquainted with members of a theatrical troupe and joined them—with what purpose we do not know. He had become interested in drama while in college, perhaps through the humorous dialogs and dramas which were a regular feature of the frequent student exhibitions, and he and E—— had often talked of writing plays. Probably his love of adventure—the puzzle instinct—stimulated by his travels and the wonders of New York, helped to interest him in the players and their plans. The company went on the road, and traveled from place to place for two or three weeks, giving their performances. It was a rather wild and reckless adventure. Judson's name was frequently misunderstood as "Johnson," so he allowed the mistake to stand and went under that name. According to the story which Henry Gouger, his friend and fellow prisoner in Ava, reported that Judson told him, the actors lived a sort of vagabond life, slept where they could, and not infrequently skipped without paying their bill. But Gouger said that later, before Judson sailed for Burma, he went back over the route they had traveled, and scrupulously reimbursed all the inn-keepers for their losses.[4]

He soon had enough of the actor's life, and returned to his uncle's home in Sheffield to get his horse and resume his journey to the west. His uncle was not at home, and his place was occupied by a visiting minister, who talked of spiritual things with young Judson in a kindly though serious way. Judson was deeply impressed; but he did not allow this to disturb his anticipations of the pleasure trip ahead of him.

Leaving his uncle's home by the banks of the Housatonic he headed westward again. Thrilled as he had been by the majestic glories of the Hudson, doubtless he was now quite as much stirred by the picturesque beauty of the Berkshire Hills. As he rode across the level valley the wooded slopes of Mt. Everett rose at his left, bright with the rays of the morning sun. Gradually he made his way along the winding road up into the hills, where the magic fingers of frost had already begun to decorate the foliage with its wondrous autumn colors. Brooks made their boisterous way down slopes, and mosses and ferns and late flowers added beauty to the wildness. Here and there an opening in the hills revealed far-stretching valleys, with an occasional farmhouse and cultivated fields. The woods and the orchards sent forth their fragrance, and the tang of the mountain air gave zest to the journey. Happy and contented, Judson rode all day through the hills, until at evening he came to a country inn and stopped for the night.

After a good supper the landlord lighted him to his room, which he explained apologetically had to be next to one occu-

---

[4] Henry Gouger, *Personal Narrative of Two Years' Imprisonment in Burmah,* p. 179.

pied by a young man who was very sick—indeed he might be dying. Judson expressed his sympathy, but said that he would not be disturbed.

But he *was* disturbed—very much disturbed. The partition between the two rooms was a thin one, and again and again he heard the sick man groaning and the attendants moving about. Judson was very restless, and his mind grew more and more agitated—not by what he heard but by what he thought. The landlord had told him that perhaps the sick man might die. Was he prepared to die? Judson listened and thought in the darkness of the night. What the minister at his uncle's home had said to him came back to his mind. But he was ashamed at his question. Prepared to die? A future life? Sin? God? Why, he had given up all those ideas! What would his old friend E—— think of him and his weak notions?

But the question would not down. Again and again it rose before him. The young man might die—would he enter into a bright immortality, or was he going out into the dark? What if he was an infidel like himself? And he could not help thinking how it would be with him, Adoniram Judson, if he were lying where that young man was now lying.

So the weary night wore on—a wretched night. At last the morning came, and he hunted up the landlord.

"How is the sick young man?"

"Dead."

"Dead!"

"Yes, poor fellow, he is gone."

"Who was he? Do you know his name?"

"Yes, he was a fine young fellow from Brown University, named E——."

E——! His own friend! Dead! And an infidel! He was stunned. Lost! Lost! The words rang in his ears till it seemed as though they must be echoing through the hills around—Lost! Lost!

After a time he recovered sufficiently to settle his account and start once more on his westward journey. But all the delightful anticipations of his trip were gone. He could think of only one thing: God and his own eternal future. He had a more important matter in hand than his trip. He had a problem to solve. And abruptly he turned his horse's head toward home. On September twenty-second he was back in Plymouth.

And now what should he do? How could he solve his problem? Was the Bible true? Was salvation necessary? Could he himself be saved? Was Christ the Way? His mind was crowded with questions. Most of his infidel philosophy had faded away with the death of E——, and he set himself to discover the truth.

Just at this critical juncture Professor Stuart and Dr. Griffin, representing the new theological seminary at Andover, came to Plymouth. Earnestly they tried to help Adoniram with his problem. Finally the suggestion was made that he come to Andover. There he might find help. He was undecided for a while. At first he thought of resuming teaching, and took a position as assistant in a school in Boston. But he had scarcely arrived in that city when there came into his hands the old book by Thomas Boston, *The Fourfold State*. This decided him; and on October twelfth he entered Andover. A new epoch in his life had begun.

What sort of a man was Adoniram Judson at this turning-point in his career? What did he look like? What were his habits? What were his mental and spiritual qualities?

He was of medium height and build, perhaps a little slender, but with an erect and commanding figure, especially when speaking to an audience. His complexion was fair, and he had a wealth of curly chestnut hair, brushed back in a way that revealed his high forehead but left a curly lock over each temple, and long side-burns that came well below his ears. He had prominent features, with a rather long and sharply pointed nose. But a miniature of about this time shows an attractive, pleasant face, with a faint smile, that often must have broadened out into hearty laughter. His eyes were somewhat dreamy, but they and his mouth had a suggestion of self-satisfaction, independence of spirit, decision of character and quiet authority. Immaculately neat, dressed in the long black coat and trousers worn by the young men of his day, with well set stock, he was one who would command attention—as indeed he did.

When Judson entered Andover the two qualities that were most outstanding were his passion for excellence and his enthusiasm for life. Full of gayety and vivacity, tremendously enthusiastic, noted for his quick wit, easily at home where social grace was needed, a fascinating conversationalist, he was ready at all times to get the best out of life. But that best never meant indulgence in anything vicious; he had too much self-respect for that. His kindliness and generosity drew him to others and won their affection, and he had a stately courtesy that gained respect. So it is not strange that he easily won friends.

His passion for excellence revealed itself in a powerful am-bition, one of the principal factors in his success. His father had encouraged this ambitious spirit. When he gave him the arithmetic puzzle-book he patted his head and said,

"You are a very acute boy, Adoniram, and I expect you to become a great man."

And Adoniram intended to be great. As a boy he had extravagant dreams of success as an orator, or a poet, or a statesman. But he was a natural leader, and his ambition to be first was easily attained. In Brown he took the lead in studies and intellectual life. In Andover he assumed and was readily accorded the place of leadership in the missionary plans. He could have echoed General William Booth: "Have you no ambition? Because I have; I intend to do something great; I don't mean to belong to the commonalty." [5]

He wanted to be number one, to be sure. But his desire to excel went deeper than that. He wanted to know. He had a genuine thirst for knowledge—languages, literature, mathe-matics, effective speech—and a keen memory as well. But it was his indomitable purpose that kept him studying so hard. He had no patience with laziness. He believed that success came to the one who worked for it. So he worked, persistently, term time and vacation time. Like most leaders, he had un-shaken confidence in his own judgment and did not look to others for advice. He was always ready for argument and abundantly confident in his argumentative and intellectual powers. He was certainly not an imaginative dreamer; he was a man of action, impetuous and eager.

---

[5] Gamaliel Bradford, *Dwight L. Moody*, p. 124.

On the platform Judson was an attractive and convincing speaker. He used no notes, but spoke in a glowing, impassioned manner, with dignity of style but little of studied ornament, yet with strong feeling that gripped his hearers. By the time he was completing his Andover course he had been selected by Dr. Griffin, then pastor of Park Street Church— "the largest church in Boston"—as the man to be his associate.

When Judson entered Andover he was a marked man, known for his intellectual ability and his scholarship, welcomed in social circles for his keen wit and his conversational powers, bearing a reputation as a speaker of unusual force and persuasion, and eager for the place of leadership that he knew he could fill.

CHAPTER II

THE STAR IN THE EAST

It was on Wednesday, October 12, 1808, that Judson arrived in Andover, only a month after the seminary was opened. Andover was already an educational center, for here Phillips Academy, famous as the first incorporated academy in the state, had been teaching boys for thirty years. And here on Andover Hill, across the road from the academy, the new theological seminary, the first in New England, had been founded in 1807, and was now ready for students, with a faculty consisting of Leonard Woods, professor of theology, and Eliphalet Pearson, professor of sacred literature. The latter served but one year, and was succeeded in 1810 by Moses Stuart. Edward D. Griffin came in 1809 as professor of sacred rhetoric, remaining two years. Professors Woods, Stuart and Griffin, especially Stuart, were to be important influences in Judson's life.

Judson was admitted at once into classes of the second year, sufficient evidence of his scholarship; though perhaps in this first year of the seminary the requirements and the grading were not so exact as would be true later. Not being a candidate for the ministry, nor even a confessed Christian, he was enrolled simply as a special student.

He gave himself faithfully to his studies, but his overwhelming interest was in the problem that had brought him to Andover. Light did not dawn immediately. He was not sure of the historical basis of the Christian faith, nor of the truth of the New Testament teachings. But gradually his doubts were satisfied and his questions answered, and towards the end of November he was able to accept Christ and to "entertain a hope." On December second he solemnly dedicated himself to God. And on the twenty-eighth of the following May, when he returned home at the close of the seminary year, he united with his father's church in Plymouth.

What led him to become a Christian? First of all, the fine
Christian influence of his home. The Judson family through
several generations provided men for the Christian ministry;
Adoniram's father was not the least in this succession. And
Adoniram had in his father and mother two noble Christians
whose sincerity and genuineness he deeply respected. Through
them and their fathers, through the home life in Wenham and
Braintree and Plymouth, and through the books in his father's
library which he eagerly devoured, came one line of influence
that helped to bring him into the Christian life.

A second influence, of course, was that which came from
the death of his friend E—— and the sudden and dramatic
ending of their comradeship. It is of the keenest interest that
E——, who in his life had led Judson away from Christian
ideals, should by his death turn him toward the very ideals
and life that he had derided.

A third influence came through Andover. In the quiet of
the hilltop, in the calm stillness of the adjoining woods, in the
sympathetic classroom discussion of Scripture and the deep
things of Christian faith, and in the friendship and example
of wise teachers and fellow students, Judson heard the answers
to his questions and was led into the light that was never to
grow dim.

The final factor was God. For God had made choice of
Judson for a mighty work. He was His chosen vessel and He
was preparing him for His own use.

Judson's impetuous spirit was not evident in his conversion.
He did not go through any of the excruciating spiritual struggles so common in his time. Nor on the other hand did he
have the ecstatic experiences that might have been expected of
one with so enthusiastic and ardent a temperament. There was
nothing striking about his conversion. But of its reality he
was absolutely certain. "He felt as sure that he was an entirely
new creature . . . as he was of his own existence." Never once
afterward did he ever raise a question as to his acceptance by
God. President Francis Wayland, who knew him well, and
who had exceptional opportunities for frank and intimate conversation with him on the inner experiences of his life, says

almost categorically, "From the moment that he fully believed, I think he never doubted."

While this great revolution was taking place within him, influences were being set in motion on the other side of the world that were to transform his life still further.

The British East India Company, which ruled India, had never been favorable to missionary work, though they had permitted it in moderation so long as they could keep the control in their own hands. But about the turn of the eighteenth century the first of a series of notable and powerful chaplains joined the company, whose deep missionary interests made them outstanding factors in the establishment of the missionary enterprise in India. One of these was Claudius Buchanan.

Buchanan had returned to England in 1808, and in Bristol he preached a sermon on the text: "We have seen his star in the east and have come to worship him" (Matt. 2:2). The title of the sermon was "The Star in the East," and the preacher told how the Christian gospel had made its way to India, and recounted graphically the achievements of Schwartz in his nearly fifty years of missionary service. The sermon was published, and copies came to America and to Andover.

One day—it was in September, 1809—Judson read this sermon. That day changed his life. Exactly a year before, the dramatic experience had occurred in the little country inn which led him out of infidelity into Christianity and the Christian ministry. Now there took place another of those dramatic events that crowd his life, the reading of the little pamphlet that was to transform his plans once more, and through him was to change the course of Christian history. He began to consider the question of becoming a foreign missionary.

The idea was a new one. It took powerful hold on his imagination. A mission to India! And to other lands! How stupid not to have thought of foreign missions. But now the idea seized upon his impetuous nature, and he could think of nothing else. He could not study. His imagination ran riot as he thought of those far-away lands and pictured a missionary's life. The romance of it gripped him, and he went from room to room talking about foreign missions with any of the boys who would listen—few of them would. It was all very extravagant, but quite in keeping with his vigorous, enthusiastic temperament. His excitement soon quieted down. But Buchanan's sermon had left a permanent impression and a very deep one. "The star in the east" was shining in his firmament, and he had to decide whether he would follow it.

He devoured everything on which he could lay his hands that had to do with the subject. He read Symes' *Embassy to Ava,* and this turned his attention to Burma. Thenceforth that country was uppermost in his thought. He talked with other students about the project. Gardiner Spring, whose father was to give the charge to Judson and his companions at their ordination, says he often talked with him. But none of his fellow students seemed interested. He consulted neighboring ministers, but they gave him no encouragement. Five Brown graduates were at Andover with him—Seth Chapin, Benjamin Rice and Ezekiel Rich of the class of 1808 at Brown and now his classmates at Andover; and Joshua Dean and Jacob Ide of the class of 1809, who had just entered the seminary. But Judson's interest at Brown had been far away from Christian things, and now he had apparently no influence over these men. What if he had been a Christian at Brown? What if he had seen the missionary vision there, as Mills and Rice and the others did at Williams? But it was too late for that. The Brown men who were at Andover had lived in another world from his. And now, "condemned by all and not infrequently ridiculed and reproached," [1] he faced his problem alone.

It was five months before he came to a decision. Finally one cold, crisp day in February he was walking alone in the woods back of the seminary building,[2] deep in meditation and prayer, uncertain whether to go ahead on the path that seemed

---

[1] His own words, in his *Letter Relative to the Formal and Solemn Reprimand.*

[2] Part of the grove still remains. On a hillock at one end, across the pond from the old seminary building, is a massive stone with a commemorative tablet reading: "In the 'Missionary Woods,' once extending to this spot, the first missionary students of Andover Seminary walked and talked one hundred years ago, and on this secluded knoll met to pray. In memory of these men, Adoniram Judson, Samuel Nott, Samuel J. Mills, Samuel Newell, Gordon Hall, James Richards, Luther Rice, whose consecrated purpose to carry the gospel to the heathen world led to the formation of the first American society for foreign missions, in recognition of the two hundred and forty-eight missionaries trained in Andover Seminary, and in gratitude to Almighty God, this stone is set up in the centennial year of the American Board 1910."

to be opening before him or to give it all up. Suddenly the Great Commission—"Go ye into all the world and preach the gospel to every creature"—came into his mind. He had thought of it often, but now it came with such clearness and power that then and there he decided to become a foreign missionary. Immense difficulties stood in the way—he could see that plainly —but he must obey Christ's command at all costs. Whatever others might do, he had settled the question for himself. From that moment he never hesitated in his plans or in his faith. He knew that this was God's plan for him.

What were the factors that led to his momentous decision? Buchanan's sermon, "The Star in the East," was of course the thing that opened his eyes to the question and led him to think about it. But several elements entered into his decision. First, the international interest that prevailed in New England. Contrary to a common opinion, New England, while sectional in relation to other parts of the country, was much broader in its interests than other sections, due to its large shipping business and foreign trade. In Massachusetts, Salem was the headquarters for foreign shipping. Judson had been brought up in that part of the state, near the coast, where he must have heard frequent talk of India and China and the Indies. Probably he had visited Salem and seen the ships. Unconsciously he would grow up into a large world of thought and interest. Providence was the other chief New England center for foreign trade, and Judson lived there during the three most important years of his youth. Nicholas Brown, whose name Rhode Island College had taken just as Judson entered, was the head of the great shipping firm of Brown and Ives, whose vessels from Calcutta and Bombay and Canton and Batavia were often to be seen at the wharves along the river toward India Point. He was perhaps the most prominent citizen of Providence, and his name and face and far-sailing ships must have been familiar to Judson, and a constant reminder of the great eastern world. Without doubt this wide international interest was a factor in the development of Judson's thought of a Christian foreign mission.

A second influence in his decision was what he read—not much about missionary work but much about mission lands.

Just what he read besides Symes' story of his *Embassy to Ava*
we are not told. Doubtless the *Massachusetts Missionary Magazine* was to be had at Andover, and he would read its news of
Carey and his Bible translating and other work. A few other
periodicals with like information were available, and there
were secular magazines with stories of life in other lands. Such
reading fed the flame.

A third factor was the Bible. On his visit home in 1845 he
urged the members of the Society for Missionary Inquiry at
Brown to discover the path that heaven had marked out for
each of them. "To find that path," he said, "try all your
schemes by the unerring word of God." Doubtless he had
done that for himself.

A fourth factor was himself. He told the society at Brown
not only to search the Scriptures for light, but to look for the
developments of God's providence in their own characters, and
in the circumstances in which they were placed. Probably
Judson considered his own qualifications and abilities, and,
with the self-assurance which characterized him, believed he
could make a success of the difficult task.

And finally there was prayer. It was while he was praying,
as he walked in the woods, that the light broke and the meaning of all that he had read and thought became clear. The
chief factor in his missionary decision, as was said of his conversion, was God. God spoke to him, and it was while he was
speaking to God that he heard God's voice.

It should be noted that among these factors no mention is
made of the influence of other men who had already decided
to give their lives to missionary service. The fact is, Judson for
some time knew of none who had made that decision. James
Richards of the haystack group at Williams College came to
Andover about the time that Judson read *The Star in the East,*
but he remained silent on the subject until Samuel J. Mills
came. The latter entered in January or early February of
1810.[3] Both he and Judson were so eager to talk about for-

---

[3] In a letter of Dec. 20, 1809, Mills said he thought he would go there soon, or
within four or five weeks (Wayland, I, p. 43). In an undated letter (Spring, p. 32)
Mills refers to a letter of Jan. 24 expressing sympathy with him in the death of his
mother, and speaks of having left Andover in the vain hope of seeing her alive.

eign missions with everyone who might be interested that
if he arrived before Judson's decision it is likely that they discussed the subject together, especially as he had heard that
Judson was seriously considering the question. But if Mills
talked with Judson it was scarcely more than a casual conversation, for Judson did not mention any aid from Mills in telling
how he came to his decision.[4] Samuel Nott was there from
Union College, but though he had long been considering a
missionary life he did not decide for it until after Judson's
decision. Samuel Newell of Harvard was a classmate of Judson, but his decision followed that of Nott. Probably Judson
talked with these, perhaps also with Mills. But in making his
final decision he faced the question alone. His own account
makes that certain. His decision was entirely independent,
with no conscious influence from anyone else.

Three phases can be noted in the development of the
American foreign mission enterprise. First, the wide extent of
missionary interest. From earliest days evangelists had gone
to neglected settlements. Not a few had been missionaries to
the Indians. The Presbyterian General Assembly had a missionary committee from its organization in 1789. The Warren
Baptist Association sent out missionaries in 1778, and the
Shaftesbury Baptist Association had missionaries as far away
as Upper Canada. Methodists, Baptists, Episcopalians and
others were vigorously at work in the new western settlements.

Missionary societies had arisen in large numbers. The New
York Missionary Society had begun its work for the Indians in

---

Spring says she died Dec. 30, 1809, which might suggest that he was at Andover
before that date; but Mills' biographer, Rev. T. C. Richards, informs me that the
date on her tombstone in Torringford is 1810, so this letter does not help. Gordon
Hall writes Feb. 19, 1810, that he had visited Mills, but "Samuel J. had left for
Andover" (H. Bardwell, *Memoir of Gordon Hall*, p. 19). Nott mentions a memo-
randum of a conversation he had with Mills and Judson Mar. 11, 1810 (Wayland, I,
p. 60). From these items, all I have been able to discover, it seems evident that
Mills came to Andover shortly before Feb. 19, 1810. Judson made his decision
that month, whether before or after Mills came we do not know.

[4] This appears from Judson's own statement in Wayland, I, p. 52. Mr. Richards
writes in a letter to the author: "My theory is that Judson was already converted to
the foreign missionary idea when Mills talked with him. Buchanan's sermon was the
great factor in Judson's decision. While Judson was very independent, it is my feeling that after his conversations with Mills Judson publicly and finally committed
himself to foreign missions."

1796, uniting Presbyterians, Reformed and Baptists in an inter-denominational fellowship. In 1798 the Connecticut Mission-ary Society (Congregational) set out "to Christianize the heathen in North America, and to support and promote Chris-tian knowledge in the new settlements within the United States." In 1799 the Massachusetts Missionary Society was formed, and soon other Congregational societies elsewhere in New England. Baptists had formed the Massachusetts Baptist Missionary Society in 1802, to provide preaching "in the new settlements within these Northern States, or further if circum-stances render it proper." Other Baptist societies had rapidly followed.

The women, too, had organized for the great enterprise. In the last year of the old century Congregational and Baptist women had formed the Boston Female Society for Missionary Purposes. A "Cent Institution" arose the next year. The Bap-tist Mite Society was organized in Providence in 1806. Before 1814 there were fifty mite and cent societies among Congrega-tionalists and Baptists.

The work of William Carey and his associates in India had aroused keen interest in America. William Staughton of Phila-delphia had been one of the little epoch-making group who had formed the English Baptist Missionary Society, and was a zealous promoter of Carey's work. Captain Benjamin Wickes, who had carried Marshman and Ward to India in his ship in 1799, arrived in Philadelphia in 1805, and at his suggestion Bap-tist, Presbyterian, Episcopalian and Methodist pastors united in a call for funds for Carey's Bible translation work. More than $18,000 were sent to India before 1814.

Robert Morrison's visit, on his way out to China, must not be overlooked. Many ministers and other prominent men, like Madison, then Secretary of State, met him and caught his en-thusiasm. It is clear that American Christians were not only sending missionaries to far distant places and peoples on their own continent, but were becoming informed on the interna-tional missionary enterprise and were already sharing actively in that enterprise by their gifts.

The second phase in the development of the enterprise was the stirring of the hearts of young men here and there regard-

ing their personal duty in the matter. It was inevitable that the
widespread missionary interest should ultimately lead some to
consider this question. It was natural, too, that this challenge
should come first to Congregationalists. They had been foremost in organizing missionary societies, their churches were
principally in New England, where international interest was
most in evidence, and they were stressing education above most
others. Nor was it strange that the fire began to burn independently in several different places—Williams, Harvard and
Union.

At Williams there were the men of the haystack. As the
tale is told by Gardiner Spring, a classmate of Samuel J. Mills,
the latter had entered Williams with a purpose already formed
to devote his life to missionary service, and was eager to awaken
a similar interest in others. One day he took a few fellow
students into a meadow not far away, where by the side of a
haystack they sat down and talked together of missions. Another tradition is that they were meeting in a grove, when a
thunder storm came up and they took shelter under the haystack. Mills discovered that he was not alone in his missionary
interest; others had a similar purpose, especially Gordon Hall
and Luther Rice. The result was that in September, 1808, five
students, Mills, James Richards, Luther Rice, Ezra Fisk and
John Seward, formed a society, The Brethren, to "effect in the
person of its members a mission or missions to the heathen."

At the same time Samuel Newell at Harvard was pondering
his duty in the matter. At Union Samuel Nott, Jr., had for
some months been considering the question. And at Andover
Judson was deep in study and prayer as he tried to reach a decision. The men in these four institutions had no relations with
one another; all were considering their duty independently and
simultaneously, as God spoke to each one.

The third phase in the development of the foreign mission
enterprise was the organization of a society to send out those
who were ready to go. The Williams men had made some
attempt to arouse missionary interest elsewhere. But neither
they nor Nott nor Newell had any plans for the actual organization of the enterprise, nor for making their way to the

mission field in connection with an English society. This development came at Andover.

So that the inscription on the Haystack Monument at Williams College—"The Birthplace of American Foreign Missions"—while commemorating a significant event, is scarcely true. If one place were to be thought of as the birthplace of American foreign missions it would be Andover. For there the interest took form that led directly to an organized movement.

Adoniram Judson was a man of action. Having decided that he ought to be a missionary he lost no time in making his purpose a reality. Largely through his influence, apparently, Nott and then Newell were definitely recruited for missions. They and he, with Mills, Richards and Edward Warren, and Rice who came to Andover late in the spring, joined forces and talked eagerly and often. The Williams men had thought mostly of a mission to the American Indians. But Judson was committed to missions in Asia—"foreign missions and missions for life" was his motto—and he brought the others over to his plan and purpose.

Newell, Nott and Judson were in the senior class, Rice would be ready the next year, while Mills, Richards and Warren had still two more years. The group consulted with their professors, especially with Dr. Griffin. He promised to write to the London Missionary Society to learn whether the young men could be sent out as missionaries of that society. But Judson was impatient. "Wishing *myself* to receive a letter *immediately*" (the italics are his)—he wrote in April to the director of the London Society's seminary in Gosport for the keenly desired information. No other student was ready to join with him in this letter. Three months later Dr. Griffin also wrote. Judson received an encouraging reply, with an invitation to come to England to meet the board of the society. But before this answer arrived the American Board of Commissioners for Foreign Missions had come into being.

In the early summer Gordon Hall arrived at Andover. He was preaching at Woodbury, Connecticut, and had received a call to the pastorate, when Judson learned that he had been purposing to become a missionary. He wrote him a letter immediately, and Hall promptly left for Andover to consult with Judson and the others. The result was that he declined the call to Woodbury and remained at Andover to prepare for foreign mission work. And now there were eight eager young men pressing toward the great adventure.

Monday, June 25, 1810. It is a date to be remembered. On that Monday Professor Stuart had a meeting of high significance at his home. Professor Griffin was there. Dr. Samuel Spring of Newburyport and Rev. Samuel Worcester of the Tabernacle Church of Salem had driven over to be present. A few other carefully chosen pastors also attended. And there was one important layman, Jeremiah Evarts. They had met to consider this new missionary movement that was assuming such commanding proportions in the life of the seminary. Judson and his fellow missionary students had been invited to come and present the matter. The fathers listened, and talked long and earnestly. It was a "solemn, intellectual and devotional" conference. No wonder it was solemn; no such proposal had come before a group of Christian leaders in all the history of America. Some doubted. One thought the young men were infatuated. But Samuel Newell's presentation of their case won the support of the majority. The General Association of Massachusetts Proper, recently organized and representing the evangelical Congregationalists of the state, was to meet in annual session in Bradford that week, and the students were advised to present a memorial to that body concerning their project.

From Andover to Bradford is nearly ten miles. In 1810 that was quite a journey by horse and chaise, over the rough, dusty country road. Mr. Worcester and Dr. Spring stayed over in Andover, and on Wednesday started early on their rough trip, so as to be in Bradford by nine o'clock. The country along the way was as beautiful then as it is now, but they were not thinking of the scenery. What they thought about and talked about was the astonishing proposal of the young Andover students two days before. It gripped their imagination. How could it be carried into effect? They discussed ways and means, and before they reached Bradford the whole scheme of a Board of Commissioners had been worked out.

On the second day of the meeting, Thursday, June 28, Judson and five or six others of the students walked over from Andover to Bradford. Besides Judson there were Nott and Newell, Mills and Richards, possibly Hall (who had reached Andover that week),[5] and perhaps one or two others. They were going to the meeting of the Association to present their memorial, as they had been advised to do.

Judson had written the memorial. That was natural and to be expected. His literary ability might have turned the attention of his associates to him. But in any situation he was likely to be the leader, and in this missionary project he assumed and was readily accorded the place of leadership, though next to Nott he was the youngest of the group. He was a member of the senior class, to be sure, but so were Newell and Nott. Judson, however, had been the first at Andover to decide to enter missionary service, at least to make the decision known. And what is more important, he had supreme qualities of leadership. He knew exactly in which direction he wanted to go, and he could make others want to go with him in the same direction. Doubtless the American foreign mission enterprise would have been undertaken without him; but it would certainly not have been undertaken in 1810.

On Thursday afternoon the memorial was presented. The signers begged leave to state that their minds had been "long impressed with the duty and importance of personally attempting a mission to the heathen"; and that they considered themselves "devoted to this work for life, whenever God in His providence shall open the way." They asked whether they "ought to renounce the object of missions, as either visionary or impracticable," whether they "ought to direct their attention to the eastern or western world," whether they could expect support "from a missionary society in this country or must commit themselves to the direction of a European society," and what further preparation they ought to have. All the questions that had been discussed among them were included. The hand of Judson is visible throughout. Judson, Nott, Mills, and Newell signed the memorial. Originally Rice and Richards

---

[5] But Judson did not recollect his being present.

had also signed, but six were more than the most sanguine of the fathers could believe would be supported; so these two names were omitted, being the last on the list. Probably it was felt that they could be restored later.

The appearance of Judson and his associates produced a profound impression. "Gray hairs were all weeping" as the young men spoke of their plans and answered the many questions that were asked. A committee of three was appointed; Dr. Spring and Mr. Worcester were two of the three, so success was all but assured. The next day, Friday, June 29, the Association unanimously adopted the committee's report, recommending the formation of a Board of Commissioners for Foreign Missions. Though the action was unanimous it was not without misgivings on the part of many. But the strong determination of the group who had met at Andover, especially Jeremiah Evarts the layman, with the evident conviction of the students, carried the day.

And now what would the board do? Would they appoint the applicants and send them out? Judson doubted whether they would act promptly enough to make unnecessary their going out under the London Missionary Society. As for himself, he was going anyway.

But as they tramped along the road toward Andover that Thursday afternoon Judson had more to think about than the fate of the missionary petition. He was thinking of his own fate. For that day he had lost his heart to Nancy Hasseltine.[6]

During the noon intermission the ministers had gone over to the hospitable home of Deacon John Hasseltine for dinner. Judson was also invited. Ann, or Nancy as she was always called, waited on the guests with her older sisters. As she did so she was not too busy to steal a frequent glance at this young Andover student whose bold proposal to go as a missionary had been talked about in her home. His brilliant qualities of leadership, his ready conversation, his easy social grace had all been mentioned. But Nancy was surprised to notice that instead of being so sparkling in conversation as she had heard, he was very quiet and kept his eyes down, apparently quite

---

[6] The story is fascinatingly told in *Ann of Ava*, by Ethel Daniels Hubbard.

absorbed in what he was eating. The fact is, when he entered the Hasseltine house and his eyes fell upon Nancy—beautiful, active, restless, warm-hearted, vivacious Nancy—his heart gave a bound, and he was thrilled with a strange new feeling, that drew his heart to hers. And Nancy would have been even more surprised than she was if she had known that this brilliant, pious Mr. Judson, so disappointingly quiet, was at that very moment composing a stanza of poetry in her honor. So as he and his fellow students walked along the June road toward Andover his thoughts kept interrupting the conversation. They talked about the Association and the petition and the probability of their being sent out as missionaries. He thought of the Hasseltine dining room and Nancy and wondered when he should see her again.

So Judson was busy with something else besides his studies after that June day in Bradford. True to his impulsive nature, he lost no time in making Ann's acquaintance. And in less than two months he had asked her to be his wife and to go with him to a foreign shore. It was a momentous question that she had to decide. No woman had ever gone from America as a foreign missionary. Probably Adoniram had told her pretty frankly what she was likely to face, just as he had told her father when he wrote asking for her hand:

"I have now to ask whether you can consent to part with your daughter early next spring, to see her no more in this world? Whether you can consent to her departure to a heathen land, and her subjection to the hardships and sufferings of a missionary life? Whether you can consent to her exposure to the dangers of the ocean; to the fatal influence of the southern climate of India; to every kind of want and distress; to degradation, insult, persecution, and perhaps a violent death? Can you consent to all this, for the sake of Him who left His heavenly home and died for her and for you; for the sake of perishing, immortal souls; for the sake of Zion and the glory of God?"

John Hasseltine was a hero to let his daughter go after receiving a letter like that! But he was a genuine Christian; Nancy had won him and her mother to her Saviour. And Judson must have had consummate confidence in himself, or have been rapturously carried away with his missionary enthusiasm, to hope for a favorable reply. He had both the confidence and the enthusiasm.

Ann Hasseltine was herself of heroic stuff. Her father was one of Bradford's leading citizens, and had joined with others in founding Bradford Academy. All his seven children studied there, and Ann was a leader among the students. She was a great reader, and was ready to leave almost anything else if she could settle down in a corner with a book, of which there were plenty in her home. So it is not strange that, young as she was, she taught between terms in Salem, Newbury and across the river in Haverhill. She loved to wander in the fields and along the river paths, and her restless spirit led her mother to exclaim one day, prophetically, "I hope, my daughter, you will some day be satisfied with rambling!" But outstanding was her love for every sort of a good time. Her father had finished a hall in their large house for his children and the other young people of the village, and Ann was always at the center of the merrymaking. She was the gayest girl in Bradford, full of fun, clever and beautiful—"where Ann is no one can be gloomy or unhappy," said one of her friends.

The high moral standards of New England dominated the Hasseltine household, and all went to church regularly, though neither of Ann's parents was a Christian. When she was fifteen two books turned her attention to spiritual things, Hannah More's *Strictures on Female Education* and Bunyan's *Pilgrim's Progress*. But during the winter of her sixteenth birthday (December 22, 1805) books and disturbing thoughts were forgotten, and days and nights were given over to balls and gay parties. In her heart was a restless spirit that she could not hush, though she tried to drown it in a wild and reckless gayety that led some of her friends to say that something terrible would surely happen to her if she kept on. When spring came evangelistic meetings were held in the church, and her spirit was stirred like the tumultuous river near by. She passed through the tragic mental and spiritual experience so common even among young people in those days, and her father and mother could give her no help. At last, through the wise help of the principal of the Academy, she came into the light and yielded her heart to Christ, and united with the Congregational Church. And now, glowing with a new purpose, she was ready for a great adventure for Christ.

"For several weeks past my mind has been greatly agitated," Nancy wrote in her diary on September tenth of this year 1810. But already—not yet twenty-one—she had decided the great question which had agitated her, and had pledged her life to Adoniram and to God for the venture of faith as a foreign missionary. Henceforth for sixteen happy years the story of Adoniram Judson is the story of Ann Hasseltine as well.

In May Judson had been licensed to preach, and on Sundays he often preached in the towns around Andover. In September he completed his Andover course. Early in the same month he had received the degree of Master of Arts from Brown. During at least a part of the autumn he stayed on at Andover. And he wrote to Nott, "I have done nothing scarcely since I saw you, beside . . . riding about the country with Nancy. Pretty preparation, this last article, for a missionary life—isn't it?"

The American Board held its first meeting in September, organized, prepared an address to the churches, appointed a Prudential Committee, and adjourned. Nothing was done about appointing any missionaries. The Prudential Committee met, but were in doubt whether money enough could be secured. At last they decided to consult the London Missionary Society to see if some joint arrangement might be made, and to send one of the students to London to inquire about the project. Naturally Judson was chosen. He was already in correspondence with the London Society, so the mission suited him exactly; and suited his adventurous spirit as well. Moreover the London Society had invited him to come. He had to advance the money for the voyage, but friends of the cause offered to refund what he might spend.

So it was that on December twenty-fifth—Christmas Day was not a day of festivity in old New England—he and Newell, Nott and Hall were examined by the committee and approved, and early in January, 1811, he sailed on the *Packet*. He was instructed to inquire whether he and his associates might be supported for a time by the London Missionary Society without being wholly under that society's direction; and whether in any case it would join with the American Board in their support. It was a bold proposal in view of the threat of war between England and America, but intelligible in the light of New England's friendliness for the mother country. And probably the recent correspondence with the London Society by Judson and Dr. Griffin had considerable weight.

Judson's voyage went well until a French war vessel, *L'Invincible Napoleon,* hove in sight. They could not escape, and the *Packet* suffered the common fate of neutral ships at the time: it was captured and all the ship's company were made prisoners. Judson had little money and he could not speak French. No consideration was shown him and he was ruthlessly thrown into the hold with the crew. He had always had comforts and respectful attention, and he shrank from the associations of the dirty hold and resented the degradation to which he was subjected. He was homesick. To cap the climax he was seasick. Could suffering be worse!

Then it came to him that all this was a temptation to be overcome. So he prayed for strength and turned to his Bible— his Hebrew Bible, which he hunted up in his baggage. It speaks volumes for his scholarly interest that he had his Hebrew Bible with him. And it is still more revealing that after reading a few verses in Hebrew in the dim light of the hold, he should rest his eyes and amuse himself by mentally translating the Hebrew verses into Latin!

The ship's doctor happened along and saw the book. What was this fellow reading? He picked up the book and carried it to the light. Hebrew! The young man must be something of a scholar—perhaps he knew Latin. So the doctor came back and spoke to Judson in that tongue. Exactly the opportunity for Judson! It was for that he had studied and spoken Latin at Brown. In a few words he explained who he was, and soon he found himself in the cabin, with a comfortable berth and a seat at the captain's table.

At last they reached Bayonne, and Judson expected to be set at liberty. Instead, all the prisoners were marched through the streets to the prison like common culprits. For a proud spirit like Judson this was too humiliating to be borne. He had picked up a little French, and he made vigorous use of it, complaining against his treatment. But the bystanders only laughed at his broken French. Then he tried English. Here he was more at home. At last a man stepped out from the crowd and walked along by his side.

"You'd better speak more quietly," he said in English.

"With great pleasure," replied Judson, "now that I have made myself understood."

Quickly he explained who he was, and found to his delight that his new-found friend was an American.

"I am going to help you," he said; "but go along quietly now."

"Oh, I will be a perfect lamb," answered Judson; "I have gained what I was after."

But when he reached the prison he was thrown into an underground dungeon, with no light from outdoors, and only a single dim lamp hung on a pillar in the middle of the room. It was cold and damp, and there was a mouldy smell that made him sick. Not a chair or stool was to be seen in the dungeon, only dirty straw scattered around by the walls.

He revolted against it all. But as he was leaning against the pillar, busy with his thoughts, the door opened and the American stranger entered. He stepped over to Judson's side but paid no attention to him. Judson saw what he was about and acted with similar indifference. Looking around the room the visitor said, "I wonder if I know any of these fellows. No, there's no friend of mine here."

Then as he moved away from the pillar he threw his great coat around the slight figure of Judson and drew him out of the dungeon, slipping some money into the jailer's hand as they went out. At the gate he did the same to the gatekeeper.

"Now run!" he said as they stepped out, and dashed off at a fast pace.

They made for the water-front, and Judson was put on board a ship for the night. Next day he was taken to the attic of a friendly ship-builder's house, where he stayed a few days until a parole could be secured. Then for six weeks he remained in Bayonne, living in an American home.

Characteristically he wanted to learn all he could about

France and the French, and went about to various places of
amusement, though taking no part in what went on. But one
night he went to a masked ball, where what he saw led him
to make some strong remarks to bystanders. Others gathered
around, and before he knew it he was speaking of the results
of infidelity in France, pointing out that Jesus Christ was the
only way of escape and appealing to his hearers for repentance.
His speech made a profound impression.

It was quite in keeping with Judson's easy gravitation toward persons of distinction, that in some way he became acquainted with members of Napoleon's suite, and was able to
travel extensively about France in a carriage belonging to the
emperor. He saw so much and gained such valuable experience that he always looked back on his dramatic adventure as
an important part of his preparation for missionary service.
At last, with some difficulty, a passport was secured and he
crossed the channel, arriving in London on the third of May,
four months after leaving America.

The officers of the London Missionary Society received him
kindly and conferred with him at length, but apparently little
was said on either side about cooperation between them and
the American Board. The subject was not mentioned in the
formal action which they took; but they voted to appoint Judson, Newell, Nott and Hall as their missionaries, with the
promise that they would be located in a station by themselves
in India. Quite likely Judson in his eagerness and independence forgot the detailed instructions given him, and thought
only of his own application and how he and his fellow students
could get to the mission field. It may be, too, that in view of
the political situation the English society avoided discussion of
the American proposal.

After conferring with the London Society, Judson visited
the seminary at Gosport and took part in several church services, everywhere making a fine impression. His voice surprised
those who saw his slight frame. In one of the London churches
he was asked to read a hymn. When he had finished the minister explained that he was a prospective missionary. "And if
his faith is proportioned to his voice," he added, "he will drive
the devil from all India!" In June he embarked for home, and

reached New York in August, eight months after leaving the
United States.

The next month, accompanied by his intimate friend Nott,
he went to Worcester to give his report at the annual meeting
of the board. This time, on the recommendation of the Prudential Committee, the board took definite action, and appointed Judson, Nott, Newell and Hall as their missionaries,
to work in Burma, as the committee advised,[7] or in Surat or
Penang. Their salaries were fixed at $666.66 if married or
$444.45 if unmarried, with outfit money equal to a year's
salary. And a notable action was the appropriation of $300 for
books for the missionaries.

One factor that led to definite action was a bequest of
$30,000 from the widow of John Norris, who had given $10,000
in silver coin to help found Andover Seminary—money that he
had saved for missions and gave to Andover to raise up missionaries. Another inducement came from Judson and Nott
themselves, who told the board frankly and in no uncertain
terms that they proposed to go out to the foreign mission field
under the London Missionary Society if the American Board
did not appoint them.[8] Judson especially was emphatic and
outspoken, so much so that the board were greatly disturbed,
and some were for dismissing him then and there. Finally it
was decided that he should be reproved, which was done in a
very kindly manner through Dr. Spring, his warm friend.
Judson was much affected by the admonition, and humbly
promised to be more careful. The gist of the matter seems to
be that the board had dilly-dallied so long that it seemed to
Judson that the only way to get action was to insist on it; while
on the other hand the board were annoyed at being forced to
appoint the four young men, at least Judson and Nott, or else
lose them to the English society—a possibility they had not
anticipated when they sent Judson to England, though they

---

[7] Luther Rice stated that Judson was the first, so far as he knew, who mentioned
Burma.

[8] Judson's independent spirit had appeared in a letter written to Nott the preceding October, telling of the London Society's rule that a missionary going to a new
station must go without his wife, waiting a year until he could determine whether it
would be wise to take his wife there. Judson adds, "So this piece of advice I intend
to keep on my hat; for I am resolved, new or old station, to take my wife with me."

must have known that Judson had already applied to London for appointment. These fathers were not accustomed to have anyone lay down the law to them as Judson did. And he was so fired with his missionary passion and was so certain of God's call that he thought only of getting to the mission field, and was evidently not so careful as he ought to have been in observing the proper formalities and courtesies.

According to Samuel Worcester the board had occasion to caution him again before he sailed. But he was so carried away with his missionary enthusiasm that the admonitions made little impression on him; and he denied vigorously that the board had "reprimanded" him, when later the insinuation was published that he had become a Baptist because of this "reprimand." It is one of the revealing things in his story, however, that nearly twenty years afterward, when his friend Nott pointed out his error, he wrote to Jeremiah Evarts, successor to Dr. Worcester as secretary of the American Board, to admit that he had probably been wrong, and humbly to confess his fault. But he did not regret his stand before the board, as he told Francis Wayland near the close of his life. For he wondered when and how he and Nott would ever have reached the mission field if they had tamely accepted the advice of the board to "wait the further intimations of Providence!" Indeed Dr. Worcester himself admitted in his report to the board at their next annual meeting that "the resolution could not have been taken at all, but for the commission which had been obtained from that society," that is, the appointment from the London Society, which assured their support in case the American Board could not secure sufficient funds.

In spite of all this, Judson retained "the warmest filial affection" for the American Board, and once said to Francis Wayland, "When I grasp the hand of Dr. Worcester in heaven I do not think we shall either of us feel called upon to settle any such differences." And the attitude of the American Board toward him as the years went by was well expressed by Secretary Rufus Anderson when he wrote to Judson, "We love to think of you as intimately related to us—having a common missionary parentage."

And now they were ready to go. Hall had taken the place

of Mills, who had still a year of study before him. Richards, too, was not yet prepared. Judson, Newell, Nott and Hall were the four. And almost at the last moment, as we shall see, Luther Rice was added.

There were three others. Nancy Hasseltine was one. On New Year's Day of 1811 Judson had written her: "It is with the utmost sincerity, and with all my heart, that I wish you, my love, a happy new year. May this be the year in which you will change your name; in which you will take a final leave of your relatives and native land; in which you will cross the wide ocean, and dwell on the other side of the world, among a heathen people." Not 1811, but 1812, was to be the year of these important events. But she had plighted her troth to Judson, and was busy preparing for the great adventure.

Harriet Atwood was another. She was a Bradford Academy friend of Nancy's, living across the Merrimac in Haverhill. One of the first things Nancy had done after she had decided the great question that Adoniram had presented to her was to go over and see her friend Harriet about it. And soon Harriet had had to face a similar question herself. For Samuel Newell had asked her to share his life and mission—sending his proposal through Nancy! Like her dear friend, Harriet had answered "Yes," though when she said it she was not yet eighteen.

The third was Roxana Peck, childhood friend and promised wife of Samuel Nott in Franklin, Connecticut, where Samuel's father was pastor—destined to spend but a few years in India, but to have a place in missionary history all her own as the first American woman to engage in foreign mission service.[9]

So now there were seven, soon to be eight, every one equipped with the best that America could give, in education and spiritual heritage—Gordon Hall, lovable, gifted, steady, quiet yet forceful; Samuel Nott, Phi Beta Kappa student, energetic, loyal, eager for pioneering; Roxana Peck, retiring, nobly faithful, unknown and without a biographer through all these years, content to be simply the wife of Samuel Nott; Samuel Newell, Master of Arts from Harvard and Yale, earnest and conscientious; Harriet Atwood his promised wife, old for her

---

[9] The Notts reached Bombay before the Judsons reached Rangoon.

years, serious and saintly, with a charm that made her seem beautiful; Luther Rice, shortly to be added to the list, giant in stature and giant in oratory, unsurpassed in energy, witty in speech, musician and preacher; Adoniram Judson, brilliant in intellect and social graces, burning with eager devotion to his great purpose, imaginative and determined, the superb leader; and Ann Hasseltine, his bride-to-be, vivacious, sparkling in conversation, resourceful, unflinchingly courageous, devoted to Adoniram, consecrated to Christ, a queenly spirit whom one has called "the woman of the century."

And now they are straining to be away, only waiting for the ship that is to carry them forth on their great venture of faith.

CHAPTER III

FROM SALEM TO RANGOON

A SHIP was not to be had. France was seizing American ships wherever found. British cruisers were blockading American ports. Naturally no ships were sailing to India. Late in January, however, it was learned that the ship *Harmony,* Captain Brown, had been authorized to sail from Philadelphia for Calcutta with passengers. But nearly $5,000 would be needed for the missionaries, while less than $1,200 was available. Mrs. Norris' legacy had not been received, as her will was being contested. At first the committee suggested that the wives delay their sailing. Then that they provide for two of the men and their wives, the other two to look, if necessary, to the London Society for support. At last they boldly acted on faith and decided to send out all four men and the wives—though they could not see where the money would come from.

This was Monday. Thursday of the following week, February sixth, was set for the ordination of the new missionaries. But now a new difficulty—or opportunity—arose: Luther Rice applied for appointment. He was one of the first men at Williams to decide to be a missionary, he was the first student elected president of the society of The Brethren at Andover, and he tremendously desired to go. But he was engaged to a young woman who hesitated to accept the great uncertainties and hardships of a life to which no American woman had yet gone, and he had been waiting in the hope that she might be willing to go. But at last she said a final "No." Then he turned to what he believed a higher duty, and promptly rushed an application to the Prudential Committee. At first the committee hesitated. But finally they yielded and agreed to appoint him—though only on condition that he could raise the necessary funds himself. Only six days remained before the ordination. But Rice was equal to the emergency. He set out at once on horseback in the depth of the New England winter, traveled day and night, and came back at the end of the six days with the full sum needed. It was a foreshadowing of the tremendous energy and power of appeal that were to characterize him in later years.

According to the plans, all the missionaries were to sail from Philadelphia on the *Harmony*. But during the week news came that the brig *Caravan*, Captain Heard, was to sail from Salem for Calcutta, and arrangements were at once made for the Judsons and Rice to take passage on her, the Newells, the Notts and Hall to sail on the *Harmony*. Immediately after the ordination, however, the Newells were booked on the *Caravan* in place of Rice, so that Ann Judson might have another woman companion on the long voyage. The *Harmony* would have other women passengers besides Roxana Nott.

The ordination service for all the five young men took place in the old Tabernacle Congregational Church in Salem. It was an event without precedent in America. That Thursday was one of the coldest days of the winter. But people came not only from Salem but from surrounding towns. Seminary and academy students tramped over from Andover, a long sixteen miles. William Goodell was one of them, later to be famous as a missionary to Turkey. He was "so thoroughly inoculated with the missionary spirit that a second inoculation has never been found necessary." [1] Rufus Anderson, later the long-time secretary of the American Board, was there with his father, and received an indelible impression that was to issue in great missionary achievement in after years. Others were equally affected.

An immense throng filled the church, not less than fifteen hundred, some say two thousand.[2] "The Tabernacle was packed like rows of new pins in a paper. The aisles could be traced only by the ridges or seams made by the people standing."

The service, including probably the examination by the

---

[1] Quoted by E. D. G. Prime, *Forty Years in the Turkish Empire*, p. 45.
[2] The scene is vividly described by James L. Hill, in *The Immortal Seven*, pp. 5f. Strangely, he nowhere mentioned Roxana Peck; she made an "Immortal Eight."

council, began at eleven and lasted till three. Five leading ministers took part. Professor Griffin, now pastor of "the largest
church in Boston," Park Street, offered the introductory
prayer; Professor Woods preached the sermon; Rev. Jedediah
Morse of Charlestown offered the prayer of ordination; Rev.
Samuel Spring of Newburyport gave the charge to the candidates; and Rev. Samuel Worcester, pastor of the Tabernacle
Church, extended the right hand of fellowship. The sermon
text was nearly the whole of that great missionary Psalm, the
sixty-seventh. The candidates sat on a wooden settee[3] in front
of the congregation, and the five ordaining ministers placed
their hands on the heads of the young men as Dr. Morse offered
the prayer that set them apart for their great work. And
listening with throbbing hearts were Ann Hasseltine, now Mrs.
Judson, and Harriet Atwood, soon to be Mrs. Newell. Samuel
Nott's bride-to-be, Roxana Peck, was probably at home in
Norwich, Connecticut. They were quite as much a part of
what was taking place as the five young men themselves.

All who were present were stirred as perhaps they had
never been stirred before. "The entire wrapt convocation
seemed moved as the trees of the wood are moved by a mighty
wind. Pent-up emotion could no longer be restrained. Eyes
overflowed with Christian sympathy at the affecting scene.
An irrepressible sighing and weeping, which broke at times the
silence of the house, attested how deeply the heart of the vast
congregation was touched." It was a service such as had never
taken place in America before, and would never take place
again.

Nott and Roxana Peck were married on Saturday the
eighth, and left immediately for Philadelphia, as did Hall and
Rice. Judson had spent his last Sabbath in Plymouth with his
parents, and early the next morning, Monday the third, before
the family were up, he set out for Boston on horseback with his
brother Elnathan. As they rode along they talked together
earnestly, and Adoniram pleaded with his brother to commit
his life to Christ. At a quiet place on the road they drew rein

---

[3] This, with other reminders of the great occasion, are now exhibited in a special
missionary room in the present Tabernacle Church.

and dismounted, and stepping behind some trees they kneeled down while Adoniram offered an earnest prayer for his brother, a prayer that was answered after many years.

The brothers parted in Boston and Adoniram went on to Bradford. There on Wednesday the fifth of February, in that same west room in which he and Nancy had first met, they gave heart and hand to each other as pastor Allen united them as husband and wife, after preaching a sermon to the assembled company on the text John 11:52—"that he might also gather together into one the children of God that are scattered abroad." Among the guests were Harriet Atwood and Samuel Newell, themselves to be married four days later. Thursday came the ordination. The next day Adoniram went to Boston, to bid farewell to Elnathan and his sister Abigail. Then he and Ann went to Beverly, close to Salem, where in the home of Ann's sister Rebecca, wife of the pastor, Mr. Emerson, they waited for the sailing of the *Caravan*.

On the day of the ordination the board lacked $3,800 of the $5,000 they needed. But those present at the ordination service were so stirred that they contributed $220. After that day money began to pour in, so that in less than two weeks the board had $6,000, ample for all needs. Letters had been sent to possible givers, and pastors and Andover students had solicited contributions. Especially energetic was Ezekiel Rich, of the class below Judson at Brown and his classmate at Andover, now deeply stirred and volunteering his services as agent for the board.

The new missionaries received innumerable kindnesses and gifts. For example, while the Judsons were in Beverly some one opened the door of the Emerson house one day and without saying a word threw in a purse containing fifty dollars. A label read, "For Mr. Judson's private use." The Salem ladies provided an ample supply of the crisp New England gingerbread, which the missionaries were still eating three months later. And many other presents came to them.

On Thursday, the thirteenth, the *Caravan* moved out from the wharf into midstream and lay at anchor waiting for a fair wind. The Judsons and the Newells were now in Salem, ready for the call to go aboard. The Newells were staying with relatives; Nancy, with her husband and her sister Abigail, was having one last visit with her former Bradford friends Eliphalet and Sally Kimball, the latter the sister of Lydia Kimball, Nancy's classmate and dearest friend.

Friday, Saturday and Sunday the weather was stormy and the *Caravan* could not sail. Monday, the seventeenth, was marked by a violent snowstorm; snow choked the streets and travel of any kind was practically impossible. Tuesday was bleak and cold, but Captain Heard thought the wind would be favorable and sent word to his passengers. Israel Putnam, a junior in Andover Seminary and a friend of Newell's at Harvard, secured a sleigh and took Samuel and Harriet Newell down to Crowninshield's wharf, where the brig was again tied up, and Captain Ingersoll, later a Congregational minister, drove Ann Judson and Sally Kimball from the latter's home. Judson preferred to walk. But before the loading could be finished the wind died down and the sailing had to be postponed. Friends had come to see the new missionaries off, and they lingered in the biting cold until dark, then reluctantly went home. Judson and Newell and their wives spent the night on board the brig, Israel Putnam and Captain Ingersoll staying to keep them company and make the last evening a cheerful one. Indeed it was no doleful occasion. Putnam said that "all was cheerfulness and even joy." And Samuel Worcester's son tells how the Judsons "appeared to the last in most marked animation of good spirits, as if no clouds could ever gather to darken their bright hopes and anticipations." [4]

The next morning, Wednesday, dawned raw and cold, a typical New England February day. But the wind was from the west, and Captain Heard saw his chance to clear the coast. Judson and Newell went ashore early, had breakfast with Mr. Worcester at his home, and hurried back to the brig. Shortly after sunrise the *Caravan* got under way, and the voyage of faith, so long anticipated, had begun. Putnam and Ingersoll stayed with their friends till the last, remaining on board until the brig had cleared the harbor. Then they went over the side with the pilot, a last "Good bye!" was called, Adoniram and

---

[4] S. M. Worcester, in his *Life of Samuel Worcester*, II, p. 142.

Ann and the Newells stood at the stern and waved for a few minutes as the *Caravan* and the pilot boat drifted apart, then the spray and the mist closed in and they were off alone on their great adventure. Three other vessels sailed from Salem that February nineteenth, but none of them is remembered. The sailing of the *Caravan* made history.

On Tuesday the eighteenth, Samuel and Roxana Nott, with Rice and Hall, left Philadelphia to board the *Harmony* at Newcastle. But the ship was delayed in getting down the river, and it was not until the twenty-fourth that they passed the Delaware Capes and were on their way to join their *Caravan* friends in India.

It was no ocean greyhound on which Adoniram and Nancy Judson sailed from Salem that wintry day. The *Normandie* of 1935 is 1027 feet long and measures 75,000 tons. The *Caravan* of 1812 was only 90 feet long and measured 267 tons. There was room for only the Judsons in one cabin and the Newells in another. Yet the accommodations, though limited, were comfortable. Food was provided in abundance and variety, though they had to become accustomed to coffee and tea without milk, and sometimes even just water gruel. But they were satisfied.[5]

How to get exercise was a problem. The limits of the deck made walking unsatisfactory. The games enjoyed by modern travelers were unknown. Finally they solved the difficulty: they took to jumping rope! Harriet tells, too, of some running on deck. And in the retirement of her cabin she even did some dancing. After all, young folks in those days were not fundamentally different from those of today, in spite of the ponderous language they used in their diaries and letters.

The weather did not favor them all the time. Sometimes high seas deluged their cabins. Once the little vessel sprang a leak and the men were at the pumps many hours before the danger was passed. But Nancy wrote, "God preserved us— enabled us to trust in Him and feel safe." On Sundays they

---

[5] Pickering Dodge, owner of the *Caravan*, wrote to Capt. Heard, "The missionaries are to dine in the cabin. I hope you will find them pleasant companions. Give them a fresh dish once a week or oftener." Pond, *Bradford—A New England Academy*, p. 89.

had service in the cabin, where Captain Heard and his officers joined them while Judson or Newell preached. And every evening they gathered for prayers in Judson's stateroom. Of course they found plenty of time for reading, using their good collection of books. All in all they thoroughly enjoyed the long five months' voyage.

While in Andover Judson had commenced an original translation of the New Testament,[6] another illustration of his scholarly interest and independent spirit. This he continued on shipboard. His study went along very smoothly until he came to the word commonly translated "baptize." Then he found himself in difficulty. For as he considered the meaning and purpose of baptism he began to wonder how he ought to treat the unconverted children and servants of converts. He remembered the instructions of the board, to baptize "credible believers with their households." The result was that he set himself to study the question, Who should be baptized? Then when he tried to get at the exact meaning of the Greek word in order to translate it, he found to his consternation that apparently the meaning was at variance with his former understanding. And his difficulty was emphasized by the recollection that in Calcutta, and perhaps other places, he would be associated with Baptist missionaries from England, who he expected (quite contrary to the fact) would be aggressive in asserting their distinctive beliefs, in which case he would wish to be prepared to defend his own position as a Congregationalist. Here was a dilemma: his presuppositions on the one side, the apparently contrary teaching of the Bible on the other. What should he do? He did as he always did in such a situation, what his intellectual honesty and his Christian loyalty compelled him to do: he gave himself to serious study of baptism and the teaching of the New Testament.

The matter first presented itself in April, when the voyage was half over. From that time until they reached Calcutta he kept at the problem. Whether or not he discussed it with Samuel Newell we do not know; evidently Newell was not troubled by the question. But Judson was troubled. The more

---

[6] So he stated in a letter to Dr. Spencer H. Cone, quoted by Mrs. H. C. Conant, *The Earnest Man*, p. 433.

he studied the more troubled he became. For as he said to Ann, he was afraid the Baptists were right, though he did not like to admit it.

Ann urged him to stop thinking of the question. "I am afraid you will become a Baptist," she said, "and what would become of us if you did? And what would our dear parents and friends think?"

So it was with consternation and dismay that they faced the possible results of his study. But Judson was not one to confront a problem and leave it unsolved—we have seen that already. Puzzle, or mathematical proposition, or the truth of the gospel record, or the mode and meaning of baptism, whatever the question he must go through with it, and go to the end. So in spite of his growing fears he continued his study of the subject until they arrived in Calcutta on June sixteenth.

It was a long, slow voyage. But it was a honeymoon trip for both the Judsons and the Newells and they were supremely happy. They had sighted several vessels, but Captain Heard had been strictly enjoined not to speak any on account of the threatening war. As they came in sight of the shores of India they hailed an American ship which they thought might be the *Harmony,* and were greatly excited at the anticipation of seeing their friends once more. But they were disappointed; it was not the *Harmony.*

Even yet the dangers of the long voyage were not ended; for as they lay at anchor at the mouth of the Hugli waiting for a pilot, a storm broke during the night and the anchor cable parted. It looked as though they were to be wrecked, and perhaps, after all, find a watery grave. But after great difficulty the crew managed to get the brig under way and out beyond the shoals, and they were safe.

The next day they were moving quietly up the river toward Calcutta. And what a change from the monotony of the ocean! "The smell is fragrant beyond description"—"we have passed the mango trees"—"the pagodas are handsomer and larger than the houses"—"we hear the birds singing"—"I have never witnessed or read anything so delightful as the present scene." So wrote Nancy and Harriet. They were all excitement. At last they had reached the land of their missionary hopes.

For a couple of days they were delayed on board while Judson and Newell went ashore and, with difficulty, secured permission to land. Then—on the eighteenth of June—they all disembarked from the *Caravan* and once more walked on solid ground. Dr. Carey cordially invited them to spend that first night at his large and comfortable Calcutta house, and they made their way in sedan chairs through the streets. They were impressed by the crowds, mostly Hindus, but now and then a European, and they wondered at the whitewashed stone houses and the large and numerous temples. In the evening they went eagerly to attend service at the Anglican church. Then the next day, at the invitation of Carey and his colleagues Marshman and Ward, they went up the river to Serampore to stay until Rice and the others should arrive on the *Harmony*.

The very first Sunday in India Judson and Newell began their missionary work, Newell preaching in the Serampore chapel in the morning and Judson in the evening. But the government did not long allow them to forget that it frowned on missions. Ten days after their arrival they received a summons to Calcutta, and at Government House an order was read to them which peremptorily demanded that they return to America—and on the *Caravan,* the very vessel that had brought them. To make the matter doubly sure, Captain Heard was refused clearance unless his former passengers were sailing with him. Their hearts fell as they heard the order. Here was trouble indeed.

What could be done? Apparently nothing. The life plans of Judson and Newell and their wives seemed threatened with tragic failure. The *Harmony* party—delayed nearly three weeks at the Isle of France—had not yet arrived and they must face the situation by themselves. Carey and Marshman did what they could, but without avail; no escape from the government order appeared possible. Again and again they were summoned to Government House and the same order was repeated: they must return to America. The Serampore family held a special prayer meeting on their behalf, which greatly comforted them in their extremity. English friends, led by

Chaplain Thomason of the Company itself, collected five hundred rupees for them. And other practical kindnesses were received.

At last the government modified its order so far as to grant permission for the new missionaries to go to the Isle of France, now Mauritius. A French vessel, *L'Enterprise,* was to sail that very week! "Would the captain take them as passengers?" "No, there were no accommodations." Again their hearts sank. At the last moment, however, Captain Chimminent changed his mind and said he could take two passengers. But which two? All four must go, but only two could go.

It did not take long to decide: Samuel and Harriet should go. For Harriet was expecting motherhood and it was imperative that she should find a settled abode without delay. It was hard for Nancy and Harriet to think of being separated, girlhood chums as they had been, and now facing the future without other woman companionship. The *Harmony,* too, had not arrived, and Harriet and Samuel would have to leave without seeing their friends. Most serious of all, Harriet must go on her voyage with no woman to attend her in her need. But to all this they had consecrated themselves when they gave their lives to the great cause. So the four met together for the last time, bravely said good-bye, and on Thursday, July thirtieth, Samuel and Harriet and Adoniram took a budgerow down the river to Calcutta, had dinner with Dr. Carey, went to church in the evening for one last service, and the next day Samuel and Harriet boarded the ship, with many profuse promises on the part of all to meet again soon in the Isle of France.

For a while Adoniram and Nancy were left to themselves. They went down to Calcutta to live, and found a very delightful home with an Englishman, Mr. Rolt, who had married the widow of Brunsdon, one of the English Baptist missionaries. And now once more the question of baptism came up. In Mr. Rolt's house they discovered many books dealing with both sides of the question, and Adoniram settled himself again to the study of this problem that would not down.

He and Ann had many a discussion of the subject. But always Ann championed the position she had held as a Congregationalist. "If you become a Baptist," she declared with spirit, "I certainly will not."

"But it is my duty to examine the subject," replied Adoniram; "and even if I have to pay dearly for it, I hope I shall not be afraid to embrace the truth."

And Ann was apprehensive, knowing how persistent and fearless Adoniram was. Indeed she herself was beginning to fear that the position of the Baptists might be stronger than she had thought; for she searched the Scriptures for herself.

The *Harmony* arrived August eighth, with Rice and Hall and the Notts. Undoubtedly Judson promptly talked over his problem with them. Samuel Worcester in presenting the report of the Prudential Committee to the American Board in 1813 said that Judson's associates did not know of his plans for baptism until they heard of them from Dr. Marshman.[7] But Judson told them to Nott at least, as the latter explicitly stated: "On the day of my arrival in Calcutta, and within three hours after my arrival, he opened to me his whole mind." And again: "From the time of my arrival in Calcutta I knew intimately the labor of his mind; and I declare my full conviction that he gave the subject the most thorough and serious examination, studying carefully the Scriptures and all the authors he could find on the subject; that he studied it religiously; and that in all his conversation upon it he seemed under a solemn and deep religious impression."[8] Hall and Rice also knew the way the matter was developing, for a week after their arrival Nott recorded in his diary a discussion of the situation by them and himself.

Finally, after close and continuous study, depressed as they faced the probable separation from their friends, fearful of the future but convinced of their duty, feeling their weakness but strong in their faith in God's leadership and care, Adoniram and Ann came to the conclusion together that "the immersion of a professing believer is the only Christian baptism."

To decide was to act. Judson immediately wrote to Carey and his Serampore colleagues, telling of their decision and ask-

---

[7] Report of Am. Bd. of Com. for For. Miss., 1813, p. 60.
[8] Nott's *Letter Addressed to Rev. Enoch Pond*, pp. 6, 9.

ing that they might be baptized. A day or two later he wrote to Worcester, enclosing a copy of his letter to Serampore and saying that he supposed that the board would feel as unwilling to support a Baptist missionary as he was to baptize "credible believers with their households," and that he assumed that his connection with the board was dissolved. It was not easy to write this letter. "The dissolution of my connection with the Board of Commissioners, and a separation from my dear missionary brethren," he wrote, "I consider the most distressing consequences of my late change of sentiments."

At the same time he wrote to Thomas Baldwin, pastor of the Second Baptist Church of Boston, transmitting copies of these letters and saying, "Should there be formed a Baptist society for the support of a missionary in these parts, I shall be ready to consider myself their missionary." He also wrote to Dr. Lucius Bolles of Salem, and Dr. Marshman wrote to Baldwin. All this before Judson and his wife had actually been baptized. The ordinance was administered to them by Rev. William Ward of Serampore on Sunday, September sixth, in Carey's Lal Bazaar Chapel in Calcutta.

Everything was changed by this decision and action. The government had given the *Harmony* group the same sort of welcome as had greeted the Judsons: they were ordered to leave the country at once. Should they all try to go together, or should they separate now that the Judsons had become Baptists? Nott held with tenacious loyalty to his old friend Judson, and seized the first opportunity to champion the latter's sincerity. But both he and Hall, and probably Rice, felt that the decision of Judson and his wife made it unwise for the two groups to carry out their plan to work together.[9]

Apparently they had all talked of this probability before the baptism actually took place. The thought was most distressing to both Adoniram and Ann. Nott and Judson had been in the group who had presented the memorial that brought the American Board into being. Judson's application to the London Missionary Society for the appointment of himself and his Andover friends had stipulated that they should all be stationed

---

[9] So Judson wrote Worcester (Wayland, II, p. 110).

in the same mission. Nott and Judson had gone together before the board with their insistent request—almost demand—
that they be sent out or be released to the London Society.
Must now their old companionship be dissolved? Ann had had
to say good-bye to her friend Harriet—must she now separate
from Roxana Nott, the only other woman in their number?

But Adoniram and Ann could not alter their decision. "If
ever I sought to know the truth," wrote Ann in her journal, "if
ever I looked up to the Father of lights, if ever I gave myself up
to the inspired word, I have done so during this investigation."
And that was true of her husband. So they faced the separation and the unknown future with the same strong reliance on
Him who led them thus far, as when they had made their
first decision to go forth from their native land as missionary
exiles. "I feel confident that Jesus will go with us and direct
our steps; and in that case it is of little consequence whether we
have more or less of society." So wrote Ann.

This insistence of Hall and Nott and Rice on separate missions for themselves and Judson has been passed by unnoticed,
or accepted as a matter of course. But it was of epochal importance. It immediately determined the policy of American
missions as strictly denominational. Judson seems not to have
thought a separate mission necessary, or at any rate a separate
field, on account of the change of denominational affiliation by
himself and his wife. Only when Hall and Nott, and perhaps
Rice, discussing the impending baptism with Judson, made
positive statements (though in the utmost friendliness) that in
their opinion Judson's decision made separation necessary, did
he accept it as inevitable.[10] He wrote to Dr. Worcester, "My
change of sentiments on the subject of baptism is considered by
my missionary brethren as incompatible with my continuing
their fellow laborer in the mission which they contemplate on
the island of Madagascar." Unfortunately he acquiesced in
their decision. Suppose all four had stood out boldly for a
united mission, or intimate cooperation in the same field—one

---

[10] The possibility of separation from their colleagues was first mentioned by Ann
in her journal Aug. 10, two days after Hall and Nott and Rice arrived. (James D.
Knowles, *Memoirs of Mrs. Ann H. Judson,* p. 76).

can only guess the result, but it is a fair guess that the sharp divisions in missions along denominational lines might not have arisen. Denominational distinctions at home might have limited the plan to cooperating missions in the same field. But conditions on the foreign field make cooperation easier than at home, and a way would probably have been found if the missionaries had laid down that policy from the beginning. Strong representations by the whole group in favor of a cooperative plan might have led to a fellowship between Congregationalists and Baptists that would have made the foreign mission policy of the American churches very different from what it has been.

There were favorable influences at home. For example, the founders of the American Board were a remarkably broadminded group, big men in the truest sense, and many of the Baptist leaders were equally broad in vision and had quite as wide an interdenominational spirit. Then, too, Carey's example and influence were powerful in America; he was eager for interdenominational cooperation, and stimulated this through his appeals, for gifts toward his Bible work. Moreover, the American Board looked to the London Missionary Society for leadership, and that society was organized on a wide interdenominational basis; this might conceivably have influenced the attitude in America favorably. It is true that denominational feeling was strong, but the considerable range of interdenominational activities shows that this was not as great a barrier as is commonly supposed. The fact is, all foreign mission work was in its beginning and its program was not fixed; the new American missionaries were formulating policies that were to determine the future. Perhaps the future could not have been different from what it has been. But perhaps it could. At any rate, the decision of Judson's associates, followed by Judson's acquiescence in that decision,[11] determined the future and made it certain that American foreign missions would be carried on upon a strictly denominational basis.

---

[11] In a joint letter to the American Board, written about twenty days after Judson's baptism, Hall, Nott and Rice said, "In consequence of this trying event it has appeared to him and to us, and to those with whom we have conversed, expedient that we should separate and labor in different fields." (Report of Am. Bd., 1813, p. 60).

While all this is true, it needs to be added that through the years since the time of which we are speaking missionary co-operation has greatly increased, and at the forefront in that movement have been the American Board and its missionaries. If Hall and Nott were in India today they would perhaps be leaders in efforts for cooperation and unity. On the other hand, the chief obstacle in any cooperative plans, as pointed out, would have been in the relations between the churches in the home land. And at that point Baptists and other denominations have had difficulty. It is too late in the day to pass unfriendly criticism on those who, with few precedents to guide them, formulated the policies of modern missions. It is ours rather to set ourselves to bring into reality the ideal of fellowship that was the early desire of that noble band.

After all, Judson and his wife were not to be alone. Luther Rice had been facing the same problem. As far back as his student days in Williams College he had engaged in a discussion of baptism with a Baptist friend, and had acknowledged to himself (with some astonishment) that his friend had presented points that he had not been able to refute. On board the *Harmony* a warm discussion of the question had arisen between him and the English Baptist missionaries Johns and Lawson, perhaps pressed by Johns, who seems to have been rather pugnacious. This led to his studying the matter assiduously during the voyage. When he arrived in India he took it up again, and learned to his surprise that Adoniram and Nancy Judson were also in not a little doubt about the question. Soon after they were baptized he went to live with them at Mr. Rolt's, and frequently tried to argue with Adoniram about baptism. The latter always declined the argument, however, and advised him to study the Bible. This he did; and he went to Dr. Carey's house one morning before that worthy gentleman was up, to borrow a Greek Testament so as to go deeper into the study. At last, like Judson and his wife, he became convinced that the immersion of believers was the only scriptural baptism, and on November first he was baptized.

The Judsons had had permission to go to the Isle of France, as has been seen, but the one available vessel had had accommodations for only the Newells. And now Rice and Hall and the Notts were with them; what should they do? The possibility of a professorship in Fort William College, where Carey was teaching, was presented to Judson, and it appealed to his scholarly interest, but he had come to preach the gospel and he promptly rejected the offer. Yet where should he go? Burma had been his preference from the beginning, and had been suggested by the board as their first choice.[12] But a mission in that country seemed impracticable on account of difficulties between the English and the Burmans, the unsafe conditions under the barbarous Burman government, and the lack of success in the missionary attempts already made by the English Baptist and London Missionary Societies. The Isle of France attracted them, partly because the Newells had gone there, partly in view of the possibility of going on from there to Madagascar, an unoccupied and very inviting field.

So they planned at first to go to the Isle of France; but no transportation was to be had. A number of other fields were considered, Ceylon, Japan, Amboyna in the Spice Islands, and even Brazil. Judson began to study Portuguese to prepare for work in the last-named country. He wrote to Mr. Chater of the Baptist mission in Ceylon to get information about opportunities in that island. Felix Carey, son of Dr. William Carey, who was a missionary in Burma, came to Calcutta in September, and urged the Judsons to go to Burma. By the next month, however, they had decided to try for Java, and had applied for a passage. But they were ready to go to Burma if prospects of getting into that empire should open.

Yet why did they not go *somewhere*? Was there no vessel at all sailing from Calcutta? The situation is obscure, and it is uncertain whether they could get no passage to any country, or whether they were trying to decide on a field that would be satisfactory for permanent work. Without doubt the serious illness of Rice was an important factor; Hall and Nott, too, had

---

[12] In Worcester's instructions to Judson and his associates he had said: "It is still the desire and hope of the board, as it is the expectation of the friends of the mission, that you will find it practicable to make your station in some eligible part of the Empire of Burmah; and we are persuaded that no light reason will prevail on you to disappoint us in this regard." (S. M. Worcester's *Life of Samuel Worcester*, II, p. 243). So Judson's final choice of Burma as his mission field carried out the original wish of the American Board.

been delayed by sickness. Ann wrote in October that her husband was making daily exertions to get away. But at any rate,
the government finally came to the conclusion that they intended to remain in India, and about the middle of November
issued a peremptory order that they should all be sent to England on one of the Company's ships which was soon to sail.
They were forbidden to leave their house without permission,
and they saw their names listed in the newspaper as passengers
in the ship referred to in the order. Hall and Nott had booked
for the Isle of France, but the vessel was delayed and they had
cancelled their passage. Now, however, the ship, *La Belle
Creole,* was ready to sail, and Judson and Rice applied for a
renewal of their own pass. This was granted, but the next day
refused—they must go to England. The *Creole* was to sail in
two days, perhaps the last opportunity they might have to get
away. The case was desperate—what should they do? They
went to the captain of the *Creole,* told their story,[13] and asked
if he would take them without a pass.

"There is my ship," he replied, "do as you like."

They talked it over with their friend Rolt, and decided to
board the *Creole* that night.[14] Rolt secured coolies to carry
their baggage, and toward midnight, when all was dark and
still, they started out. It was a solemn and mysterious procession—Judson presumably in the lead as always, then Nancy,
the coolies with the baggage, Rice, and probably Rolt. Stealth-
ily they made their way through the deserted streets down to
the water-front. The dockyard gates were closed, but some
one opened them to the fugitives, and bidding good-bye to Rolt
they hurriedly slipped in and went aboard. Promptly the next
morning the *Creole* sailed, and the passengers settled down
contentedly for their voyage to the Isle of France, happy that
they had escaped and were on their way to a mission field.

But they were mistaken. For two days they sailed peace-
fully down the river, until they reached the little town of Budge
Budge. There to their dismay a dispatch boat from the government overtook them, with an order forbidding the ship to

---

[13] See the account by Rice, in J. B. Taylor's *Memoir of Rev. Luther Rice,* p. 120.
[14] Saturday, Nov. 21st.

proceed as it had passengers aboard who had been ordered to England. Some one had betrayed them—they were undone!

There was nothing to do but to go ashore. The captain— in the employ of the French and probably eager to get the better of the English Company—obligingly anchored his ship to give them an opportunity to try again for a pass. Rice hurried back to Calcutta, but even his strong powers of persuasion failed; the owner of the vessel was angry at the delay and refused to help. And now the captain sent word that they must remove their baggage so that he could proceed. What should they do? In their anxious fear every European looked like an officer coming to arrest them. To return to Calcutta was to court certain arrest, they could not stay at Budge Budge, the only thing to be done was to go down the river to the next town, Fultah. It was not safe for Judson or Rice to board the *Creole* again, so Nancy went out for the baggage.

Meanwhile Rice set out once again for Calcutta, and Judson started down the river for Fultah in a small boat. Nancy arranged for the baggage, and came ashore at Fultah, where she went to the tavern, secured a room and sat down to wait for her husband. There she was, "a stranger, a female, and unprotected." Would the boat bring the baggage? Where was Adoniram? When would he come? How would she be treated there at the tavern? But then she remembered, "These are some of the many trials attendant on a missionary life, and which I anticipated."

Judson finally arrived. So did Rice. The latter's hazardous last trip to Calcutta had been made to get passage, if possible, in a ship bound for Ceylon which they heard was anchored near Fultah. Perhaps this was the *Commerce,* the very vessel in which Hall and the Notts were fleeing. The two groups were acting independently at the last, each trying as hard as possible to get away, willing to take any chance if only they could avoid being sent home, and could find a foothold for a mission somewhere in that wide eastern world. Hall and Nott, like the Judsons and Rice, were booked to sail to England, but no provision had been made for Roxana Nott. So she had agreed to remain in India until Samuel returned—he was sure he could find a way to get back. She was a heroine. But it was out of such heroism and faith that the modern missionary enterprise arose.

However, in some way Hall and the Notts secured a general pass on the *Commerce,* about to sail for Ceylon and Bombay, and boarded her Friday, November twentieth, the day before the Judsons sailed with Rice on the *Creole.* The *Commerce* remained at anchor several days, and they heard that the police were searching for them. But for some reason they did not come aboard, and the missionaries sailed in safety. At Fultah they passed the *Creole,* and learned that Nancy Judson had just gone ashore. But they could not stop to see their friends, for they feared arrest. Again they were apprehensive when they neared the Company's fleet at the mouth of the river. But as they approached they saw that the ships were already under way. And so they escaped, and went on to Bombay. But their adventures and trials there, and their success in laying the foundations of the first American mission in India, is a story by itself.

Rice failed to get a pass for the *Commerce,* or whatever ship it was. But the tavern-keeper thought he could secure passage for them on a vessel bound for Madras that would be down in a day or two. He knew the captain, he said, and he was sure he could arrange it. The hopes of the fugitives rose again, and eagerly they watched for the ship. It was Sunday when it came and they were spending the day in quiet. But Sabbath calm was forgotten when they saw the ship, and they hurried preparations to go aboard. Alas! the tavern-keeper returned to report that the captain could not take them. Again their hopes were dashed. They had made every effort to get passage, had applied to every boat that passed down the river, wherever it might be going, but every time without success. And now this last appeal had failed. Must they give up? Was their mission to end before it had begun? They sat down to supper that Sabbath evening with heavy hearts.

But scarcely had they taken their seats at the table when a letter was handed to Judson. Hurriedly he opened it. A pass! And for the *Creole!* Who among their friends had induced the magistrate to change his mind? Marshman? Or Chaplain Thomason? Or Mr. Rolt? Or Rice perhaps? They never knew. Enough that they had the pass. But the *Creole* had been gone three days. Perhaps it had already passed out of the river. No matter! They must try to reach it! Supper was forgotten. The baggage was still on the small boat—they would go on that. Call the boatmen! Good-bye, tavern-keeper! Now they are off—it is already dark—seventy miles to Saugur —but there is just the possibility that the *Creole* has anchored there. So pull hard—they must make it if they can! Woman-like, Nancy bears the burden of worry and passes a dreadfully dreary night. But Judson lies down and sleeps. The morning dawns and no *Creole* in sight. A favorable wind helps them along. How slowly the hours creep by! But the anxious day nears its end, and they sight ships anchored at Saugur, at the mouth of the river. Is the *Creole* among them? To be sure— there she is! And soon they are away, safe at last, headed for the Isle of France, their mission field on Madagascar or wher-ever it might be, and their dear friends Samuel and Harriet.

It was a long seven weeks' voyage, with rough weather and an uncongenial ship's company. They had prayers every eve-ning in Judson's room, and worship twice on Sundays. But neither officers nor passengers joined them. Between Sundays they read and studied French, and planned what they would do when once more they were with the Newells.

At last they reached the Isle of France, and as they came to anchor they looked eagerly for their friends. Finally Samuel came alone. And they read in his sorrowful countenance the dreadful news—Harriet was no more! Harriet, the dear friend and girlhood chum of Nancy, her earliest confidant and asso-ciate in her missionary plans—dead!

Gradually the tragic story came out. The *Enterprise* had proved a leaky, unmanageable vessel. After more than a month of sailing and drifting they were still only two-thirds of the way down the coast to Madras. Then they put in at a little port for two weeks, where Harriet had no care but what untrained Indian women could give her. And then followed three slow, miserable, weeks on the sea, full of anxious anticipation. At last, out on the Indian Ocean, three weeks before they could reach the Isle of France, Harriet's day came, and with no one to attend her but her husband she became a mother. The exposure was too much for babe and mother, and first the one and then the other succumbed. Harriet lived a few days after they arrived in port, and died, only nineteen years old, the very day Nancy and Adoniram and Luther Rice sailed from Saugur.

In spite of his sorrow Newell held to his missionary purpose, and in February sailed for Ceylon, and thence to Bombay to join the Notts and Hall. Judson and Rice engaged in Christian work, preaching to the soldiers and visiting in the hospital. But it was soon evident that the Isle of France offered no adequate missionary opportunity. Madagascar was closed to them. Burma seemed impossible. Finally they decided on Penang, in the Straits of Malacca. "O when will my wanderings terminate?" asked Nancy of her journal. "When shall I find some little spot that I can call my home?"

And still another trial faced them. It was determined that Luther Rice should return to America. He had suffered seriously from liver trouble—in Calcutta it had brought him near death—and he still had no relief. A few months at home under skilful medical care would probably cure him. And there was another most important consideration. Someone must stir up the Baptists at home to support and develop the mission which they, the Judsons and Rice, had thrown upon their hands. Who could preach this missionary crusade so well as Rice, giant preacher and orator and organizer? So on the fifteenth of March Rice sailed for America, and Adoniram and Ann were left alone. No wonder that in their loneliness Ann wrote to her sisters, "I want one of you with me very much." Yet neither she nor Adoniram faltered; faith drew them on.

No ship was sailing direct to Penang, so they dared the Company once more and took passage for Madras, arriving in June. A warm welcome was given them by the newly-come English Congregational missionaries, Mr. and Mrs. Loveless. But they knew that their arrival would be reported to the government at Calcutta, and they must get away with all haste. Their friends in Bombay were already feeling the heavy hand of the Company—so they were told—and it would surely fall on them, too, unless they could escape to Penang.

But not a ship for Penang was to be had. Nor a ship for any port whatever—with just one exception. There was a "crazy old vessel," as Judson described it, about to leave for Rangoon. Rangoon! Burma! The very field they had chosen at the beginning. But they had come to think of Burma with feelings of horror. Yet now they had no choice. It was Burma or England. Their Madras friends tried to dissuade them, remembering what they had heard of Burma and noting Nancy's condition. But they commended themselves to God and decided for Burma. Perhaps they could go on from there to Penang. Even if that proved impossible, there was some satisfaction in the thought of a mission to Burma itself, in spite of the probable privations and dangers. No translation of the Bible had been made into Burmese, and might not Judson be able to give it to the people? And would they not be in a land of immense opportunity and need? Besides, their wanderings would at last be at an end. So on June twenty-second they embarked on the *Georgiana,* bound for Rangoon.

Nancy was expecting motherhood, and it was as important for her to have care and speedily find a home as it had been for Harriet Newell. The Lovelesses arranged for a European woman to accompany her on the voyage. But just as the ship was getting under way this woman was suddenly taken ill and fell to the deck, and in a few minutes was dead. It was a terrible shock, but not even this could turn them back. No other woman attendant was available and they sailed without one.

It was a voyage on which they always looked back with horror and sadness; and they had ample cause. They had no cabin, nothing but an apartment made by stretching curtains of canvas. The captain was the only other person aboard who could speak English. The vessel was dangerously unmanageable. Before the trip was more than half over Nancy was prematurely confined and they buried their firstborn in the waters of the Bay of Bengal. Nancy was left dangerously ill and near death's door. The ship was carried far off its course and was threatened with wreck on a cannibal shore, as they passed between the Little and Great Andamans. But this passage saved both the ship and Nancy. For the calm channel relieved her, and on the easterly side of the islands they found favorable winds which quickly carried them on to Rangoon.

On Tuesday, July 13, 1813—it is a historic date—they sailed up the river and dropped anchor off the city of which they had heard so much. At last their long journeyings were over. They had reached their mission field. Their dream had become a reality.

CHAPTER IV

THE STRUGGLE FOR A FOOTHOLD

ADONIRAM and Nancy had dreamed of Rangoon. But they must have thought their dream a nightmare when they looked out on the city that July day. All around the country was flat and uninteresting. Rangoon itself was a wretched-looking place. Heavy rainfall had flooded the city, and from the river it seemed hardly better than a neglected swamp. In front of the city stretched a mud flat. Here and there a few tumbled-down shacks stood up in the mud on posts, with bamboo walls and thatched roofs. A little back from the river there was a stockade of timbers, perhaps eighteen feet high, with a few useless cannon lying at the gateways. Beyond the stockade, in the city, could be seen two or three larger brick houses, two Roman Catholic churches, an Armenian church, and scores of sharply pointed spires of pagodas, large and small. In the distance, rising out of the trees beyond the city, towered in glittering splendor the gold-covered Shwe Dagon Pagoda. Everywhere else there was only a miserable jumble of irregular streets and low, ramshackle huts and houses, a dirty, dismal prospect.

Adoniram went ashore at sunset to take a nearer view of the place which was to be his home and Nancy's. He tramped through the muddy streets and picked his way along the few stretches of brick pavement. He saw and smelt the refuse under the houses, where a confusion of dogs and chickens and crows disputed possession of the feast. Everywhere he was stared at by the people and snarled at by the dogs. Finally he located the mission house where Felix Carey lived. Then he made his way back to the river and the *Georgiana*, with feelings as downcast and dejected as the face of Rangoon itself. As Nancy lay in her berth and they listened to the tinkle of the pagoda bells, they thought of all they were likely to face

63

in this Buddhist land. They talked the situation over, and it all seemed so dark, so cheerless, so unpromising, that they marked that evening down as the most gloomy and distressing they had ever passed. One consolation comforted them: they probably would not last long there, and heaven would be a happier place! But they were wise enough to turn to the One who had led them thus far on their pilgrimage. And talking with Him and of Him brought peace and renewed faith. So they retired to rest contented.

The next morning they went ashore, visited the custom house and were searched, then made their way out of the city to the mission house, some distance north of the stockade. The original mission house had stood not far from the place where the refuse of the city was thrown, with the public execution ground near by, and the enclosure where dead bodies were burned. In 1809, however, a new house had been erected in a different location farther from the city.[1] Close around was a thick growth of trees and vines and bushes that made an ample lurking-place for robbers and wild beasts. But the house itself was pleasantly situated, surrounded by a two-acre garden filled with shade trees, mangoes and other fruit trees. And the house, though unfinished, was large and comfortable. Felix Carey was not at home when the Judsons arrived, but Mrs. Carey gave them a warm welcome. Here for the next few months they all made their home together.

The Judsons, it will be seen, were not the first Christian missionaries to Burma. Indeed, as early as the sixth century Nestorian Christians were reported in Pegu, and Roman Catholic missionaries arrived in the sixteenth century. In 1807 William Carey had sent two missionaries to Rangoon, Chater and Mardon, the latter giving place to Felix Carey later in the year. Chater had retired to Ceylon after four years, and Felix Carey was now in the employ of the government. Another Serampore missionary, Kerr, had also been in Rangoon for a short time, and the London Missionary Society had experimented with two missionaries, Brain and Pritchett. But Brain

---

[1] S. Pearce Carey, in a letter to *The British Weekly*, July 2, 1931.

died soon after his arrival and Pritchett returned to India within a year. It is almost true to say that nothing at all had been done by Protestant missionaries, and as for the Roman Catholics, though they had a considerable following they were required by the government to limit their efforts to the remnants of the early Portuguese population and those of mixed blood. Judson had a clear field among the Burmans.

The first business was learning the language. Felix Carey had done something on a grammar and a dictionary, and these, though unfinished, were a considerable help. In less than a year both Adoniram and Ann could read, write and converse in Burmese with ease, and frequently spent a pleasant evening with Burman friends.

But ordinary fluency would not satisfy Judson. He would have to preach in the language in a way that would be easily understood by the common people. He would have to reason effectively with subtle thinkers concerning the metaphysical and theological teachings of Buddhism and Christianity. He looked forward to translating the Bible into the Burmese. For all this he would need the most thorough knowledge of the language that he could gain. So he put into the task of mastering this foreign tongue the same persistent thoroughness, the passion for excellence, that he put into everything else that he undertook. He gave it first place in his plans. He acquainted himself as widely as possible with Burman literature. There were no printed books, only dried palm leaves, on which the writing was scratched as one continuous word, without break or punctuation. He saturated himself with Buddhist legend and poetry, so that he might understand the language and its thought. For six months he did nothing but transcribe a Pali dictionary, in order to recognize and understand the words brought over by Buddhism from that ancient tongue. Then he went to work on a Burman-English dictionary, to gain and conserve the most complete knowledge of Burmese words. Not for six years did he attempt to preach in public. No wonder that it could be said: "For feeling his way into the heart of a language, and following out its innate principles of development, till the whole structure stood in characteristic form before his eye—in this he has had few equals, and probably no superiors." [2]

Nancy pictures him at his study: "Could you look into a large open room, which we call a veranda, you would see Mr. Judson bent over his table covered with Burman books, with his teacher at his side, a venerable looking man in his sixtieth year, with a cloth wrapped round his middle and a handkerchief round his head. They talk and chatter all day long, with hardly any cessation." But after two years and a half all Judson had to say was, "I just now begin to see my way forward in this language, and hope that two or three years more will make it somewhat familiar!" Yet it was just this untiring drilling, "from sunrise till late in the evening," that made him the master that he became.

Not long after their arrival Judson made a formal call on the viceroy of Rangoon, thinking an acquaintance with him might be advantageous in case any difficulty should arise. But the viceroy scarcely deigned to look at him. When he reported his visit to Ann they were at first apprehensive. But Ann's spirits rose quickly.

"After all," she said, "English *men* are no uncommon sight here in Burma. But an English *female* is quite a curiosity. Leave the matter to me."

So a few days later, with the aid of a French woman, she gained an introduction to the viceroy's wife. The latter received her cordially, seated her on a rug by her side, and talked with her in a friendly way for some time, meanwhile smoking a long silver pipe. Ann even captivated the viceroy himself, who came in carrying an enormous spear, but spoke courteously to her and even asked if she would not have some rum or wine!

Adoniram was waiting for her, and she told him with glee of her pleasant reception.

"Never fear," she said; "if we should get into trouble I can see her, even if you cannot get at the viceroy himself. And I am sure that a small present will secure almost any favor from her."

---

[2] Mrs. H. C. Conant, *The Earnest Man*, p. 152.

So they felt safer and more encouraged.

Later this viceroy was succeeded by one who was very friendly. He gave a dinner one day for all the Europeans in town, including Adoniram and Nancy. Skilful musicians played native instruments like the boat-shaped harps, and the wonderful circle-framed *kyi waing*[3] and *saing waing*,[4] while other performers entertained the guests with dancing and similar attractions. Nancy was asked to show how Americans danced, but pointed out that it was not proper for wives of priests to dance, to which the viceroy's wife agreed. It was evident that the viceroy wanted to be friendly. They taught English to his son for a year, hoping to win him to Christ, but without success.

But they knew that their usefulness would be mostly among the common people, and they were eager to become as closely acquainted with these as possible. Living where they were, however, outside the town and off the road, they had few visitors. Moreover, robbers were infesting the country and were daily growing bolder, making the location dangerous. So after six months they moved to a house inside the walls. But they had been settled in their new home scarcely two months when one Sunday, while they were out at the old mission house spending the day in quiet, a servant came running in excitedly to report that a great fire had broken out. Sure enough, a fire was rushing toward the city and threatening to burn the whole place. Fortunately, they managed to get into the city in time to carry their goods to a safe place, and then moved out once more to their former home in the mission house. Here they continued to live as long as they were in Rangoon.

Felix Carey arrived in April from Calcutta, and delighted Judson and his wife with letters and news from their friends. But he was soon ordered to the capital by the king, and in August started up the Irrawaddy River with Mrs. Carey and

---

[3] Twenty-two gongs or bells hung on a circular frame, placed horizontally, within which the performer sits; or sometimes on a vertical triangular frame, with the performer standing.

[4] Eighteen kettle drums arranged like the *kyi waing;* very carefully tuned, and used for melody playing.

the children. They had not gone far on their journey when the boat upset and all were drowned except Carey himself. News of this tragedy emphasized the sense of isolation which the Judsons felt, increased yet more by the long wait of two years and a half after their sailing from Salem before they had a single letter from home. No wonder they were lonely and often homesick. Occasionally a ship captain would call, but they met few other Europeans. Sometimes they would ride out to the Great Pagoda, and climb to its high platform to look out at the many pagoda spires scattered over the city—they reminded them of the meeting house steeples back in New England. All by themselves they observed the Lord's Supper, and then they were particularly lonely. It cheered them to remember their friends the Notts and Newell and Hall, and correspondence with Newell made them less lonely. But they longed for the return of Luther Rice, and they wrote him often, urging him to come out and join them.

But they had no regrets for coming to far-away Burma. "I do feel thankful that God has brought me to this land," Nancy wrote in her journal. And Adoniram wrote to the Emersons in Beverly, "If 'the world was all before us, where to choose our place of rest,' we should not desire to leave Burma." And to Dr. Baldwin: "I know not that I shall live to see a single convert; but notwithstanding I feel that I would not leave my present situation to be made a king." One can see his face light up with enthusiasm as he writes it.

At first Adoniram and Nancy thought the climate of Rangoon excellent. Nevertheless, Nancy's health soon began to fail, and a voyage to Madras was agreed upon. So that in February, 1815, less than two years after she and her husband had fled from that city, she found herself there again with their friends the Lovelesses. On this trip, as always, she made friends. The Rangoon viceroy allowed her to take a Burman woman with her as an attendant, though the law forbade native women leaving the country. The ship's captain gave her free passage. The doctor in Madras returned the money she sent him. And the Lovelesses and others overwhelmed her with gifts and supplies when she left for Rangoon. Perhaps few things contributed more to Adoniram's success than this friend-making ability of Ann's.

In three months she had regained her health and was back home once more, and with her a little orphan girl, Emily Van Someren, seven years old, whose guardian, a cousin, was a warm friend of all missionaries. Emily brightened the Judson home for six years, rambling among the trees and flowers in the garden, playing with Ann and Adoniram, studying with Ann, and helping about the house, only returning to India in 1821, when Ann went to America.

Five months after Ann's return to Rangoon, on September 11, 1815, a baby came to gladden their home, to whom they gave the great name Roger Williams; Adoniram served as doctor and nurse. But Roger did not stay. Eight months of joy, and then he slipped away to a better land. The Portuguese priest, who had a little medical skill, did his best to save his life, but without avail. He was buried the afternoon he died, in a little grove of mango trees in the garden of the mission house. Many Burmans and Portuguese attended the funeral to show their sympathy, for he was the only legitimate child of foreign parents in Rangoon, and had been of unusual interest to everyone. The wife of the viceroy shared in the general sympathy and friendliness and came with all her retinue, two hundred in number, to comfort Ann. And a few days afterward she invited Ann and her husband to spend a day in the country at a garden of the viceroy's, "that their minds might become cool." The garden was a beautiful place, with fruit trees in abundance, and a wide-spreading banyan under which they sat as they talked and ate. Every kindness was shown them, but it was hard to be comforted.

Judson had no illusions about the task he had undertaken. The glamor of his first enthusiasm at Andover had worn away in the tough experiences through which he had passed. But his faith did not falter. He wrote to Luther Rice, "If they ask, What prospect of ultimate success is there? tell them, As much as there is an almighty and faithful God, who will perform His promise, and no more. If this does not satisfy them, beg them to let me stay and try it, and to let you come, and to give us our bread; or if they are unwilling to risk their bread on

such a forlorn hope as has nothing but the word of God to
sustain it, beg of them at least not to prevent others from giving
us bread; and if we live some twenty or thirty years they may
hear from us again." Years after, on his visit to America, he
made a similar reply to one who asked, "Do you think the
prospects bright for the speedy conversion of the heathen?"
answering promptly, "As bright as the promises of God!"
Francis Wayland put it in a nutshell when he said of Judson's unwavering faith, "He believed that Burma was to be
converted to Christ, just as much as he believed that Burma
existed."

Rice did not come. But on October 15, 1816, three years
and more after Judson and his wife had landed in Rangoon,
George H. Hough and his family arrived, the first recruits for
the mission. It was a red letter day for Adoniram and Ann.
Hough was a printer, and Judson welcomed him eagerly. For
he had two tracts waiting to be printed, one *A View of the
Christian Religion,* which he had written, the other a small
catechism prepared by Ann; and a few chapters of the Gospel
of Matthew were ready in Burmese. The Serampore missionaries had generously sent over to Burma a press and a font of
type, and inside of six months Hough had the tracts in print,
with the first sheets of Matthew.

And now Judson was eager to begin public preaching. But
he felt the need of a Burman Christian associate. One might
be found in Chittagong, he thought, over on the west coast,
where the Baptists of England had carried on a brief mission.
So he decided to take a trip over there, combining mental rest
with an effort to secure a helper or two. A ship, probably
Burmese or Indian, was to sail for Chittagong and return
immediately, a rare occurrence, and he would be away from
home only about three months. So on Christmas Day of 1817
he sailed.

But the ship was unmanageable and the winds were contrary. After a whole month they were still a long distance
from Chittagong. Then to Judson's dismay and bitter disappointment the captain changed his plans and headed across
the Bay for Madras. But the wind and current carried them
off their course and they sailed up and down for another whole

month without being able to reach that city. Then they made
for Masulipatam, farther north. But again they were disappointed, and spent still another month in a fruitless effort
to make port.

By this time their provisions were exhausted and they were
reduced to what they could beg from passing vessels, mostly
mouldy rice and water, and little enough of either. Judson
had been attacked by fever, and lay in his berth half delirious.
At last they managed to get into Masulipatam, twelve weeks
after leaving Rangoon. An English officer took Judson ashore
and cared for him in his own home, and after a few days he
was ready to continue his voyage. But what was his dismay
to learn that his ship was not to sail again for several months.
The only thing to do was to get to Madras, three hundred
miles down the coast—traveling by sedan chair, the only means
of transportation. But on his arrival at Madras he was further
dismayed to find that no vessel had sailed to Rangoon that
year and no one knew when one would sail. There was nothing to do but wait—the hardest thing in the world for Judson.
But the Lovelesses welcomed him to their home once more.
So did Chaplain Thompson of the Company. And they cared
for him so well that he was almost loath to leave when at last,
after more than three months in Madras, he was able to secure
passage on a small English vessel for Rangoon and home.

And what of Ann? She had expected Adoniram back in
three months. But he did not come. Then a boat brought
news from Chittagong that Judson's ship had not been heard
from. After that no further word for four long months. Hope
alternated with despair. Was her beloved husband alive or
dead? She could only hope.

Other troubles added to her anxiety. Hough was ordered
to the courthouse, in hope of extorting money from him. It
was not deemed fitting for a woman to visit the viceroy in his
wife's absence, but Ann courageously broke through custom
and went in person with her appeal; only then was Hough
released. Then cholera broke out, and the death drum could
be heard all day long. To cap the climax, rumors began to
run around that Burma and England were about to go to war
with each other. One after another the English ships in the

river sailed away, until just one was left. Hough became panic-stricken and insisted on fleeing from the land. He urged Ann to go too, pointing out the dangers that would face her if she stayed. She was in a fearful quandary. Was Adoniram alive? Then he was in India and she might find him there. But what if she left and then he were to come and find her gone. She refused to go. But the Houghs insisted, and at last she yielded.

Fortunately the ship's sailing was delayed and she could think the matter through again. This time her courage and faith reasserted themselves and she determined to stay in Rangoon. Hough and his wife did their utmost to dissuade her, but in spite of their appeals she returned alone with Emily to the city and to her deserted home. How large and empty the house seemed! "I know I am surrounded by dangers on every hand, and expect to see much anxiety and distress; but at present I am tranquil, and intend to make an effort to pursue my studies as formerly, and leave the event with God." So she wrote in her loneliness. But her brave, determined stay in Rangoon was of more importance than she could know. It is not unlikely that her decision saved the mission and made possible all of Judson's great work for Burma and the Burmese. The event proved her wisdom, for the Houghs returned from the ship, and at last, on August second, she heard to her infinite joy that her long-lost Adoniram had arrived at the mouth of the river.

But the Houghs persisted in their plans, and shortly afterward left for Calcutta with the press. Once more Adoniram and Nancy were alone. Yet not for long. The very next month, September, 1818, four new missionaries arrived, James Colman and Edward Wheelock with their wives, "four lovely young persons, in every sense of the word," as Judson said.

That was high praise, for Judson had very definite ideas as to the qualifications for missionary service. When he and his friends offered themselves to the American Board the qualifications stressed were good education and deep religious experience. Judson's years as a missionary led him to broaden these simple tests. Only three years after he reached Rangoon he wrote to Luther Rice, "In encouraging other young men to come out as missionaries, do use the greatest caution. One wrong-headed, conscientiously obstinate fellow would ruin us. Humble, quiet, persevering men; men of sound, sterling talents (though perhaps not brilliant), of decent accomplishments and some natural aptitude to acquire a language; men of an amiable, yielding temper, willing to take the lowest place, to be the last of all and the servants of all; men who enjoy much closet religion, who live near to God, and are willing to suffer all things for Christ's sake without being proud of it, these are the men." But he did not underestimate educational qualifications. He urged that "whatever of mental improvement, or of literary or scientific attainment, is desirable in a minister at home, is desirable in a missionary." He urged both a college and a theological course; "for the better the mind is disciplined and stored with knowledge, the more efficient workman he may humbly hope to become." And finally, after costly experience, he added to these qualifications sound health, which in the early days was scarcely thought of at all.

Colman and Wheelock did not measure up to this last qualification, but their coming gave Judson and his wife new courage and enthusiasm.

How had Judson been supported during these five years? What was his relation to the churches back in America? It is time that we recalled Luther Rice, who left Adoniram and Ann at the Isle of France to return to America.

Rice was warmly welcomed by the Baptist leaders, Thomas Baldwin and Daniel Sharp in Boston and Lucius Bolles in Salem. He found that on the very day after the ordination in Salem the Baptist church of that city had initiated a plan out of which had grown the Salem Bible Translation and Foreign Mission Society, probably the result of a suggestion Judson had made to Bolles at the service of ordination. And Baldwin and Sharp, immediately on hearing from Judson that he had become a Baptist, had taken steps to form a society to support him and his wife, the Baptist Society for Propagating the Gospel in India and Other Foreign Parts.

The trustees of this Boston society had promptly appointed Judson and Ann as their missionaries. At first, like the Congregationalists, they had thought of a cooperative mission with the English, and had proposed to the Baptist Missionary Society of England that that society appoint Judson as their missionary, to work with the Serampore group and under their direction, their salaries and expenses being paid by the American Baptists. Fortunately the English Baptists advised the Americans to form their own society. Word of his appointment by the Boston society did not reach Judson until nearly a year and a half after his withdrawal from the American Board. Meanwhile all the expenses of the mission were provided by Serampore. Without the aid of the English mission, with its ample resources, their situation would have been hazardous in the extreme. The Serampore missionaries added also a spiritual contribution, for once a month they met in prayer for the new mission in Burma.

If Judson was the leader in the mission abroad, Rice was as great in its leadership at home. He has been seriously underestimated, on account of the financial failure of the educational enterprise[5] with which he and the board became connected. But to him more than to any other man was it due that the Baptists of the United States became a denomination. And to him more than to any other was it due that they caught a vision of their world task and opportunity. What he did grows in magnitude when we remember that Baptists were not concentrated in one section of the country, but were spread from Massachusetts to Georgia. Rice was the man for the hour, and it was providential that he came home, and that he came when he did. In place of the local New England society as the promoter of the new mission he proposed a national organization, and gave himself to the stirring of the Baptists of the country with a thrilling enthusiasm and a tireless persistence that have never been surpassed in like service. Commanding in presence, impressive and powerful in public speech, daring in his conception and presentation of Christian duty, persuasive and compelling in personal influence, with social and conversational qualities that made him welcome everywhere, Rice went up and down the land from Massachusetts and New York to Virginia and Georgia, preaching and pleading, organizing and collecting, until he had aroused the churches, had led them in

---

[5] Columbian College, now George Washington University, Washington, D. C.

the formation of The General Missionary Convention of the Baptist Denomination in the United States of America for Foreign Missions, and had placed the mission of Judson upon a permanent and secure foundation. It was a disappointment to Judson that Rice did not return to the mission field. He intended to do so, and wanted to go, but he was too much needed at home. And that was his place. Among the factors that made Judson successful in Burma must be reckoned Luther Rice in America.

The Board of Foreign Missions of the Convention appointed Rice and Judson as its foreign missionaries. But it was not until September of 1815, sixteen months after the action had been taken, that Judson learned of his appointment.

Judson had welcomed every opportunity to speak of Christ and the Christian faith. From time to time people made their way out to the mission house, in spite of its isolation, to inquire about the new religion. Sometimes he would have quite a company present, and he would explain clearly and in no un-certain terms the difference between his faith and Buddhism, and tell with eagerness the story of Christ. Ann likewise had frequent visitors, sometimes fifteen or twenty, to whom she read the Bible and talked about God and Christ.

But now Judson was prepared to begin the proclamation of the Christian message in public. He was the only one pre-pared. Hough had left the country. Rice had not been able to return. Colman and Wheelock had come, but neither could yet use the Burmese. And inside of a year Wheelock left for Calcutta in hopes of better health and in a delirium jumped overboard and was drowned. Judson had appealed vigorously for reinforcements—"five men is the smallest number that will possibly answer"—but only Colman was now with him. He himself must certainly begin to preach.

For the proclaiming of his religion Judson adopted the method of the Burmans themselves: he built a zayat. This is a kind of building found in almost every Burman village, where the men may gather to talk and smoke, or travelers may sleep, or a Buddhist monk or teacher may talk to his followers or lead them in the reciting of their prayers. Adopting this idea, Judson determined to have a Christian zayat, where he could converse with those who might come, and hold regular services of worship. A place of this sort was especially needed in view of the retired location of the mission house. Fortunately he was able to secure a piece of ground adjoining the mission premises, and fronting on Pagoda Road, one of the main streets, which was lined with small pagodas and homes and led out to the great Shwe Dagon Pagoda; here he built his zayat. The street was always crowded with passers-by, men in their gorgeous silk waistcloths, white jackets and brilliant turbans; women in their skirts of red or green or gold, their bright-colored scarfs, and their red or white flowers tucked attractively into their black tresses; yellow-robed monks making their way solemnly along, with hands under their begging bowls and eyes fastened on the ground before them; immigrants from India and wild visitors from the frontier; sometimes, too, Buddhist processions with their bands—drums, clappers, cymbals and flageolots. Judson would not lack for people.

Compared with most of the zayats of the city his was a very modest one. Some were elaborate, with carving and decoration and a succession of roofs rising one above another. But this first Protestant Christian gathering-place in Burma was very simple, only twenty-seven by eighteen feet in size, with three small rooms. The front room was really a large veranda, nine feet deep and the full width of the zayat, and was entirely open to public view. Here Judson could sit at his little table, bought by Rice at the Isle of France, read the scripture to any who would stop to listen, and explain the new religion to those who would come up and sit with him. Back of this was a larger room made of whitewashed boards, in which worship could be held and a boys' class could meet. At the rear was a small room or entry, leading to the garden of the mission house, and here Ann might hold her women's classes. Sunday, April 4, 1819, marked the beginning of a new era for the mission, for on that day Judson called together some of the neighbors and held the first worship and preaching service in the zayat. Three weeks later he took his seat on the veranda for the first time and began to invite the people to come up and talk with him about the Christian religion.

The first congregation consisted of fifteen persons besides a number of children. It was a disorderly crowd, very inattentive, and not at all promising. But in just a month there was a convert—Maung Nau, the first evangelical Christian in Burma. Two years before this Judson had told with glee of the first genuine inquirer, and since then others had considered the teaching seriously, both men and women. But Maung Nau, almost from the first time that he visited the zayat, was ready to become a Christian. He was about thirty-five, a man of moderate ability, with no family and quite poor, an employe of a timber merchant. He was quiet and reserved, modest and teachable, and day after day came to the zayat and sat for hours listening to Judson. Finally he wrote a letter to the missionaries, confessing his faith and asking for baptism; and on June twenty-seven, after the usual Sunday service at the zayat, the little company of seven retired to a large pond near by, and there among the lotus and the water lilies, with a great image of the Buddha silently looking down from the bank, the first Burman convert confessed his Saviour in baptism. It was the beginning of the Protestant church in Burma. The next Sunday, July fourth, Burman and American Christians sat down together at the Lord's Supper. The hope of years was fulfilled.

It was a motley procession of visitors that Judson had from day to day. Once several Moslems came in, one a mufti. A number of times Buddhist priests visited him. A keen doctor came again and again. And one night during Buddhist Lent a virulent opposer brought a large crowd, and they made a great uproar with their threats and denunciations.

Slowly the number of converts grew. Maung Tha Hla was the second, a rather superior and well-read man. Another was Maung Bya, a middle-aged man who had learned to read in the evening school at the zayat. Others, too, were inquiring.

In spite of crowded days at the zayat Judson kept on with the translating of the New Testament. Ephesians followed Matthew, then The Acts. He was as thorough in this as in everything that he did, and it was exactly ten years, less one day, from the landing in Rangoon to the completion of the New Testament: July 12, 1823. Meanwhile he prepared an Epitome of the Old Testament, largely in the words of the

Bible itself, for use until he could provide the whole. The dictionary, too, was finished.[6] Ann turned her attention to the thousands of Siamese in Rangoon, and learned their language well enough so that by 1819 she had translated the Gospel of Matthew, the *View of the Christian Religion,* and her catechism.

All this looked as though they were gaining a foothold. But any progress meant a constant struggle. Every convert had to face the possibility of persecution, perhaps death. And Judson knew perfectly well that if it became known that Burmans were turning from Buddhism to Christianity through his efforts, he and Ann might have to suffer as well. They had experienced more than one annoyance from the underlings of the government. And a prominent Buddhist teacher, meeting them one morning as they were taking their customary ride out to the mineral tank beyond the Great Pagoda for their daily bath, had peremptorily ordered them not to ride there again or they would be beaten—an order which Judson afterwards learned had issued from the the viceroy himself at the instigation of this influential Buddhist leader.

More important, however, was the persecution which threatened the converts. The danger grew increasingly evident, and everyone became afraid to talk with Judson in the presence of others. Maung Shwe Ngone, a notable inquirer, was accused of heresy, and when the viceroy ordered, "Inquire further about him," he hastened to put himself right with those at the top and kept away from the zayat for some time. All were afraid. And with good reason. Persecution was sure. Death was probable.

It began to be whispered to Judson that he had better not stay in Rangoon and talk to common people, but go directly to the king, "the lord of life and death." If he approved, the new faith would spread rapidly. Without his approval what hope was there? Judson was none too sanguine of a favorable result from an appeal to the king. But a new monarch, Bagyidaw, had ascended the throne and might prove tolerant; and

---

[6] It was published in 1826, but was unsatisfactory and only preparatory to his greater work later.

certainly there was no prospect of success under conditions as they were. Secretary Baldwin had been consulted and he had approved an appeal. Finally Judson and Colman decided to go up to the capital and present their case to the king. So they applied to the viceroy for a pass "to go up to the golden feet and lift up their eyes to the golden face." Of course a present had to be taken—nothing could ever be expected from any official, however friendly, unless one first gave him a present —and a copy of the English Bible was decided upon, in six volumes, each enclosed in a rich wrapper and covered with gold leaf. This for the king. For other officials there were less elaborate gifts.

On the twenty-first of December, 1819, they pushed off from Rangoon, soon rounded Pagoda Point, and the city was left behind. At first they passed through a thick jungle. Then this disappeared and the country stretched away on either side in a flat plain, with here and there paddy fields, banana plantations and orchards, and a scattering of dillenia trees with their showy flowers. Along the river banks were tall rushes or cane brakes eight or ten feet high, full of pestiferous mosquitoes, as they soon found out. Occasionally they passed a thatched roof house, standing up on its posts as if on stilts. After they came out from the Rangoon River upon the Irrawaddy their way wound among islands of sand, while on either hand could be seen indigo fields and groves of mango and peepul trees or clumps of bamboo. Ducks and geese appeared along the banks, with occasionally a crocodile; while parrots, green wild pigeons, peacocks and other birds of brilliant plumage flitted across the landscape. Often deer could be seen skipping over the fields, and monkeys swung from trees on the bank. As they neared Prome the hills closed in upon the river, and the rocky banks rose abruptly two or three hundred feet, overhung with trees of variegated foliage. Above Prome there were tall palmyra trees with their graceful drooping fronds, and a glimpse now and then of a small monastery almost hidden in a grove of tamarind or peepul. Travel was slow, only ten miles a day, but Judson keenly enjoyed the scenery, and even the threat of robbers at one place did not spoil the trip. At Pagan, the ancient capital, they stopped for a day to view the remarkable array of ruined temples and pagodas, stretching eight miles along the river, and Judson climbed to the top of one temple a hundred feet high to take in the extensive view. Numerous towns and villages were passed, and Judson thought of the people and longed to tell them the wonderful story of Christ. At last they passed Old Ava, and on January twenty-fifth, after five weeks on the river, they reached Amarapura, or New Ava, then the capital.

The next day they called upon the former viceroy of Rangoon and asked leave "to behold the golden face." That night they lay down in sleepless anxiety. "Tomorrow's dawn will usher in the most eventful day of our lives. Tomorrow's eve will close on the bloom or the blight of our fondest hopes. Yet it is consoling to commit this business into the hands of our heavenly Father—to feel that the work is His, not ours. . . . Thy will, O God, be ever done; for Thy will is inevitably the wisest and the best." So wrote Judson in his journal.

The next morning they made their way along the broad, tamarind-shaded streets to the palace, where they were ushered into the presence of Maung Za, one of the private ministers of state. He was to introduce them to the king. They told him their mission, gave him their petition, and he was reading it when someone announced that "the golden foot was about to advance." Only then did they learn that they had happened on an unpropitious day for presenting their petition. For his majesty was about to view a celebration in honor of a recent victory of the Burmese arms, and was not likely to be interested in an appeal from foreigners and potential enemies. But it was too late to alter their plans. King Bagyidaw came in and they knelt with the others. Every head but theirs was in the dust, but theirs they held erect, with their eyes on him. At once they attracted his attention, holding up their heads as they did, and dressed in long white surplice-like gowns, and he asked who they were.

"The teachers, great king," replied Judson.

"What! you speak Burmese? When did you come? Are you teachers of religion? Are you like the Portuguese priest?"

It was a rapid barrage of questions that the king threw at them, and Judson answered them all. Then their petition was read aloud by Maung Za, requesting permission to preach their religion, and toleration for Burman converts. The king took it and read it for himself, then handed it back. As he did so Judson gave Maung Za an abridged copy of the tract, *A View of the Christian Religion,* which the king took and began to read. Now Judson was all anxiety—"Have mercy on Burma! Have mercy on her king!" The king read only the first two sentences: "There is one Being who exists eternally. . . . Besides this, the true God, there is no other God." Then with disdain he threw the tract on the ground. A Burman assistant opened one of the volumes of the Bible and held it up, but the king took no notice.

That was the end. "Why do you ask for such permission?" said Maung Za, interpreting the king's attitude. "Have not the Portuguese, the English, the Moslems, and people of all other nations, liberty to worship according to their own customs? In regard to the objects of your petition, His Majesty gives no order. As to your sacred books, His Majesty has no use for them; take them away."

So ended their high hopes. They were hustled out of the palace with little ceremony. Then to the home of the Portuguese priest, who served as the king's physician, to discover whether they had any medical skill that might be useful to his majesty. Finally they returned through the sun and the dust to their boat.

Even after this failure of their plans they were not discouraged, but tried again the next day, assisted by a friend, Mr. G——,[7] formerly collector of the port at Rangoon. They went to see Maung Za, and G—— urged every argument, but without avail. Night had fallen as they made their way back to the boat again, a weary four miles. The darkness seemed the very extinction of their hopes, and Judson in his journal that night quoted the closing lines of Milton's "Paradise Lost," adapting them to Colman and himself, driven as they were from what had seemed in imagination another Eden:

---

[7] The full name is not given anywhere. Clement *(Memoir of Adoniram Judson)* incorrectly assumes that this was Gouger, or Gauger as he spells it. But Gouger was not in Ava or Amarapura until three years after this.

"Some natural tears we dropped, but wiped them soon;
The world was all before us, where to choose
Our place of rest, and Providence our guide."

But their spirits rose again with the dawn, and Judson sent another petition to Mr. G—— to present to Maung Za. That day was the Sabbath, and they stayed quietly in their boat. Monday brought G—— and Maung Za's reply: "Tell them there is not the least possibility of obtaining their object, should they wait ever so long; let them go about their business." Even then they would not give up; they would send the tract to Maung Za. And G—— promised to do his best. As a last resort they appealed to Rodgers, a Rangoon friend who was later to be a fellow prisoner of Judson's in Ava; but he was out of favor and could do nothing.

It was useless to wait longer. They applied for a passport, and after a week of effort and present-making the desired palm-leaf was secured and they started back to Rangoon. Judson had failed in his great effort to obtain toleration. Again and again throughout his life he was to renew his effort, and always to fail. Yet neither now nor later did his faith and his hopeful spirit fail him: "Something better will turn up tomorrow," he wrote in his journal.

But on the way down the river one of those brief fits of depression overtook him into which he was so prone to fall— reaction from his intense enthusiasm. What hope was there? The king had forbidden them to preach the Christian faith. No Burman would dare to come near them, much less accept Christianity. Would it not be best to leave Rangoon and go to Arracan, where, under the protection of the East India Company's government, they could preach to the Burman population without molestation?

But when he reached Rangoon and presented the plan to the little group of converts they instantly rejected it. "Stay with us a few months," they urged. "Stay till there are eight or ten disciples. Then appoint one to be the teacher. We shall not be concerned with the result after that. If you should leave the country then the religion would spread of itself; the king himself cannot stop it." And some who were not yet members of the church joined in the plea.

So strong was their urging that Judson yielded. Colman and his wife should go to Chittagong and establish a new station, so that if Rangoon had to be given up they could go there. But he and Ann would stay. Once more they took up their work, and the next Sunday resumed worship in the zayat—though with doors closed. A month later the Colmans left for Calcutta and Chittagong,[8] and again Adoniram and Nancy were alone.

Yet they were not alone. There were three baptized converts. And a week after the Colmans left a fourth was baptized, Shwe Ba, under cover of the darkness. Of their own accord, the disciples went to the zayat and held a prayer meeting. By July the number had increased to nine. One of them was Maung Ing, a fisherman, whose devotion and faithfulness during the terrible Ava days were to save their lives. Another was Ma Min Hla, the first woman convert. She was of unusual ability, and had spent ten years trying diligently to find God, but in vain. Then she had learned to read in order, if possible, to discover in the sacred Buddhist books the help she sought. Finally she had happened on one of Judson's tracts and had found her way to the true Saviour.

Perhaps the most interesting disciple was Maung Shwe Ngone, a teacher of high standing, outwardly a Buddhist, but very liberal, half deist half sceptic. He had thought deeply along philosophical and metaphysical lines, and was keen and subtle in argument. Judson spent whole days discussing with him such fundamental questions as the existence of an eternal Being, the idea of the atonement, and the authority of the Christian scriptures, and found that his own thorough learning, skilful logic and mastery of the Burmese tongue met a keen test and proved their worth. After months of study of the new faith, going at it from every possible angle, Maung Shwe Ngone accepted the teaching and became a Christian.

When the day came for Judson and his wife to sail for Calcutta there were ten baptized converts and nearly a hundred

---

[8] Colman died in 1822, while Judson and Price were at Ava.

other disciples and friends to see them off. For they found they must go to Calcutta for medical aid for Ann, on whom liver trouble had laid its hand. They sailed in July of that year, 1820, and spent "a very quiet and happy sojourn" of two months in Serampore with the Houghs, besides a month in Calcutta with the Lawsons, fellow passengers of Rice on the *Harmony,* and Mr. and Mrs. Townley of the London Missionary Society. Ann rapidly improved in health, and in November they set sail once more for Rangoon, on a crowded, dirty little brig. After a long, distressing voyage of six weeks they were happy to catch sight of the Elephant, the well-named grove at the mouth of the Rangoon River. Shortly they were home again, eagerly greeted by the disciples.

The former friendly viceroy was back in Rangoon once more. And an incident that soon occurred encouraged them to hope for toleration under his regime. The priests and officials of Shwe Ngone's village made a conspiracy to destroy him, and Shwe Ngone, learning of their plans, prepared to flee for his life. Finally his enemies went to the viceroy and complained that Shwe Ngone was trying in every way to turn the priests' rice pot bottom upwards.

"What of it?" replied the viceroy. "Let them turn it back again."

The conspiracy evaporated at once, Shwe Ngone breathed freely once more, and all the disciples felt that they were safe.

Other advances could be reported also. Ma Min Hla opened a school in her own home, to keep the boys and girls from going to the Buddhist priest's school. The Tuesday and Friday evening prayer meetings were resumed. The zayat was reopened, with good congregations. An English service was begun, for the few European residents. Judson was able to continue his translating of the New Testament and to begin a revision. And he spent many an evening with the new converts, reading the Bible and showing the location of biblical scenes on a map which he had made.

But Ann's liver trouble had returned, and in spite of continual salivation she rapidly grew worse. Adoniram was faced with the alternative of sending her to America or losing her altogether. So on August 21, 1821, she embarked once more for

Calcutta, taking with her Emily Van Someren, who was going back to her former home in Madras. It was with pathos as well as humor that Judson wrote to Hough, "I send you herewith Mrs. Judson, and all that remains of the blue pill and senna, and beg that you will see the articles well packed and shipped for America by the earliest safe opportunity. . . . For ten days or a fortnight we were laid by with fever, unable to help one another; and since we became convalescent I have been occupied in making up my mind to have my right arm amputated, and my right eye extracted, which the doctors say are necessary to prevent a decay and mortification of the whole body conjugal."

They were indeed one. Adoniram Judson cannot be mentioned without Ann. Apart from her his story would have been very different. Her adventurous nature had been a source of worry to her mother in her childhood days, but it was one of the qualities that made possible her joining so gladly with Adoniram in his missionary enterprise. Again and again it gave her courage when both sorely needed courage. And she never lost her happy, vivacious spirit, in spite of trials and discomforts and sorrows. Her winsomeness and attractiveness often won an opening when the future looked like a solid wall, and she was always the magnet that eagerly drew Adoniram back to his home. She had a radiant joy in her religious life, and a deep and genuine faith, well expressed in a letter to her sister Mary: "A little sacrifice for the cause of Christ is not worth naming; and I feel it a privilege, of which I am entirely undeserving, to have had it in my power to sacrifice my all for Him who hesitated not to lay down His life for sinners. I rejoice that I had a pleasant home, dear friends, and flattering prospects to relinquish, and that once in my life I had an opportunity of manifesting my little attachment to the cause of Christ."

Her visit to America revealed again her remarkable ability to make friends. Francis Wayland, who became intimately acquainted with her during this visit, says that he never remembered meeting a more remarkable woman—such clearness of intellect, such powers of comprehension, such intuitive sagacity, such womanly delicacy, such impressive religious feeling. She had a quiet reserve; but when she talked about her beloved Burma, "her eye kindled, every feature was lighted up with enthusiasm, and she was everywhere acknowledged to be one of the most fascinating of women."

From September, 1822, to July, 1823, she was in her home land. But the rigors of the New England climate and the excitement of meeting the many old friends so exhausted her strength, that after only six weeks in her dear Bradford she found that she must go south if she was to have any hope of regaining health and returning to Burma. Adoniram's brother Elnathan invited her to come to Baltimore, where he was a naval surgeon, and take a course of treatment under his direction. She accepted, and went by way of Providence. There she met "Mr. B.," undoubtedly Nicholas Brown, who invited her to his home, took her to her boat in his chaise, and offered to give her and other missionaries free passage to India the following spring in one of his ships, which he expected would be sailing then. So through Ann, Adoniram comes back to two of the sources of his interest in India and the east, Providence and Nicholas Brown.

In Baltimore she scarcely left her room throughout the winter. But she was able to finish an account of the Burma mission, in the unique form of letters to her English friend and benefactor, Mr. Butterworth, in whose home she had stayed on her way to America. In the spring she went to Washington to oversee the printing of her book, *A Particular Relation of the American Baptist Mission to the Burman Empire,* and remained to attend the sessions of the Triennial Convention. There undoubtedly she once more met Luther Rice. What a day of days that meeting must have been for both of them!

At last in late spring she went north to prepare for sailing. Her health was only partially restored, and many urged her to remain in America another year, or to go to England. But she was insistent on returning, whatever might be the result to her. She had some almost prophetic forebodings. But what if she had not returned to Burma!

On Sunday, June twenty-first, with the newly appointed missionaries Jonathan and Deborah Wade, she sailed from Boston on the ship *Edward Newton,* Captain Bertody, and on

October nineteenth reached Calcutta. Friends in that city entreated her not to go to Rangoon on account of the threat of war between India and Burma. But she pressed forward, and on Friday, the fifth of December, she and the Wades arrived at the city of the Great Pagoda. Who could not share Adoniram's feelings after the long separation: "I had the inexpressible happiness of welcoming Mrs. Judson once more to the shores of Burma." And he wrote with delight to a friend, "It is the Ann Hasseltine of other days!"

CHAPTER V

THE TRAGEDY OF AVA

JUDSON had spent four busy months in Rangoon after that August day when he waved good-bye to Ann. In December, Dr. Jonathan Price and his wife and child arrived. Price was a tall, raw-boned fellow, with hair and ideas that bristled in every direction. Mrs. Price lived only five months, then was laid to rest beside baby Roger in the garden of the mission house. In January Hough and his family had returned from Calcutta, and he and Judson and Price eagerly made plans for the future.

Dr. Price picked up the language rapidly, and began at once to practice medicine. He specialized in eye surgery, and his success in removing cataracts gave him a fame that soon reached Ava. The king heard of this new wonder worker, and sent him a summons to come to the capital, which meant that Judson would have to go too, as Price was new to the country and the language. However, there was just the chance that Price's medical knowledge might open the way for the toleration for which Judson prayed night and day. So leaving the Houghs in charge in Rangoon, Judson and Price set out on August twenty-eighth for Ava, the new capital, in a boat provided by the government, and a month later reached the golden city.

Price was given a hearty welcome by the king. But not Judson; for several days he was not noticed. Then one day the king asked him,

"You in black, who are you?"

Judson told him. And then——

"Have any accepted your religion?"

The question he had feared! What would be the consequences when the king heard that some had renounced their national faith for Christianity? But he had to tell the truth, and replied,

"Some foreigners and some Burmans."

Judson trembled. The king was silent a minute or two, then went on with other questions. Nothing happened. Was toleration coming? But it was several weeks before the king noticed him again.

With his usual ability for getting close to people of high station as well as low, Judson soon made the acquaintance of members of the court, and secured a piece of land on the bank of the river, just outside the city, where he put up a small temporary house to show that he intended to stay. Price, too, was assigned land, across the river in Sagaing, and built a home for himself. The king gradually grew friendly with Judson, and invited him to bring his wife and settle in Ava. A number in the court and among the common people began to show a real interest in the Christian message. By January (1823) Judson had accomplished all he had planned, and felt that he had been able to lay a good foundation for future work. Promising the king that he would soon return, with his wife, he bade good-bye to Price, and after a fast seven days' trip reached home on Sunday, February second. There he threw himself once more into his translating, and on the twelfth of July he completed the New Testament.

Everything was ready for the return to Ava when Ann arrived on the fifth of December, and a week later she and Adoniram were on their way. Those were not idle tales that Ann had heard in Calcutta about a possible outbreak of war. The Burman king had charged the English with protecting political fugitives, and war was indeed imminent. So when Judson and Ann arrived in Ava in January of 1824, they found things very different from what they had been when he left but a short time before. Dr. Price was out of favor. All foreigners were under suspicion. The king treated Judson coldly. And the queen, who had expressed eagerness for Ann's coming, paid no attention to her at all. What this might portend they could only guess. The best they could do was to begin missionary work, build a permanent house, and thus, if possible, convince the government that they had nothing to do with the threatening war.

In two weeks they had finished a wooden house with three

small rooms and a veranda, built up on posts four feet off the ground in accordance with the custom. Here every evening they held worship in Burmese. Here Ann opened a school for girls, teaching them to read and sew, the nucleus being two daughters of the convert Shwe Ba, whom she named Mary and Abby Hasseltine, after her sisters; one was supported by the Judson Association of Bradford Academy. On Sundays they went over to Dr. Price's house in Sagaing and had a service in English, Judson doing the preaching. A welcome member of the little congregation was Henry Gouger, a young Englishman of twenty-five, who had recently established himself in trade, and was much attracted to Judson and his wife. He and Judson quickly became friends, and through him they secured from time to time the money they needed from the board's agent in Calcutta.

But conditions were threatening. On the way up the river Judson and Ann had passed a fleet of golden war boats, crowded with soldiers. Each boat was eighty to one hundred feet long, with fifty or sixty rowers, who were singing their war song as they rowed—a thrilling but disturbing sight. And they had seen the army of the chief general encamped on a road leading to the British province of Arracan. Soon after their arrival in Ava a gorgeous celebration was held, when the city was formally dedicated as the capital in place of Amarapura, and they had joined the gay throng in the palace grounds, hoping that the occasion would make the king friendly. But to their dismay he had ordered that no foreigner should enter the palace except Lanciego, the Spanish collector of the port at Rangoon. Judson and his wife could not help being anxious.

Such was the situation on Sunday the twenty-third of May when Judson and Ann and Henry Gouger went across the river to Sagaing for their customary worship at Dr. Price's home. The service was unusually impressive. The tinkling pagoda bells made them think of the churches at home. The retirement of the place, the great river which they could glimpse through the trees, the insignificant number of their little company, the dark storm that they knew was gathering about them, and the uncertainty of the future, all combined to make them feel the need for wisdom and help from above. So they entered with deep feeling into the worship.

But just as the service ended, their quiet was rudely interrupted. A messenger rushed in with the woeful tidings that an English fleet had bombarded Rangoon and had taken the city. The war had begun!

Here was a threat for every foreigner in Ava. There were many, Chinese, Indians and others, but only nine Europeans. Two were Englishmen, Gouger and Rodgers. The latter was a former officer on a Company ship, who had had trouble with his superior and had fled to Burma, and for forty years had been in the service of the king. A third was a Scotchman, Captain Laird, formerly commander of a vessel engaged in local trade, but now a lumber agent for the king's brother, who had had him arrested and brought to Ava when war threatened. A fourth was Lanciego the Spaniard, recently come to the capital with his annual return of Rangoon port duties. A fifth was an Armenian, Arakeel, a young merchant. A sixth was Constantine, a Greek, rather old and afflicted with leprosy. The three others were Dr. Price and the Judsons. Ann was the only white woman. Rodgers had an Anglo-Burman wife, and Price had married a native woman of Siamese extraction. Judson and Ann knew all of the Europeans except Arakeel and Constantine. But Gouger was the only one who was sympathetic with the missionaries. He spent many an evening at the Judson home, and had an admiration for both Judson and his wife which was to grow steadily through the months that were to come.

Events moved rapidly. As soon as news of the British attack reached Ava a second army was organized and sent off with singing and dancing and a great hurrah. Then Gouger, Laird and Rodgers were examined and put in confinement. Judson and Price were given a searching examination, but were allowed to return home. Finally Gouger's accounts were looked into, and it was found that Judson and Price had received money from him. Ha! they must be spies. "Arrest them!" ordered the king.

That was Tuesday, June 8, 1824—Judson never forgot the date. They were just about to sit down to dinner when in rushed a dozen men. The officer in charge carried an ominous looking black book. One of the men had a round spot or ring tattooed on each cheek—"Spotted Face" Ann called him— marking him as a criminal turned executioner.

"Where is the teacher?" demanded the officer.

"Here I am," replied Judson, stepping forward.

"You are called by the king," said the officer—and Ann trembled, for the words meant "You are arrested."

Instantly Spotted Face seized Judson, threw him on the floor, and began to bind his arms tightly behind him with a small cord. Ann seized his arm.

"Stop!" she cried. "I will give you money."

For she knew how terrible could be the torture of that cord, drawn back so tight that one could scarcely breathe, often dislocating the shoulders, sometimes making the sufferer's blood run from nose and mouth, a torture that frequently ended in death.

"Take her too!" was the officer's answer.

But Judson pleaded that she might remain till further orders came. Spotted Face did not reply, but pulled Judson to his feet, disregarded the entreaties of Ann and her offers of silver, and dragged his victim off, amidst the shouting and confusion of the crowd outside, the crying of the little Burman girls, and the silent astonishment of the two servants.[1]

"Take this money! Save the teacher from torture!"

And Ann hurriedly dispatched Maung Ing to follow his master, and help him if possible. But soon he was back, to report that the money was refused, that Spotted Face had thrown her husband on the ground and drawn the cord tighter, that the gang had dragged him before the governor at the court house, that the king's order had been read committing the teacher to Let-ma-yoon prison, and that he had been hustled over to the prison, thrown inside, and had been seen no more.

Let-ma-yoon! "Hand-shrink-not!" It was the terrible name of the death prison. Judson had been taken there! O,

---

[1] The sources for the story of the experiences in Ava and Aungbinle are Ann's letter to Judson's brother Elnathan (Wayland, I, p. 334), reminiscences told by Judson to Wayland (Wayland, I, p. 374), and Gouger's *Personal Narrative*. Price wrote an account, but this adds nothing to the others.

what possible hope was there? Why had they come to this dreadful place? Had not Henry Gouger been right in insisting that they were courting martyrdom in staying there? Ann could only go into her room and try to get some peace of mind by committing Adoniram and herself to God and imploring strength for whatever trial might be awaiting them.

But soon she was interrupted. The magistrate was on the veranda with a crowd of followers, calling to her to come out and be examined. Hurriedly she seized all her letters and journals and all other writings that she could find and destroyed them, so that the magistrate might not find anything that he could use against her or Adoniram. Then she went out and answered one after another the searching questions that were hurled at her. At last the officer went off, leaving ten of his men in charge, with orders to let no one go out or in.

Ann passed a terrible night. She barred the doors, but the ruffians demanded that she unbar them and come out or they would break the house down. Ann, on her part, threatened to report them to the magistrate. They retaliated by seizing the servants and putting them in the stocks. Their cries of pain were too much for Ann, and she promised money in the morning if the guards would release them. They finally agreed. But all through the dark night she had to listen to their wild carousings and diabolical language, while constantly she thought of Adoniram and his possible fate.

It was hardly light the next morning when she called Maung Ing, and succeeded in sending him off to find out about Adoniram and carry him food. Before long he returned, with the news that not only Judson but Dr. Price and all the other white foreigners except Lanciego were in the death prison, each manacled with three fetters. And she herself was a prisoner and could not help! Throughout the day she made repeated efforts to leave the house in order to appeal to some member of the government, but without success. She sent a note to one of the king's sisters, enlisting her aid, but without avail. Then another dreadful night, though a little quieter than the previous one, as she tactfully provided tea and cigars for the guard and they did not disturb her. But she could not sleep.

The next day she sent a message to the governor—"governor of the north gate of the palace"—asking that she might be allowed to visit him with a present. At once he sent orders to let her come. He received her pleasantly, but explained that he could not release the prisoners.

"But my chief secretary here"—nodding his head to an evil-looking man near by—"can make the teachers more comfortable."

Ann turned to him. "What must I do?" she asked.

"Pay me two hundred ticals,[2] two pieces of fine cloth, and two handkerchiefs, and I can relieve your husband."

"I have some money with me," said Ann, "but nothing else, and my house is two miles away."

At last the rapacious secretary agreed to take the money without the cloth or handkerchiefs, and promised to make the teachers less uncomfortable.

When Judson was shoved through the gate of the prison yard he was met by the chief jailer—everyone called him "Father"—who led him to a block of granite, where three pairs of fetters were pounded on his ankles, and he was shuffled along to the prison house. Here a savage-looking underling conducted him to the darkest corner, where he found Gouger, Laird and Rodgers. Soon Price came in. And a day or two later Constantine and Arakeel joined them.

The prisoners lay on the floor until it was nearly dark, when the "father" came in, and taking a bamboo pushed it between the legs of each man. Then it was raised until only their shoulders rested on the floor, their feet hanging by the fetter chains from the bamboo. The young savage in charge lighted the pipes of those who wanted to smoke, and thus they were left hanging for the night. Judson tried to sleep, but the pain and discomfort, the awful uncertainty about Nancy, the mournful drizzle of the rain on the roof, and the conviction that he and his fellow prisoners were to die, made sleep impossible.

At last the morning came. Some of their Burman fellow

_____

[2] $100.00.

victims greeted it with the plaintive intoning of a Pali prayer. Many times were they to hear this Buddhist matin chant, so often that the melody became fixed in their memory. The "father" came in and counted his prisoners, and lowered the bamboo to within a foot of the floor. Then Judson had an opportunity to look around.

He was in a wooden building about thirty by forty, with a sloping roof covered with tiles. There was no window, and the only light and air came through a closely woven bamboo door, and holes in the walls. Some forty or fifty men and women were lying about, most of them with chains on their legs, some fast in the stocks. Decayed remains of cast-off animal and vegetable matter were scattered around, the juice of chewed betel strewed the floor, other nameless abominations were here and there, the whole place was teeming with creeping vermin, and all in a temperature of nearly a hundred. Sight and smell were almost unbearable—yet they had to be borne.

During the morning Judson and the other prisoners were taken out into the yard in groups of a dozen or so. Only five minutes were allowed in the open air, then they were hustled back inside. But how they enjoyed those five minutes, in spite of the rain and the mud. Maung Ing's breakfast package came, and Price and the others were likewise provided for by their servants—woe betide any luckless prisoner who had no one to bring him food, for the government gave him nothing. Gouger was on one side of Judson and Price on the other, with Rodgers and the rest strung on the bamboo further along. As they lay there they discussed their situation, talking quietly in Burmese, as English was taboo that first day. But towards three o'clock everybody began to grow strangely silent. When the gong sounded in the palace yard not far away a deathlike stillness prevailed. Judson listened, wondering what it all meant. Just then the door opened, and a spotted-face jailer came in, strode across the room to two Burman prisoners, and led them out of the room. Not a word was spoken. All knew, or quickly came to know, that if anyone was to die on that day three o'clock was the hour. No wonder that Judson and Price and their companions listened day after day in breathless apprehension as the fatal hour approached, and shuddered as the gong sounded, each asking himself, "Is it my turn?"

Ann's visit to the governor secured an order for her admission to the prison yard to see her husband. But when she saw him she was so shocked that she hid her face in her hands and gave way for a few minutes to uncontrollable grief. And well she might. For he had been fastidious in his habits, always neat and clean; but two days in that loathsome, filthy place, with the rough and savage treatment he had received, had so changed him that she scarcely knew him. Time was allowed her for only a brief word about her plans, then the jailer harshly ordered her out. But her plans worked, for that evening Judson and his companions were released from the abominable prison room and housed in an open shed in the yard, a boon that cost them each a bribe of three hundred ticals ($150).

Meanwhile officers had searched Gouger's house and seized all his property. As they passed Ann's house they told her they were coming to visit her the next day. That gave her time for preparation, and she hurriedly hid a good many small articles, including most of her silver. The following morning the governor, with forty or fifty secretaries and underlings, came to seize her possessions. But Ann, with her marvelous force of personality and exquisite tact, seemed almost to dominate the situation. She invited the officers to sit down, and regaled them with tea and sweetmeats, with the result that she was able to keep a good deal of her property,—clothing, books, medicines, and her prized little work table and rocking chair, together with other things that proved of inestimable value later.

The royal treasurer asked her how much she had paid the governor and his officers. When she told him, he demanded it from the governor, who fell into a rage and ordered the prisoners sent back into the prison house. Ann went to see him the next morning and he began to berate her.

"Why did you not say you gave me nothing?"

"But I cannot tell a lie," she replied; "my religion forbids it. If you had held a knife over me I could not have done it."

"That is right," interrupted the governor's wife; "what else could she have done?" And thenceforth she was a loyal friend of Ann.

The governor was placated with a beautiful pair of opera glasses Ann had received from friends in England, and Judson was allowed to stay outside. But in spite of her pleadings Dr. Price and the others were kept in the inner prison.

Day after day Ann visited different members of the royal family or leading officials, pleading for her husband's release. All she got for her pains were empty promises, except that she made friends—she was sure to do that—who secretly gave her food for Adoniram, and used their influence to remove the suspicion that he was a spy. But demands were continually made for money, or cloth, or handkerchiefs. Sometimes the prisoners would be ordered not to speak to one another. Or the servants who brought their daily food were not allowed to deliver it until an extra fee had been paid. Days at a time Ann could not enter the prison till after dark, and then had two miles to travel through the dangers of the unlighted streets before she reached her home. "O how many, many times have I returned from that dreary prison at nine o'clock at night"—so she wrote to Elnathan—"solitary and worn out with fatigue and anxiety, and thrown myself down in that same rocking-chair which you and Deacon L. provided for me in Boston, and endeavored to invent some new scheme for the release of the prisoners."

One day the loud booming of a gun from the river-side broke into the monotony and suspense. "What is that?" asked the prisoners of one another. It proved to be a signal. Guns were to be fired when a battle had been fought—one gun if without success, two if a victory, three if the invaders had been driven into the sea. Today they heard only one gun, and anxiously they waited. What would happen to them? Three o'clock passed and their heads still remained on their shoulders, so they took courage. But every time they heard the gun —it was seldom more than one—their anxiety was renewed.

And no wonder; all the chances were against them. And the terrible uncertainty hung over them like a sword of Damocles. Rodgers was old and infirm, and was certain that the advantage lay entirely with the Burman army. Gouger was young and strong, with no family, and he was constantly hopeful. Judson had an uneven temperament, usually enthusiastic and optimistic, but subject to occasional reaction which threw him into despondency—"he was at this time better fitted to do than to endure." So with differing attitudes they discussed the situation day after day. Try as they would they could never see how escape was possible. Probably (humanly speaking) they would not have survived but for Ann. Even she felt certain that Adoniram would be put to death and she would become a slave. But never for a moment did she relax her efforts, nor hesitate at anything that held the slightest hope of success. She even dared to appeal to Bandula, the chief general, who had returned from Arracan flushed with pride at a victory he had gained, and presented a petition that Judson in some manner had been able to write. The governor was amazed at what he termed her rashness and thought it would mean the death of all the foreign prisoners. Perhaps it might if Ann had not accompanied the petition. As it was it did no harm, though it did no good either—Bandula replied that as soon as he had driven the English out he would release her husband and the others.

One day the door opened, and what was their astonishment to see a big Irishman enter, led in with a heavy chain like a dancing bear. He beamed with delight when he saw some white—or erstwhile white—faces, and expressed himself vigorously in his Irish brogue until the savage keeper threatened him with a club. He was a captured soldier, and all eagerly plied him with questions. But they gained little news from him, and in a day or two he was taken away and they never saw him again. Another time a woman was brought in covered with smallpox pustules. They drew back in alarm. Dr. Price looked as helpless as all the others. How could they possibly escape infection? Fortunately she was removed the next day and no one took the disease. Gouger was sure they were saved by the tobacco that everyone smoked.

On another day three hundred Sepoys arrived who had been taken by Bandula's army in Arracan. Fetters for all these new victims were not to be had, so some were borrowed from Judson and his companions, leaving them manacled to each other, two and two, a bit of a relief, as at last they could stretch their legs a little. Judson, fortunately, escaped the horror of being manacled to the leprous Greek, Constantine. That was reserved for Gouger—but he suffered no bad results. A hundred of the Sepoys were crowded into the inner prison, and Judson and his companions watched with dismay and alarm as all these new prisoners came in. How could they possibly survive! The floor was packed solid, so close that they were crowded against one another. The room had no ventilation except through small cracks in the wall. Soon they were wet with perspiration. Then they began to breathe hard. At last desperate cries arose:

"Air! Water!"

At that the jailers became alarmed and opened the wicket door, which with the cracks in the wall let in just enough air to save them. But it was a terrible night. The next day the Sepoys, or most of them, were taken away, and the three fetters were pounded on the ankles of the white prisoners again.

Ranged along two sides of the prison yard were a number of small cells, five feet wide and about six feet long, and Ann succeeded in getting permission for the white prisoners to occupy these. Here they were freed from some of the sights and sounds of the inner prison. But not from all. One night, for example, they were awakened by terrible cries from the prison house, and Gouger managed to crawl out of his cell and peek through a crack in the inner wall just in time to see the heavy boot of a jailer crash down on the face of a young fellow who lay on the ground with his feet in the stocks. Again and again this horrible cruelty was repeated, until the poor wretch's cries were stilled, and then the savage took a club and ended his life entirely. At another time, just at midnight, a prisoner was dragged out and put to death by having his back broken. Ugly deeds like these made Judson and the others think of their own fate, and their breath came quickly as they talked of what they had seen and heard.

Ann sent food for Adoniram every day, or carried it herself when she could, so as to spend a little time with him. Sometimes there was plenty, sometimes for weeks only rice and *ngapee,* a rather unpalatable preparation of fish. Once she tried to surprise him with something that would brighten his spirits and remind him of home. Maung Ing and Moo-chil the cook were brought into the secret. Some buffalo meat was obtained, with plantains and other ingredients, and out of them Nancy concocted a mince pie! She could not carry it herself that day, so sent Maung Ing. Judson opened the package, expecting to find the usual fare, and behold, a mince pie! What visions of his New England home that brought back—his mother and father, his chummy sister and his brother. And Nancy's well-spread table at Bradford. How different their situation now! How much Nancy was suffering! And she was alone. It was too much; he rested his head on his knees and gave way to grief. And handing the pie to Gouger he went off by himself to be alone with his thoughts.

For a while Nancy and Adoniram sent letters to each other through a messenger. But they were soon found out and the messenger was beaten and put in the stocks. Ann had to pay ten dollars to quiet the jailer, and she spent two or three days in an agony of fear for Adoniram and herself. Then she wrote to him on a flat cake which she baked and hid in a bowl of rice, while he replied on a piece of tile on which the writing was legible when dry but invisible when wet. Finally they adopted the plan of rolling up a note and inserting it in the long nose of his tea pot.

So the weary days slowly dragged themselves along. "O that we could have had the unspeakable relief of a few books!" wrote Gouger. And how much more they would have meant to Judson. But no books were to be had, nor anything else. Ingenuity came to their aid. Judson liked chess; so did his friend Gouger. Probably they had played together in Judson's home. What more natural than to suggest a game there in the prison. But how could they play? They had neither chessmen nor board. Dr. Price came to their aid. He had a piece of bamboo which he had begged from a jailer, with a lump of clay, out of which he had planned to make a prison clock! The clock had never evolved, so now he used the bamboo to carve a set of chessmen. Marvelous chessmen! One can imagine that it took a day or two to tell a king from a pawn, or a knight from a rook. Yet they did very well. But what could they play on? An old buffalo hide turned up in a corner of the prison, and by holding this over the oil lamp that dimly lighted the dark room they made some blotches that looked like squares. It was a strange-looking chessboard, with ludicrous chessmen. But many an hour Judson beguiled as he and Gouger lay or squatted at their game on the dirty floor, free for a while from thoughts of themselves and their fate.

Dr. Price occupied his time with efforts along mechanical lines such as the clock. He tried a little surgery, too. One of the jailers had a troublesome growth on one of his eyelids, and Price longed for his instruments. But all he had was a penknife with just the stump of a blade. Somehow he persuaded the jailer to let him try to remove the growth. Judson and the others were alarmed. The operation could not possibly succeed, and what would happen to them if he failed? But the doctor set to work and hacked out the tumor, and to the wonder of all the wound healed—though to be sure the poor victim found that he could not open his eye.

"Never mind," said the nonchalant doctor, "the eye will keep all the better. When you want to use it, just raise the eyelid with your finger, and when you are through with it let it drop again!"

One can readily surmise that Judson and Price did not team together very well. Gouger tells that though Judson "aimed at quietism he had not altogether attained it," and once in a while his rather high-strung temperament betrayed him into a burst of impatience. This showed itself one night in a way that amused the other men, though the amusement was lost on Judson. He and Price were sleeping next to each other in the crowded room. Price had a habit of drawing his raw-boned knees up in front of him as he lay on his side asleep, and not infrequently had bad dreams. This night he had some of his dreams, and every once in a while something in his dream made him drive his knees, heavily weighted with manacles, into the back of the soundly sleeping Judson. Judson stood it as long as he could, then burst out,

"Brother Price, you are a public nuisance! I insist on your sleeping as other people do."

A warm argument followed, which Gouger says he ended by making Price move over so he could lie between them.

But Judson genuinely tried to attain to the ideal of quietism to which Gouger referred. He had read, and made his own, many of the verses of Madame Guyon, and often he would repeat them during these days in prison. And his faith was unwavering that Burma would yet be won for Christ.

"Gouger," he would say, "this war is going to turn out to the advancement of the kingdom of God in Burma. Here I have been ten years preaching the gospel to timid listeners who wish to embrace the truth but dare not, and beseeching the emperor to grant liberty of conscience to his people but without success, and now when all human means seem at an end, God opens the way by leading a Christian nation to subdue the country. It is possible my life will be spared; if so, with what ardor shall I pursue my work; and if not—His will be done; the door will be opened for others who will do the work better."

One of the first things about which Judson asked Ann when she came to see him in the prison was the manuscript of the New Testament. Was it lost? No, Ann had buried it with the silver and other valuables under the house. But it would soon be ruined there. They hit on a bold plan. Each of the white prisoners had been allowed a pillow. Ann brought the precious manuscript and sewed it into Judson's pillow, taking extra care to make it so hard and lumpy that even the most greedy jailer would not want it. That was the most valuable pillow that ever a man's head rested on. The manuscript was safe, for a time at least.

Ann visited the governor every other day, keeping up his interest by telling of things in America that he was eager to hear about. And toward cool weather she prevailed on him to let her make a little bamboo room for Adoniram in the prison yard. There she was sometimes allowed to spend two or three precious hours with him. In the yard he could occasionally enjoy the grateful shade of an ancient wide-spreading tamarind tree. And he could look off over his prison walls to the high city watch-tower in the distance. But neither he nor Ann could free their minds from fear and dread.

As if all the anxieties which Ann and her husband were bearing were not enough, there was added still another—she was anticipating motherhood. In that city of terror, with her husband in prison and daily facing death, with hostile officials on every hand and no one daring to be a friend, Ann was to become a mother! With Judson every hour was an hour of foreboding. And he was helpless; Ann must face her hour alone. But she faced it with the same faith and courage with which she faced every other hour. And perhaps she was not alone. Some Burmese mother, it may be, won by Ann's loveliness, came to her aid in this hour of need. And the faithful Maung Ing and the equally faithful Moo-chil, who had come with her from Bengal, were with her. On January twenty-sixth Maria Elizabeth Butterworth was born.

Twenty days later Ann brought her little Maria to the prison, and the savage jailers crowded around, wondering at this first white child most of them had ever seen. Judson was thrilled at the sight of his baby and his wife. And after they had gone he composed some verses in honor of his infant daughter, though it was a long time before he could write them down:

> "Sleep, darling infant, sleep,
>   Hushed on thy mother's breast;
> Let no rude sound of clanking chains
>   Disturb thy balmy rest.
>
> "Sleep, darling infant, sleep;
>   Blest that thou canst not know
> The pangs that rend thy parents' hearts,
>   The keenness of their woe.
>
> "Sleep, darling infant, sleep;
>   May heaven its blessings shed,
> In rich profusion, soft and sweet,
>   On thine unconscious head!"

Tuesday the first of March. Judson was living in his bamboo shed and his companions were occupying their little rooms in the prison yard. Each had a mat and a pillow, nothing had happened for some time to arouse their apprehensions, and they were as comfortable as conditions would allow. They even joined in occasional laughter, as Judson with his keen sense of the ludicrous called attention to something or someone ridiculous.[3] But suddenly their laughter was quieted and they

---

[3] Gouger, *Personal Narrative*, p. 174.

were thrown into the depths of despair. At an order from the head jailer, a spotted-face came to each cell and led his man to the now well-known granite block in the middle of the yard. No one spoke. Not even the usual threats came from the savage jailers. One after another Judson and his companions were motioned to the stone, and two pairs of fetters were added to the three already there. Then back they staggered into the inner prison. And there in a dark corner they were left, without mat or pillow, to ask themselves and one another what it all meant.

That was a dark night for them all. Judson heard some of the Burman prisoners say they were to be killed. He could heard the spotted-faces sharpening their knives. So they were not to be strangled as some had been—that was a relief. Three o'clock in the morning was named as the hour. He would not be able to say good-bye to his dear Nancy or his little Maria— he thought of it with a sharp pang of regret. His death would be a terrible shock to her. But she would rise above the calamity and with her resourceful nature she would find some way of getting to the English. Perhaps it would even be a blessing to have him go. It might be that he would not be put to death in the prison yard but would be taken to the execution ground —then he would pass his own house and he could bid her good-bye in his heart as he went by the place where she was sleeping. He thought of Burma. Whatever happened to him, Christ was sure to win Burma. His manuscript—would Nancy find it? Even in that hour he remembered one or two passages where he might improve the translation.

Three o'clock! The time must be near. It was a solemn hour. The distant pagoda bells seemed to call them to prayer. And they bowed their heads as Judson calmly and quietly lifted up his voice in prayer for them all and for those they loved. Then each man prayed—some had never prayed before. Then they waited. Three o'clock was long in coming. Or had it come? Was it possible that they had been mistaken? Perhaps it would be at four instead of three. Suddenly the door opened—and morning had come! They sank down in relief. They were to live!

Ann learned about it the next day. Maung Ing brought

the news when he returned from taking food to the prison. She hurried over to the governor's house but he was not at home. She went to the prison. It was as quiet as a graveyard and the guards refused to admit her. At night she went again to the governor's house, determined to see him, and found him in his audience room.

"Your lordship has treated us with the kindness of a father," she said to him. "You have promised that you would stand by me to the last, and though you should receive an order from the king you would not put Mr. Judson to death. What crime has he committed to deserve such new punishment?"

The old governor broke down and wept like a child.

"I pity you, Lady Teacher"—he always called her that—"for I will tell you what I have not told you before. Three times the queen's brother has ordered me to assassinate all the white prisoners privately, but I would not do it. And I repeat what I have told you; even if I should execute all the others, I will never execute your husband. But I cannot release him from the inner prison, so do not ask it."

The governor had put the prisoners out of sight to save them from a worse fate. But their situation was distressing. The hot season was beginning, and more than a hundred men and women were crowded into the unventilated room. Ann pleaded with the governor almost every day, but gained nothing, except permission for Adoniram and the others to eat in the yard. And this was soon revoked. Even their five minutes of exercise had to be taken after dark.

News now came that Bandula had been killed and his army defeated. And they were amazed to learn that the king had appointed in his place one of their own fellow prisoners in the Let-ma-yoon, a high officer who was known for his deadly hatred of foreigners. The first thing this new commander did was to arrest Lanciego the Spaniard, who had done all in his power to alleviate the sufferings of Judson and his companions, and after the most terrible torture, throw him into prison. And now there were eight prisoners. They began to understand the remark of the "father" to one of his underlings:

"My son, be sure you have never wrung a rag so dry but that another twist will bring another drop."

But surely there was nothing to wring from them now but their lives.

A month in the stifling inner prison brought Judson down with a fever. To be near both her husband and the governor, Ann had a small bamboo hut built in the governor's enclosure, across the street from the prison, and here she began a siege of the governor to secure Judson's release from the inner prison house. Finally she wore him out by her unceasing pleas, and he gave the order, with permission for her to go in at any time to care for her husband. She lost no time in having him moved outside to a little bamboo cell or hut. There he had a mat, and once again the hard pillow containing the manuscript—exchanging a better pillow for this one, to the wonder of the jailer who had seized it. But his fever hung on and kept him weak. And every night he could hear his enemy the new general call out as he passed the prison,

"Are the white men safe? Keep them tight."

One day—it was the second of May—Nancy brought Adoniram's breakfast to him but found he could not eat it on account of his fever. So she stayed and talked with him. As they were talking together an urgent message came from the governor asking her to come at once. Judson was alarmed, but she went. The governor was very pleasant, and apparently only wanted to consult her about his watch, though he detained her quite a while. At last she started back to the prison, but had gone only a few steps when she met a servant coming on the run, his ghastly face telling of new disaster.

"All the white prisoners are carried away!" he burst out.

With blanched face she hurried back to the governor. He knew her errand before she spoke.

"Yes, Lady Teacher, I heard of it, but I did not want to tell you."

Then out on the street again, looking this way and that, running down this street, then that one—but the prisoners had vanished. Nor did anyone seem to know where they had gone. Again she returned to the governor.

"He has been sent to Amarapura—why, I do not know. You can do nothing more for him. Take care of yourself."

They were ominous words, but she was helpless. There

was nothing she could do but make her dreary way back to her little hut, hearing again and again those words of the governor, "You can do nothing more for him. Take care of yourself." It was a day of terrible suspense. What should she do? What *could* she do? That night she decided to follow her husband. So the next morning, leaving the house in charge of Maung Ing, she started for Amarapura. Ann and her little three months old Maria, the Burman girls Mary and Abby Hasseltine, and Moo-chil the cook—these made up the party. A short boat-ride on the river, then two miles in an open cart in the hot sun, and they came to Amarapura. But the prisoners had gone—had been taken on four miles further to Aungbinle. Another hour in the burning sun waiting for a cart, and at last they reached Aungbinle and Judson's new prison.

It had been almost a death's journey for Judson and the others. Ann had scarcely left Judson's cell when a jailer rushed in, pulled him roughly out to the granite block, tore off all his clothes except shirt and trousers, knocked off his manacles, tied a rope around his waist, and dragged him with the other white men to the court house. There they were tied in couples, and were driven along the road two and two, with a spotted-face behind each pair, carrying a spear and holding the rope, like children playing at driving horses. They headed toward the execution ground, and all were sure that this was the end. But soon they turned and took the road to Amarapura. All were barefoot, and had no covering for their heads. It was nearly noon in one of the hottest months of the year, and the sun poured down on them in all the fury of its tropic heat. Tramping on the dry, parched ground was almost like walking on a sheet of hot iron. Judson had not gone half a mile before his feet became blistered. And the sand and gravel worked into the blisters and made every step the most excruciating torture. Before they had traveled a mile Constantine, leprous and over-fleshy, gave in and sank to the ground. He was beaten and prodded by a spear and managed to get up and go on a little way, then fell helpless. The guard put him in a cart, but too late; he died before they reached Amarapura.

As they were crossing a small stream Judson was sorely tempted to throw himself into it and end his sufferings. But

he could not have done it without Laird's doing it too, for they
were tied together. Judson's feet were now one mass of blood
and raw flesh. He was ill with fever and had eaten no breakfast. Laird took pity on him and for a mile or so let him take
hold of his shoulder, until he himself began to weaken with
the added burden. Just then Gouger's Bengali servant overtook them, and seeing Judson's distress he took off his turban
and tore it in two, giving half to Judson and half to Gouger,
to bind around their feet. Then he allowed Judson to rest his
weight on his shoulder. And so they managed to get through
to Amarapura.

They were to be taken on to Aungbinle that day, but threats
and entreaties had no effect—they simply could not go on. All
threw themselves on the ground, some in a shed, some under
a cart. The wife of the officer in charge took pity on them and
brought them fruit. And the next morning rice was given
them, and carts were provided for the four miles to Aungbinle.
At two o'clock they came to their new prison, a dilapidated
wooden building standing alone in a wide cultivated plain. It
had no door, the roof had partly fallen in, and the space under-
neath was filled with dry sticks. They decided at once that
they were to be burned to death in the old shack—as indeed
had been rumored in Let-ma-yoon. Perhaps their thought was
due to inflamed imagination—perhaps there was real ground
for their fears. But the next morning they were told that the
sticks were stacked under the prison to prevent escape through
the rotten floor!

When Ann arrived a jailer took pity on her and gave her
one of the two rooms in his house, just a grain room. No other
place was to be had, and here for six months she and her brood
lived, without furniture of any kind except the bags of paddy
and such minor conveniences as her ingenuity or that of Moo-
chil could provide.

The first day after Ann's arrival Mary Hasseltine came
down with smallpox. Little Maria caught it from her. Ann
herself was taken with a disease common to the country and
almost always fatal to foreigners. For some time she was entirely unable to care for herself or look after her husband, and
both might have died but for the faithful care given by Moo-

chil, who never hesitated to go anywhere or do anything to relieve their necessities. Baby Maria suffered even more than the others. Ann's illness deprived the little one of its food, and no milk was to be had in the village near by. But now the jailers, removed from the exacting demands of the palace officers (and stimulated by bribes from Ann), showed a bit of humanity, and allowed Adoniram to leave the prison and take his wan baby around through the village, begging nourishment from one mother after another. Sometimes he was permitted to go to Ann's small hovel. Then again his keepers would be iron-hearted and pay no attention to pleas or bribes. After it was all over Ann wrote to Elnathan, "The annoyances, the extortions and oppressions to which we were subject during our six months' residence in Aungbinle are beyond enumeration or description."

Another prisoner was added to the seven one day, when Ignatius Brito arrived, a Roman Catholic priest, a native Burman of Portuguese extraction. He knew no English, so joined but little in the conversation. But he was fond of music, and often sang Latin hymns to the Virgin Mary, or varied the tune with a dance which he composed and called "Deliverance from Prison!" Gradually he lost his mind; though after his release he recovered. It was a motley company of prisoners: two American missionaries, a Burman-Portuguese Roman Catholic priest, a Spanish revenue officer, an Armenian trader, a Scottish sailor, an English adventurer, and a British merchant.

And one night still another prisoner arrived. Judson and the others were trying to sleep, when they heard rumbling sounds like distant thunder. The rumbling came nearer, and they began to distinguish the creaking of cart wheels and the voices of men. Then every once in a while, drowning out all other sounds, came the terrific roar of some great animal. The new prisoner proved to be a huge lioness, confined in a cage, which was drawn into the yard and placed close to the prison house. Judson and his friends listened with horror to her roaring, and wondered if they were to be thrown into her cage to be torn to pieces. For some time no one, not even the jailers, knew why the beast was there. Indeed, no explanation was ever given. But the poor brute was slowly starved to death.

Then an idea struck Judson. What a fine retreat the empty cage would make for him! Through Ann's meditation it was granted to him, and he lived in it for several months.

As he lay in the cage he thought many times of his hard pillow, with its New Testament so valuable, and wondered what had become of it. It had gone, with everything else that he had, the day he was so unceremoniously hurried away from Let-ma-yoon. Only when he was back in Ava did he learn that one of the spotted-faces had pulled off its mat covering and thrown the hard roll away, and that Maung Ing, searching around some hours later for anything that his master had left, came upon the pillow and carried it home. Again the precious manuscript was saved.

One day after they had been in Aungbinle six months, Judson and Ann were thrown into a transport of joy when an order came for Judson's release and removal to Ava. Once before, all the prisoners had been taken to Ava for a day, to translate a message from Sir Archibald Campbell the English general. Now Judson was to be sent to the Burman camp as translator and interpreter. But the greedy jailers at first refused to let Ann go, and thus lose the treasury of enrichment she had been to them. Only with difficulty did she and her family get permission to leave. Judson had just a few minutes with Ann in his old home, and then started down the river for Maloun. There on the hot sand between the camp and the river he was given a little windowless hut made of bamboo mats, and in spite of a raging fever was compelled to work on the papers that were brought to him. The fever overcame him for a time, and he lay for several days unconscious. Finally, after six weeks of illness, cold, poor food, hard work and continual abuse, he was taken back to Ava and put under guard in an old shed.

Here Maung Ing found him. Judson noticed that he acted strangely, and that he answered rather vaguely when asked about his mistress. After he had gone Judson began to think about it, and the more he thought the more he worried. Something was surely wrong with his dear Nancy. He could not sleep for thinking about it. Slowly the long night dragged itself away. Then came morning—and freedom! For the friendly governor sent word that he had become surety for him and that he was free. And now his one thought was to get to Nancy.

There was ample cause for his worry. Two weeks after his departure for camp Nancy had been seized with spotted fever, or cerebral spinal meningitis. She knew at once what it was, and had no doubt that it would prove fatal. Providentially, the very day she was taken sick a Burmese nurse came and offered to care for Maria. Nancy rapidly grew worse and went into a delirium, and before long was so near death that neighbors said,

"She is dead. If the King of angels came in he could not recover her."

But Providence intervened again. On the very day that she reached the crisis Dr. Price was set free, and hurried to her home. When he saw her he was shocked, and had no thought that she could live more than a few hours. But through his care and that of the loyal Moo-chil, and certainly through the prayers of Adoniram and the many others in Burma and India and far away America who remembered her though they could not know her need, she slowly began to recover.

When Judson reached his house the door was open and he entered. In the front room he came upon a coarse-looking Burman woman squatting on the floor by the side of a pan of coals, holding his little Maria, whom he did not recognize in its pallor and dirt. Hurrying into the bedroom he found Nancy lying across the foot of the bed, ghastly pale and thin, her black curls gone, and bed and room looking wretched in the extreme. She woke to see her Adoniram bending over her, and looked up at him with her wonderful smile! At last she and Adoniram were reunited. And now she steadily grew stronger, and after some days was able to be removed to the governor's house; there they stayed as guests until they left Ava.

The English army had pressed north, and the king and all the people were thoroughly alarmed. Soldiers set to work to fortify the city. The Judsons' house was torn down and cannon mounted where their beautiful little mission compound had stood. Dr. Price and Dr. Sandford, a captured British surgeon, were sent off to mediate with the English general, but accomplished nothing. Then Judson was seized on the street and was rushed away with Burman officers in a last effort to stop the advancing army, but without avail.

At last gold and silver were hurriedly collected, all the prisoners were released, the indemnity was hurried down the river, and on Tuesday, February 21, 1826, Judson and Ann, with the governor, went down to their boat, and bidding the governor a really affectionate farewell, they left the city to which they had come with such happy anticipations two years before.

One evening long afterward a number of friends were in Judson's home and were telling anecdotes to show what they considered the highest enjoyment.

"Pooh!" said Judson. "I know a much higher pleasure than that. What do you think of floating down the Irrawaddy on a cool moonlight evening, with your wife by your side and your baby in your arms, free—all free? But *you* cannot understand it; it needs a twenty-one months' qualification. And I can never regret my twenty-one months of misery when I recall that delicious thrill. I think I have had ever since a better appreciation of what heaven may be."

On the twenty-first of March Judson and Ann reached Rangoon and their old home. Two years and three months they had been gone. The tragedy of Ava was ended.

CHAPTER VI

ZAYAT AND GARRET

RANGOON was to remain a Burman port. Only Arracan, between the mountains and the west coast, and Tenasserim, the long narrow territory in the east stretching south from the Salween River, were to be retained by the Indian government. Little success could be expected for some time in Rangoon under the despotic Burman ruler. But Tenasserim was now British, and there missionaries and Burman converts would have full religious liberty. To the new province Judson and Nancy would go.

Not since their arrival in Burma had the prospect seemed so promising. The civil commissioner for the new territory, Mr. Crawfurd, invited Judson to accompany him on an exploring expedition to select a site for the capital of the new province. Judson was delighted and accepted eagerly. It was a welcome relief from the experiences that had crowded the past months, and he threw himself into it with the spirit of a boy. "Out early in the morning with the animation of new discoverers," he wrote in his journal. On a peninsula at the mouth of the Salween they chose the site for the new city, and named it Amherst after the governor general. Here, on the beach under a bold cliff, the ship's company gathered, the English flag was hoisted, a military salute was given, Judson read the sixtieth chapter of Isaiah and offered prayer, and they took possession in the name of King George and the Honorable East India Company.

The Houghs and the Wades, after thrilling adventures in Rangoon, had withdrawn to Calcutta. Again Judson and his wife were alone. And now with his usual impulsiveness Judson decided that he and Ann should be the first settlers in Amherst. So taking down the old Rangoon zayat to use as a temporary house, and packing up their belongings, they left their old home in the mission house, and on June twenty-ninth sailed for Amherst. The spot they chose for a new home was wild and uninviting, but the view was inspiring, with the far hills of Bilugyun Island, and the bold outlook to the sea. Here they would begin their mission work once more.

But a new problem interrupted their planning. Crawfurd proposed to Judson that he go to Ava with him as his interpreter and assistant, to help negotiate a commercial treaty. Back to Ava? To that terrible city? Give up his promising new work in Amherst? Leave Nancy? He promptly refused. But Crawfurd had been ordered to consult with Judson and he repeated his request. Again Judson refused. Finally Crawfurd offered the most tempting bait possible: he promised to make every effort to get into the treaty a clause guaranteeing religious liberty. That was more than Judson could resist and he agreed to go—though with the greatest reluctance. Ann strongly urged him to go. She would be comfortable in the home of Captain Fenwick, the civil superintendent, who kindly vacated it for her accommodation. And Judson would be back in three or four months. So two days after reaching Amherst he was off again for Rangoon and Ava, he and Nancy parting with cheerful hearts and looking forward with glad anticipation to the new home and work that would soon be theirs.

Judson's services with this commission were recognized by Crawfurd and the other commissioners as of the highest value, and they commended him to the Indian government in warm terms. The expedition was delayed in getting away from Rangoon, and the three or four months lengthened to six. They had scarcely arrived in Ava before it was found that no toleration clause could be hoped for, and with all his heart Judson wished himself back with Nancy. But he knew nothing of the great catastrophe that was coming upon him.

Nancy's last letter, written September fourteenth, had told of the new house into which she had moved, and how happy she would be if he were only there. She spoke of Maria:

"When I ask her where Papa is, she always starts up and points toward the sea. . . . May God preserve and bless you, and restore you in safety to your new and old home, is the prayer of   Your affectionate Ann."

But early in October a violent fever had seized her, and from the first she had a presentiment that she would not recover. The army surgeon did his best, and a European woman was secured as nurse. But nothing could stay the progress of the dread disease, and on Tuesday, October 24, 1826, she passed on into rest. She was laid away beneath the hopea tree near their home and Gouger's, looking out on the restless sea that was such a symbol of her life—restless on its wind-tossed surface, quiet and calm in the unseen depths below. Beautiful, vivacious, winsome, loving, fearless, with tact and resourcefulness unsurpassed, an example to all future generations of nobility and faithfulness, devotion and strength, "she appears on the page of missionary history as an illuminated initial letter."[1] All that one might like to say of her is summed up in Wayland's high tribute: "One of the most remarkable women of her age."[2]

Judson was left alone. All the life plans and guiding influences of which Ann had been the center were torn asunder. The Wades returned from Calcutta about a month after Ann's death, and Mrs. Wade took little motherless Maria to her home and heart. Judson took up his residence with them, in a bamboo house that Ann had built. On April twenty-fourth Maria went to join her mother. A week before Maria's death George Dana Boardman and his wife had arrived, but shortly removed to Moulmein, which had been chosen by General Campbell as his military headquarters and was rapidly becoming the chief city of the province. In August Judson went to visit the Boardmans, and in October he decided to remain in Moulmein. The next month the Wades came, and henceforth Moulmein was the center of the mission. In March of the following year,

---

[1] B. J. Lossing, quoted by Wyeth, *Ann H. Judson, a Memorial,* title page.
[2] Wayland, I, p. 329. Ann's influence still continued widely after her death, through the *Memoir* by Knowles, published by authority of the mission board. It had a remarkable circulation. The first edition was printed in 1829. Within two years three editions had been issued in America, totaling 12,500 copies, besides three or four editions in England. In 1831 a fourth edition was printed in a smaller size, to secure a still wider reading. Of the Memoir the board said in its 1831 report: "Persons who have thought little of their duty to the heathen, upon reading it have been convicted of neglect and been aroused to action. Some have offered themselves for missionary work, and others have generously given of their substance."

1827, the Boardmans moved to Tavoy, and Judson and the Wades were left as the missionary force at Moulmein.

The next three or four years form an abnormal period in Judson's life, in which he gave himself to a strange mortification of flesh and spirit, entirely contrary to his ordinary attitude and habit.

He had spent twenty-one months in prison, under torturing conditions of body and mind. They were conditions that made the mind of one of the prisoners (Brito the priest) lose its balance. Gouger, though but twenty-five when the imprisonment began, and strong and care-free, said that "another year of the same sort of imprisonment would most likely have brought on a state of settled and irrecoverable melancholy." [3] What wonder that Judson should have felt the effects of those twenty-one months! Then came his return to the scene of his sufferings, with the keen reminder of them all and the disappointing failure to secure toleration. Finally came his crushing loss in the death of Ann, then that of his little Maria, and shortly afterward the news of his father's death. He met these catastrophes as we would expect him to meet them: "Faith decides that it is all right, and the decision of faith eternity will soon confirm." But he could not avoid their inevitable effect. And this was intensified by the habit of introspection that he had cultivated, long stimulated by his study of Madame Guyon's writings.

He had received for his services to the Indian government 5,200 rupees; also gifts amounting to 2,000 rupees. He had also brought with him from America money of his own which, with accumulations, now amounted to $6,000. He had recommended to the board certain regulations, one of which was that "No missionary shall appropriate to himself the avails of his labor, or the compensation he may receive for service of any kind; but all avails of labor, and all presents or payments made in consideration of services performed, shall be placed to the credit of the board: provided, that nothing in this article shall be construed to affect private property, inheritances, or

---

[3] *Personal Narrative*, pp. 255, 304.

personal favors, not made in compensation of service." [4] In accordance with this rule, but going considerably beyond it, he now gave his whole property, nearly $10,000, to the board—"or rather," as he wrote, "to Him who loved us, and washed us from our sins in His own blood." Then he, with Wade, joined in giving up a twentieth of their salaries, as a challenge to ministers at home, and later he reduced his salary twenty-five per cent more. Thus he would cut out of his life the love of money.

Love of fame, too, needed radical measures. Brown University had conferred on him in 1823 the degree of Doctor of Divinity. Now, five years later, he sent a communication to the *American Baptist Magazine,* asking his friends in referring to him not to use the title, "which," said he, "I hereby resign." Oddly enough, apparently he did not send his declination to the University, and he still remains a Doctor of Divinity of Brown.[5] In order further to cut the bonds of fame and pride, he directed his sister to destroy all his letters. And all correspondence that he himself had he ruthlessly destroyed, including many important documents.

Judson had an unusual facility in gaining the friendship of leading men, officials of the government and others; this we have had occasion to notice. Since the war he had become intimately acquainted with a good many British officers, civil and military, and was a frequent guest at their tables. An intimate friend said that "perhaps his most remarkable characteristic to a superficial observer was the extent and thoroughly genial nature of his sociableness." [6] But he came to the conclusion that this social intercourse was taking time from the work that was his supreme duty, so he gave it all up. His son Edward Judson said that there was a spice of truth in the sneering remark of a fashionable woman that "Judson abstained from society not from principle but from cowardice—he was like the drunkard who was afraid to taste lest he should not

---

[4] The complete regulations, adopted by the board with slight modification, appear in Wayland, I, p. 409.

[5] Later he gave up his objection to the use of this degree, as is evident from the fact that his wife Emily often used it, not only in referring to him in letters to others, but even in correspondence with Judson himself.

[6] Quoted by Edward Judson, *Life of Adoniram Judson,* p. 322.

know when to stop." And Francis Wayland, who perhaps knew and understood him better than anyone else in America, said, "No one enjoyed intelligent and cultivated society more keenly than he; and he surrendered it only in obedience to those principles by which he designed to govern his life." [7] In later years he modified this practice somewhat; but now he cut himself off resolutely and absolutely from all society.

He went farther than that. He built a hermitage for himself in the woods a short distance from his house, and here he lived and worked for a year and a half, within sound of a bell which called him to meals with the Wades, or when the mood suited eating there alone. At one time he sought a still more retired refuge, and went over the hills back of Moulmein into the jungle to a place frequented only by tigers! A Burman disciple built a rough bamboo shelter for him, and there, near a neglected moss-grown pagoda, he sat day after day for forty days reading his Bible and praying, eating no food except a little rice.

Not content even with this, he had a grave dug, and for several days sat by its side, thinking how he would look when he should be lying there. This he did to free himself from a morbid fear of death—not a doubt of his acceptance with God nor a fear of the world to come, but a shrinking from the corruption of the body in the grave. He considered this the result of pride, and boldly and frankly faced the worst that it might hold, to gain complete victory over the dread and the fear.

All these things were abnormal, "the outcome of a transient and superficial mood rather than of his real and underlying character," as his son Edward Judson afterward pointed out. He was seeking a perfection of character that he realized he had not attained, and took this way of reaching toward it. In later years he saw that he had been walking in a perilous path. But he did not regret the experience, and his closest friends ascribed his self-possession, his trust in God in discouraging situations, and his constant sense of the reality of the eternal life, to the discipline of these years. He made no attempt to

---

[7] Wayland, I, p. 447.

force his ideas and practices upon others, only commending Madame Guyon's writings to some of his intimate friends. He simply chose that way for himself, as best fitted to his mood and to the purpose he had for his own life.

Judson's efforts toward spiritual perfection stand out with special vividness in this period, but it must not be thought that they were confined to these few years. In a letter to Ann written on New Year's Eve, 1810, he had said, "Perhaps the secret of living a holy life is to avoid everything that will displease God and grieve the Spirit, and to be strictly attentive to the means of grace." And just thirty-two years later he put the same thought into a resolve: "December 31, 1842. Resolved to make the desire to please Christ the grand motive of all my actions." Through all these years to please Christ was his unfaltering purpose. He was never so busy with translating or planning that he did not take ample time for the cultivation of his spiritual life. On the momentous day back in 1819 when he opened the zayat in Rangoon, he adopted for himself a set of rules, which he found so helpful that later he revised and readopted them several times:

1. Be diligent in secret prayer, every morning and evening.
2. Never spend a moment in mere idleness.
3. Restrain natural appetites within the bounds of temperance and purity.
4. Suppress every emotion of anger and ill will.
5. Undertake nothing from motives of ambition or love of fame.
6. Never do that which at the moment appears to be displeasing to God.
7. Seek opportunities of making some sacrifice for the good of others, especially of believers, provided the sacrifice is not inconsistent with some duty.
8. Endeavor to rejoice in every loss and suffering incurred for Christ's sake and the gospel's, remembering that though, like death, they are not to be wilfully incurred, yet like death they are of great gain.

The emphasis on daily secret prayer appears in other similar sets of resolutions that he adopted later. He was accustomed to walk up and down his room while he prayed, and in his

Moulmein home his children always recognized the heavy, quick, measured tread and would say, "Papa is praying." He liked, too, to pray and meditate during his rapid walks in the open air.

One cannot read his letters or his journal without feeling that prayer was a natural and necessary part of his life. Almost every letter ends with a prayer or a request for prayer. He was confident that prayer is more important than work. " 'Nothing is impossible to industry,' said one of the seven sages of Greece. Let us change the word *industry* for *persevering prayer,* and the motto will be more Christian." He remembered in his prayers all the multiplied interests and people related to him. Of course he prayed for his children, and towards the close of his life he added their children and their children's children, and saw in imagination "a long unbroken line of descendants before the throne of God." He spent a definite period each day in prayer for the Burmans, and urged the observance of secret prayer seven times during the day. No wonder that one of his colleagues who was sometimes admitted to those prayer seasons said, "I shall never forget those hallowed hours"; or that a friend who was reporting one of his public prayers said, "I can only describe it by saying it was one of *Judson's* prayers."

But Judson had not become an ascetic. He had not withdrawn from the world. On the contrary, during this time he generally spent his evenings in social visits with one of the missionary families.[8] And he was never more active in his work. No reference to the practices described appears in the journal which he sent to the board. Rather he wrote enthusiastically about the mission work and its development in the new province. While he was engaged in self-mortification for his own spiritual enrichment, he was throwing himself with keen ardor into all the work and fellowship of the mission.

Soon after he went to Moulmein he arranged a large room in the front of his house in the manner of a zayat, and there he took his seat as in the old Rangoon days, to talk about Christ and the gospel with any who would come up and sit with him. Wade likewise put up a zayat in another part of the city. And

---

[8] Edward Judson, p. 399.

a third was erected for Shwe Ba. Sometimes Judson's zayat would be crowded from morning to night. Take a look at some of his visitors.

Maung Noo, a neighbor, comes to call on a Sunday afternoon, stays to evening worship, is struck by what he hears and comes again in a day or two. Maung Bo comes every day from his house across the road—formerly a Buddhist, then a deist, and now beginning to pray in secret. A Buddhist priest comes often, and frequently speaks favorably of the missionaries to his friends. A blind man gropes his way into the zayat to find the light. Occasionally a woman comes in and listens. Others come to the house to talk with Mrs. Wade. A Hindu convert (named McDonald!) brings another Hindu, Pandar Ram, soon joined by two others. More Hindus come later and a Hindu church is organized. And there are many others, men and women and girls from the school.

Judson could not forget Rangoon. The war had scattered the disciples. Some had died. Several had come to Moulmein. All but two had remained faithful. One, Tha E, on his own initiative had begun to preach, had won a number of converts, and had been ordained to the ministry, the first Christian pastor among the Burmans. He had what Judson considered the proper qualifications for the ministry, steadiness and weight of character, wide knowledge of Burmese literature, and humble devotedness to the work. "He is as solicitous and busy as a hen pressing about her chickens," said Judson. "It is quite refreshing to hear him talk on the subject, and see what a nice, careful old shepherd he makes. The Lord bless his soul and the souls of his flock!"

"Someone should go to his aid," thought Judson. The coming of the Bennetts, in January of 1830, gave Judson his opportunity, and before long he was in Rangoon.

The old mission house where he and Nancy had spent so many happy days was gone. On his return from Ava with Crawfurd's embassy he had climbed to the roof of a high house and looked out toward his old home (the city was besieged by the Peguans), but all that was left was a few posts and a bit of the roof. Now these too had disappeared. For a while, therefore, he took up his abode in town with the Wades, who

had also come to Rangoon. There was plenty to do in the
city. But he thought of the great unevangelized interior, those
hundreds of cities and villages with no one to tell of the Saviour. They called him with a voice of appeal that he heard
day and night. Finally he could stand it no longer. So leaving
the Wades to carry on in Rangoon he took Maung Ing, Maung
En, and three other helpers, and set out up the Irrawaddy for
Prome, the chief city between Rangoon and Ava.

Always he was looking to the regions beyond. He believed
in spreading out the missionary force among the people, rather
than concentrating it in one station. He did indeed spend
most of his years, whether translating or preaching, settled in
one place, Rangoon or Ava or Moulmein or Chummerah. But
he recognized the challenging responsibility that rests upon
the Christian church and the missionary to give to all people
the opportunity of hearing and accepting the Good News—the
purpose expressed in the Student Volunteer watchword, "The
Evangelization of the World in this Generation." In this
twentieth century we have come to appreciate so keenly the
importance of thoroughness in the development of Christian
life and service that we have almost forgotten the far-stretching
fields that are still so largely unoccupied, and the great company of those who as yet have scarcely heard the gospel. We
have applied the principle of thoroughness in one direction but
have neglected it in the other. Judson held the two ideas in
balance. On the one hand he would have a strong central
station, with church and school and press. But on the other
hand he would remember the peoples out beyond—the millions
of Burmans, the Karens, the Shans, the Chins, the dwellers in
Arracan, and the rest—and keep in the main station only those
missionaries actually needed, sending everyone possible out to
build up centers elsewhere. So now he was eager to preach in
Prome.

He carried along a good supply of tracts, and went ashore
the first afternoon at a river village, got into conversation with
some of the people, and gave away a dozen copies. He could
have disposed of a hundred. The boatmen were especially
eager for them. And when at sunset he came aboard his boat
again he could look out on other boats anchored around his

or drawn up on the shore and see here and there large groups
squatting about one who held a tract, listening intently as it
was read to them. It was an inviting picture.

At another village a regular procession followed him back
to the boat, begging for tracts. Many came to the bank of the
river and called out,

"Teacher! Are you asleep? We want a writing to get by
heart."

And some climbed out in a canoe that was moored to the
bank and pushed out a long pole, in the end of which Judson
inserted tracts for them. The captain left the boat during the
evening, and on his return thrilled Judson with what he told
him:

"They are all reading! In almost every home I passed there
is someone at a lamp, reading one of your papers."

At another village the people pursued his boat in a canoe.

"Teacher! Here is a present! Rice and beans! Give us a
tract!"

That was the story all the way up the river.[9] At last he
reached Prome, where he received a hearty welcome from the
one European in the city, and an invitation to stay in his house.
This was a poor shack, as Judson found out the next day, Sunday, when the rain fell in torrents and beat in on every side.
But Judson's spirits were not dampened, and he eagerly went
out to hunt up a house for permanent headquarters. There he
struck a snag. Many houses were vacant but there was none
for him. The owners were afraid of him. They did not want
to have anything to do with a foreigner. In fact Judson found
that the country was full of fears and rumors. The very face
of a white man spread alarm. The situation was not quite so
promising as he had anticipated.

At last he came upon a pagoda in the heart of the city, with
an old unused zayat in front of it. This he was able to secure,
and partitioned off a part for living quarters, leaving an open
space at the front for visitors.

But he had not been sitting in his zayat a week before he
found that whatever might be the attitude of the common

---

[9] See Judson's own vivid account, in Wayland, I, p. 489.

people—and a good many visitors had begun to come—the authorities were suspicious. It was reported that he was a British spy. The deputy governor sent to ask his name and title. Maung Ing came in from a country trip and told him that suspicion was spreading all around. Judson had been thinking of making a tour among the many villages scattered through the country near by, but Maung Ing urged him not to go.

"Teacher," said he, "if you should go, there is not a house whose owner would dare to ask you even to sit down in his doorway!"

The first day of Buddhist Lent came, and great crowds were out on the streets. Judson was out with the others. But everyone cast dark looks at him. The smiles of the first days were nowhere to be seen. No one welcomed him. Even the dogs barked at him and were not restrained. But this worship day was too good an opportunity to be missed. So he made his way to the great Shwe Sandaw pagoda, where the zayats were crowded with devout-faced worshipers. There he found an open shed built over a brick image of the Buddha, and in it he took his place. Buddha and Christ! The old faith and the new! In spite of dark, unfriendly scowls he held to his place all day. Some small groups stopped to look at him and then to listen. In the evening a number came to the zayat to visit him. And though the day had opened with a poor prospect he could come to its close with the satisfaction that two persons at least had discovered the way of salvation.

Neither here in Prome nor elsewhere did Judson shut himself off from Buddhist worship or Buddhist leaders, nor separate himself from the religious life of the people. He read an immense amount of Buddhist literature, and collected a considerable library of the palm leaf books. He frequently visited the pagodas, as he had the Shwe Dagon in Rangoon and now the Shwe Sandaw in Prome, and watched the gaily-dressed worshipers as they bought their lotus and lilies, knelt before the shrines, and laid their fragrant flowers on the altars. More than once he attended lectures by a Buddhist teacher. And he welcomed visits from Buddhist priests. It is said, too, that in his early days at Rangoon he wore a yellow robe, as the Buddhist priests did.[10] And he took care to adapt his plans and verbal expressions to Buddhist custom. So now he mingled with the throng of Buddhist worshipers in Prome.

Not that this meant any compromise between his faith and Buddhism. He believed that only through Christ was salvation possible from the "ruin impending on their immortal souls." Christ and Christianity were sufficient, and the Christian gospel was a complete gospel. But he knew Buddhism well, and made full use of it in opening the way for his own message.

The next day, and every day of his stay in Prome, he and his helpers scattered to different sections of the city, Maung Ing and Maung Dwe distributing tracts in one quarter, Maung En meeting the people who came to the house, and Judson preaching or teaching in a public zayat near the great pagoda or by the brick idol in the open shed. Crowd now succeeded crowd. Some were outrageously angry and had to be placated. Some were deeply philosophical and challenged the keenest logic and strongest argument. Some were dull and the story had to be told again and again.

But there was something tangible to show for the work. U Myat Pyu, sixty-nine years old, timid and retiring, is confident that this is the true religion. Maung E, a bright young man, formerly a government officer with a considerable title, has begun to pray to the eternal God. Maung Kwet Ni, secretary to the deputy governor, has repeatedly visited the zayat and has begun to attend evening service. One or two others also are hopeful prospects.

So much for three months' effort. But the enemy has been busy too. Judson hears, as he has expected, that his arrival has been reported to Ava. Many begin to send back the tracts they have received. Attendance at the zayat falls off. And one day Judson is summoned to the courthouse and undergoes a long examination regarding all his past life in Burma. Then Maung Kwet Ni suddenly disappears. U Myat Pyu sends word that he reads the writings daily but begs that no one be told that he visited the teacher. Maung E leaves town without

---

[10] Wayland, II, p. 384.

giving any reason. Fear! Judson had never seen so much of it before.

It was this fear of the government that made the people draw back from Judson, not unfriendliness. The opposition that he met, here or elsewhere, came mostly from officials or priests. It is worthy of note that in Ava, and Rangoon, and here in Prome, the Burman people themselves with scarcely an exception were friendly when they dared to be. But they were terribly afraid. And with good reason.

At last it became clear that nothing could be accomplished in Prome under conditions as they were. The prospect looked better at Rangoon. At any rate he could work there quietly on the translating of the Old Testament. So late on a Saturday evening, September 18, he boarded his own little boat, and with only his disciples for a crew pushed off from Prome and headed down the river. The sun was just setting—setting on his hopes for the great city, one might think. But he was not discouraged. Five hundred tracts had been distributed. Hundreds had heard the message of life. Some few had given him reason to hope that they had received the Saviour into their hearts. Even Kwet Ni had appeared at the last minute and had bidden him farewell with encouraging words:

"Mark me down as your disciple. I pray to God every day. Pray for me also. As soon as I can get away I am coming down to Rangoon."

So as his boat glided down the Irrawaddy that night he wrote to his fellow missionaries, "There is no period of my missionary life that I review with more satisfaction, or rather with less dissatisfaction, than my sojourn in Prome." On September twenty-fifth the glittering point of the Shwe Dagon pagoda caught their eyes, and soon he and his companions were back in the familiar scenes of Rangoon.

Judson found that the Wades had gone to Moulmein. Opposition had arisen. Guards were stationed on each side of Wade's house to threaten visitors and seize their tracts. Pastor Tha E, who had been occupying the house, had found it wise to move to a less conspicuous place. Reports were being circulated that the government had decided to make an example of the heretics. The crowds that had been coming for tracts had entirely disappeared.

But with the return of Judson the people grew bolder and were soon eager for tracts. He took copies with him on his regular morning walks along the jumbled lanes of the city, and "notwithstanding every precaution" a dozen or fifteen or forty would be taken before his return. Many came to his house to ask for them. Requests were received from distant towns and villages. Not a few priests deigned to ask for copies.

But he had come back from Prome partly to work at the translating of the Bible. And in spite of his eager and busy task of distributing tracts he set himself steadily to the turning of the Old Testament into Burmese.

His Burman colleagues occupied the lower floor of his house and received callers, while he lived upstairs—"the garret" he called it—where he could work undisturbed, or receive the more hopeful visitors. An English woman who happened to visit Rangoon,[11] and who called on him with the captain of the ship and his wife, has given a vivid picture of the garret and its worker:

"It was a Burman habitation, to which we had to ascend by a ladder; and we entered a large, low room through a space like a trap door. The beams of the roof were uncovered, and the window frames were open, after the fashion of Burman houses. The furniture consisted of a table in the center of the room, a few stools, and a desk, with writings and books neatly arranged on one side. We were soon seated, and were most anxious to hear all that the good man had to say, who in a resigned tone spoke of his departed wife in a manner which plainly showed he had set his affections 'where alone true joy can be found.' He dwelt with much pleasure on the translation of the Bible into the Burman language. He had completed the New Testament, and was then as far as the Psalms in the Old Testament, which having finished he said he trusted it would be the will of his heavenly Father to call him to his everlasting home. Of the conversions going on amongst the Burmese he spoke with certainty, not doubting that when the

---

[11] Miss Emma Roberts, quoted by Wayland, II, p. 505.

flame of Christianity did burst forth it would surprise even him by its extent and brilliancy.

"As we were thus conversing, the bats which frequent the houses at Rangoon began to take their evening round, and whirled closer and closer till they came in almost disagreeable contact with our heads; and the flap of the heavy wings so near us interrupting the conversation, we at length reluctantly took our leave and departed. And this, thought I, as I descended the ladder, is the solitary abode of Judson, whom after ages shall designate, most justly, the great and the good."

Here in his scriptorium he worked on the Old Testament, and found time to revise his translation of the Book of Hebrews as well. In February and March, however, the great annual Buddhist festival was to be celebrated, and again he turned all his attention to the circulating of tracts. Scores of thousands crowded into the city. Day and night the platform of the Golden Pagoda was thronged with worshipers. The streets were filled with people, wandering aimlessly along, or stopping at zayats to listen to monks tell stories of the Buddha, or amusing themselves with the entertainment provided for festival visitors.

Judson saw that here was an immense opportunity to spread the Christian message, and he wanted five times as many tracts as Bennett could possibly turn out from the press. "Rangoon is the key to the country," he wrote to Moulmein; "from this place tracts go in to every quarter." He grew enthusiastic: "You can't send too many. . . . Send by every opportunity. . . . I want to be laying in a good stock against the great March festival, when if things go on prosperously I shall want ten thousand on hand at the very least. . . . Send everything you possibly can, and by every other boat after receiving this."

How long he would be allowed a footing in Rangoon was uncertain, so he was eager to distribute his tracts to all who would take them. "Tuesday we gave away three hundred; on Wednesday eight hundred; on Thursday nine hundred; on Friday, the full moon, seven hundred; on Saturday eleven hundred; on Sunday eight hundred; on Monday five hundred. On Tuesday the immense crowd of boats began to move off. . . . On the same day we gave away at the house six hundred;

on Wednesday seven hundred; on Thursday, today, five hundred. . . . We have had a glorious festival, for which I feel under infinite obligation to you."

Writing to a friend in America he summed up the crowded days: "I have distributed nearly ten thousand tracts, giving to none but those who ask. Priests and people, from the remotest regions, are alike eager to get our writings. . . . Some come two or three months' journey, from the borders of Siam and China—'Sir, we hear that there is an eternal hell. We are afraid of it. Do give us a writing that will tell us how to escape it.' Others come from the frontiers of Cathay,[12] a hundred miles north of Ava—'Sir, we have seen a writing that tells about an eternal God. Are you the man that gives away such writings? If so, pray give us one, for we want to know the truth before we die.' Others come from the interior of the country, where the name of Jesus Christ is a little known—'Are you Jesus Christ's man? Give us a writing that tells about Jesus Christ.' I should have given away double the number if I could have obtained sufficient supplies."

Perhaps both curiosity and genuine interest played their part in the desire for tracts, but the story of these months reveals in a thrilling way the opportunity for the new religion, in spite of the Buddhist leaders and the dangers from the hostile government.

For the government was definitely and actively hostile. Judson knew, and the people knew, that a blow might fall on him at any moment. So no public worship was attempted, only private services at his house. Yet so long as people asked for tracts he gave these out eagerly. He had something of the imagination of a radio preacher; in his thought he could visualize the unseen, far-flung audience to whom he was telling his glorious message, as his tracts were carried out along the rivers, and into the great jungles, and up into the far mountains; and he could see scattered over the country here and there the little groups gathered around a dim lamp, or seated about a fire, listening with eager hearts as one among them read from the precious writing. No wonder he was thrilled!

---

[12] So spelled in Wayland; but probably it should be Cassay, *i.e.*, Manipur, in Assam.

After the Buddhist festival he turned back once more to his translating and revising. Early in March word reached him of the death of George Dana Boardman in the Tavoy jungle, and he wrote to Mrs. Sarah Boardman a letter that is a model of Christian comfort, revealing the richness of his sympathetic nature without overstepping the bounds of good taste. He offered to help in securing an education for her little George, or to care for him as his own son in case she should be taken away. How little he realized that in three years he would take the place of her husband, and that the young George would indeed become as his own son.

But Mrs. Wade's health had failed alarmingly, so that a sea voyage seemed absolutely necessary to save her life. Judson must care for her husband's work while they were gone. So he closed his books, sent off Shwe Doke, San Lone and Shwe Too with tracts on last trips up the country, and sailed for Moulmein. On the thirty-first of July [13] he was back in his old home once more, joyfully welcomed by the native Christians and the children of the school.

Judson had now been in Burma seventeen years. Twenty-four missionaries had been sent from America to that land, including Ann and himself and Rice. Yet only twelve remained; the others had died or withdrawn from the mission. And the twelve shrunk to two, if one reckoned only those available for evangelizing the Burmans. Mrs. Boardman and the Masons were at Tavoy, among the Karens. Mr. and Mrs. Jones were in Rangoon, but knew little Burmese as yet. The Bennetts, the Wades and the Kincaids were in Moulmein. But Bennett was putting in every minute on the press, Kincaid had taken the pastorate of the English-speaking church, and the Wades were leaving for America. Mrs. Bennett was able to lead the women's meetings. But only Judson could preach to the people in their native Burmese. [14]

---

[13] Judson's *Autobiographical Record* gives this date. His journal says August 11th (1831).

[14] Judson, like other early missionaries, had a paternalistic attitude toward his converts. C. H. Carpenter, *Self Support*, p. 133, says he did not ask them for contributions because Buddhist doctrine of merit was so ingrained in them that they might think their gifts were gaining merit with God, instead of being used by His free grace.

And now the board invited him to return to America. One can imagine how eagerly his heart responded! See the members of this Baptist board that he represented but most of whom he had never seen? Meet those with whom he had corresponded so long but had never met? Rove once more across those New England hills? Visit his old friends and classmates of Brown and Andover? Live again for a little while in the old Plymouth home with his mother and Abigail? An unutterable longing for home came over him. Indeed he was always homesick for America. He never saw a ship sail away from Moulmein for the home land without an almost irresistible desire to go home. And now all his home yearnings, his social instincts, his love of culture, his ambition to be in the center of things, came back with a rush.

But he thought of the little flock in Moulmein, he remembered the people in the jungle fastnesses, he recalled the innumerable villages from Tenasserim to China. He could not plead ill health now, the mission was short-handed, and the value of a furlough to a missionary and to the home church had not then been learned. So he turned away from thoughts of home, declined the invitation, and set himself with fresh enthusiasm and almost fierce determination to his old work of proclaiming the gospel.

Another chapter in Judson's life had begun.

CHAPTER VII

JUNGLE TRAILS

JUDSON's crowded days at Prome and Rangoon make a thrilling story. So do his jungle tours among the Karens. He had noticed small groups of these wild men in Rangoon soon after he and Ann first came. Seeing them straggle past his house, he asked who they were. "Karens," he was told; "as untamable as the wild cow of the mountains." They kept away from the city as much as possible, for the Burmans scorned them as no better than beasts, and treated them as slaves. But Judson was able to arouse the interest of his Burman converts in them, and during the war Shwe Ba took pity on one, a Karen slave whom he found in Rangoon, bought him, gave him his freedom, and after the war took him to Moulmein. There he introduced him to Judson, and the latter told him the story of his great Saviour. But he was dull of mind, and seemed a very unpromising prospect. Finally the light dawned and he welcomed Christ into his heart. Shortly afterward he went with the Boardmans to Tavoy and was baptized by Boardman. We know him as the great apostle to the Karens, Ko Tha Byu.

Reports came to Judson of the interest in the gospel shown by Karens in the jungle, as a result of a visit by Wade, and in a month after his return from Rangoon he was out in the jungle himself, with Tau-nah, the first of Wade's converts, as interpreter. He had only two weeks of touring, and then jungle fever laid hold of him and he reluctantly returned to Moulmein. But he brought three Karens from the jungle with their families, to attend an adult school that he had opened in Moulmein. Here a few selected converts were to be taught to read, and to understand the Bible; then they were to be sent back among their own people to tell them the message. For several weeks he carried on this school and cared for the mission. But the jungle called him. It was the old pioneering spirit still in his blood. It was this that had sent him out on his western trip after college days, and at Andover had fired him with enthusiasm for the foreign mission adventure. It was this that had made him the leader in the enterprise and had carried him forth into the unknown east. It was this that had kept him from discouragement, in the face of tremendous odds, and had made him press on through every hindrance and difficulty. He had pioneered to Ava, he had pioneered to Amherst, and he would be pioneering throughout his life, until he should set out on his last voyage into the unknown.

So he closed the adult school, and at the end of the year (1831) he and nine companions started out again. On New Year's Day, a Sunday, they reached Wadesville.[1] Within a few days he had his helpers out in every direction. One party went up the Dagyaing River as far as boats could go. A second went across the country to another small stream. A third traveled to the head of the Patah River. Everywhere they spread the news of the coming of the white teacher. All the twenty-seven disciples had been faithful, and they came in for Sunday worship. But they had met a good deal of opposition; and the people who three months before had seemed eager to hear the white messenger were now quite noncommittal. None was ready to cast in his lot with the little company of disciples.

The result was a new project—the Karens suggested it—a separate Christian village. They named it Newville. And a month later a second was founded, Chummerah. There a zayat was built, disciples erected their homes, and Chummerah became the central station for the jungle work.

The month that followed was as strenuous a period as Judson ever experienced. He was on the move constantly—from village to village, from home to home, sometimes traveling by boat or canoe, often tramping through the jungle on foot, making his way over rocks and sandhills or through streams that crossed the path, preaching, counseling, holding church meetings and baptizing—a month of tireless activity that tested his endurance but stirred him with boundless enthusiasm.

It was not an easy tour. Of course there were no chapels

---

[1] Named by Judson for Jonathan Wade, who had here baptized the first Karens.

in which to preach. Frequently no house was available. Often he sat on the ground as he talked to the people, or under a low mat set up by his men. If he traveled by boat he was liable to be stopped by logs that had fallen across the stream, and he and his companions would have to cut a passage for the boat. If they were crossing the country by land, they might find a river with only a bridge of slippery logs. The trail might lead, as he said, "over dreadful mountains and in the bed of a rivulet, where the water was sometimes knee deep, and full of sharp, slippery rocks, where my bare feet, unaccustomed to such usage, soon became so sore that I could hardly step." Once he was wading a stream when he was startled by a shriek from one of his men, and turned just in time to see him dragged under the water by a huge alligator. The country swarmed with tigers and it was never safe to sleep in the open. Days and nights were full of difficulties and dangers.

The church meetings that Judson held in the wilderness were very informal affairs. When anyone applied for baptism he got together as many members as he could, in a village or by a river bank, and held what he called a "church meeting." Sometimes quite a number were present, on one occasion only five. But the candidates were examined thoroughly. First their own testimony was heard and they were questioned about their experiences. Then their fellow villagers and other ac-quaintances were asked for their opinion. Finally the church members voted on the admission of the candidates, sometimes, perhaps always, voting by ballot. If the vote was not unani-mous, the candidate was asked to wait; and Judson tells with amusement of the members overruling him in some cases where he himself felt that the candidate was acceptable.

The thing that stands out is his emphasis on the church. Even among these jungle Karens he stressed the importance of church membership and church action. This he had done in early days in Rangoon, and the same emphasis characterized his later work in Moulmein. It is refreshing and stimulating to note his emphasis on evangelism and the church, for in our later missionary practice we have developed other institutions and methods more than these great fundamentals. We can have little doubt that the permanence of what he did can be largely traced to this emphasis upon the church.

His journal, written for the board at home, is naturally serious in tone for the most part. But his irrepressible good nature and his appreciation of the ludicrous come out now and then. For example, there is his picture of the long procession which he led along the path—"men, women, children and dogs." The description of the woman who presented herself for baptism is rich—arrayed in all the ornaments she could get together, twelve strings of beads around her neck, colored stones in her ears, rings on her arms and legs. So is his account of her coming next day—"the decorated lady of yesterday"— his "holding forth" before breakfast on the subject of female attire, and his amusement at the way she saw the point and proceeded to take off all the ornaments she was wearing. And one can imagine him chuckling to himself as he describes his amusing experience at one place where he tried to conciliate the children and the dogs, who were the only ones who received him, and who "cried and barked in concert!"

Judson's appeal to the decorated lady brings out his high ideal of church membership.[2] If a candidate was not ready to give up completely every evil practice he was asked to wait. Tee-pah, for example, "though convinced of the truth and giving some evidence of grace, cannot decide at once on total abstinence from rum, though he has never been in the habit of intoxication." So he was declined. Abstaining from worship of the nats (spirits), and keeping the Sabbath, were other conditions required. Likewise the putting aside of elaborate dress. For Judson saw that the wearing of such a wealth of ornaments encouraged vanity, and that by sacrificing this the new disciples were helped to give Christ the first place in their affections. He remembered, however, that American Christian women were subject to the same temptation to vanity as their sisters in Burma, so he prepared a letter on the latter addressed "To the Female Members of Christian Churches in the United States

---

[2] In his Moulmein church three applications for baptism were required. Each Sunday the applications were announced and the church voted by ballot on each name. See Appendix to his *Sermon on Baptism* for his reasons for baptizing.

of America," [3] and urged that their ornaments be sold and the proceeds be given to the work of the Lord. This was entirely in harmony with his desire that nothing should be allowed to contend with Christ for first place. But he did not press the matter, except with members of his own native churches, and he did not badger other missionaries with what was a matter of conscience with himself.[4]

The Karens did not welcome him and his message as eagerly as he had expected. In one village the chief would not even give him the usual hospitality and invite him to his house, but sent him off to a deserted old hut, so rotten and ramshackle that the floor would not support him and his helpers. But not all were indifferent. In some places crowds gathered to listen. Some heard with joy and accepted the new Saviour. Here was an old woman with her daughter and son-in-law who begged that their baptism might not be delayed. There a man eagerly followed Judson two days until the latter and his Burman disciples agreed to receive him, then went on his way rejoicing. At another village he sat down by the river bank with those interested, like Paul at Philippi, and could say of almost the whole village that the Lord had opened its heart to give heed to the things that were spoken.

The principal man at another place sent word that when the English government enforced their religion at the point of the sword, and he had seen two or three suffer death for not accepting it, he would begin to consider, but not before; however, he could not be inhospitable, so Judson could come if he wanted. Judson replied that as he loved darkness he would leave him to live therein, and at last go the dark way. But something touched the old man, and while Judson and his friends were considering what to do, they heard the sound of footsteps approaching in the dark, and a voice, "My lord, please come to the village." And he led the way back to his house,

---

[3] Given in full in Wayland, II, pp. 476f.

[4] During his furlough in 1846 some Quaker ladies in Philadelphia gave him a doll, dressed in perfect Quaker style, and asked him to persuade the women missionaries, if possible, to adopt that dress. He was embarrassed but agreed to bring it to their attention, which he did; but then eagerly gave the doll to little Sarah Stevens.

spread a cloth for Judson to sit on, listened earnestly, repeated some of Judson's prayer with emphasis, and after his visitor had gone, said to his people that it was hard to change one's religion, but that if some others would join him he would accept the new faith.

Some who heard the message became true disciples; and at the end of the tour twenty-five could be reported as baptized, with as many more who were hopeful inquirers.

On February eleventh he was back in Moulmein; but on the twenty-ninth he was off once more on a third tour, with three Karen helpers and four Talaings. This time he was gone four weeks. The tour was much like the previous one, with many villages visited, some hearers accepting the new faith, and now and then violent opposition. There were disappointments—a few promising disciples yielded to the besetting sin of the Karens and made offerings to the spirit of disease, some hopeful inquirers lost their interest, one of the Karen workers while out preaching met a Buddhist priest with his novices, and they set upon him and gave him a sound beating. But there were encouragements as well. He had to spend one Sunday in travel on a river, and meeting a boat full of men he hailed them and asked whether they would like to hear the gospel of the Lord Christ. An old man, who was leader of the party, called back that he had heard much about it and would like nothing better than to hear the teacher. Soon the boats were side by side and Judson was preaching to the man and his comrades, with happy result: "After a short engagement the old man struck his colors and begged us to take him into port, where he could make a proper surrender of himself to Christ." So they went ashore and talked for several hours as they sat together under the overhanging trees; then the boatman was baptized.

Thus it went. Judson was overflowing with enthusiasm. Quoting the words of John Wesley, he said, " 'The best of all is, God is with us,' I feel in my very soul. Yes, the great Invisible is in these Karen wilds." Thirty-six sat down together at Chummerah for the Lord's Supper. Nineteen were baptized during the tour.

These two years of touring bring out sharply the evangelistic purpose that was foremost in Judson's interest throughout his life. He was constantly eager for conversions, and his correspondence and journal are full of this longing: "You want to hear of some Burman brought to taste that the Lord is gracious; but O not more than I want to speak of it." . . . Of Maung Ing, "Lord Jesus, give him saving knowledge of thine adorable self!" . . . Of U Ya, "O that he may be brought in!" . . . To Ann, "O let me travel through this country, and bear testimony to the truth all the way from Rangoon to Ava, and show the path to that glory which I am anticipating." Again and again he would quote his own lines:

> "In these deserts let me labor,
> On these mountains let me tell
> How he died—the blessed Saviour,
> To redeem a world from hell."

He put it in words that could not be misunderstood: "The grand means of converting the heathen world is to preach the glorious gospel of our great God and Saviour Jesus Christ." It is certain that his controlling missionary principle was evangelism.

On returning to Moulmein from his third tour he was "glad yet sorry" to find that Bennett was back from Calcutta, whither he had gone for better Burmese type and printing presses. A new brick printing house had been built. All was ready for the printing of the Bible. This meant that Judson must settle down once more to translating and correcting proofs. But his mind was still in the Karen jungle. So he organized a party of evangelists, under the leadership of his former interpreter Ko Myat Kyaw, and sent them up the Salween in the mission boat ten days' journey, to the home of a celebrated Karen prophet, Areemaday, who was drawing large numbers of followers. He received the evangelists cordially, and they were busy day and night preaching to large crowds. Later, Areemaday sent messengers to Judson several times, often with presents, begging him to come and instruct him and his Karen people in the Christian faith. But Judson could not go.

In 1833 he spent three months in Chummerah, devoting

much of his time to a boarding school that he had started. In May his place was taken by Miss Sarah Cummings—"Aunt Sarah" Judson called her—who had come out as the first single woman missionary of the Baptist board, and he was glad to turn over the school to her. For in his thought schools must always be secondary to evangelism. He was critical of some kinds of schools, but his appreciation of this type of work increased through the years. In his view, schools could not take the place of preaching or the circulation of the Scriptures and other Christian literature; nevertheless they provided opportunity for reaching boys and girls and young men with the saving message and thus would help in the winning of precious souls. Schools for adults would open the way for them to learn to read, especially the Bible, and so they would be able to read to others the word of God; and training schools for Christian workers were essential and should be carefully planned and encouraged. He would not have taken Duff's attitude, that Christian education would, by undermining the nonchristian system, turn the people to Christianity; though his philosophical and metaphysical arguments with thoughtful Burmans show that he did not minimize the intellectual side of evangelism. He would not have been content with schools of any kind without full opportunity for Christian evangelism —"suffering school keeping to eat up all their time and energies," as he put it. "Go ye into all the world and preach the gospel to every creature" was the command that had brought him to his missionary decision at Andover, and all questions regarding schools were to be decided according to this standard and test.

Occasional brief visits were made to the jungle later. On September eighth, 1833, he baptized the one hundredth Karen convert north of Moulmein, all but the first fourteen having been baptized by him. After this he spent most of the time for the next five or six years in Moulmein, preaching and translating.

All his preaching to the Karens had been done through an interpreter. So also his earlier work for Hindus. These form striking exceptions to the policy which he vigorously emphasized, the use of the vernacular. He criticized strongly those missionaries "who never acquire the languages, except a mere smattering of them, of the countries to which they are sent, but beguile their time and expend their labors among their own countrymen and the country-born [5] population, under the fallacious idea that through them the Christian religion will gradually reach the masses of the native population." But no "mere smattering" for him! He set an example to missionaries of all future time. The thoroughness with which he studied both the written and the spoken tongue, and the long years in which he allowed himself to do scarcely anything else, make clear his sense of the importance of mastery of the language. It was natural, therefore, that he should advise new missionaries not to stay in Moulmein, but to "dash into Toungoo, or some other place, get the language from the living sounds," and thus fit themselves for whatever task awaited them. "Read the palm leaf, read the palm leaf," he would often say to his younger colleagues; in other words, "Get the language." So, though among the Karens he used an interpreter, yet for his work with those whom he considered his special responsibility, the Burmans, he mastered the language, as we have seen.

News reached him this year of the organization of the American Baptist Home Mission Society, a result of influences set in motion by Luther Rice. Judson was enthusiastic about the new society, and wrote to the secretary, Jonathan Going, his friend from days at Brown, expressing his warm sympathy with the project.

His broad interest is to be seen, likewise, in his attitude to the proposal made about the same time for the opening of a mission in France. Doubtless his mind went back twenty years to his experiences in that land, and he saw again the things that had so stirred his soul in the moral need of the people. He wrote home urging that the plan for the French mission be carried into effect, and said he would "heartily rejoice" in having a considerable proportion of the appropriations for Burma diverted to the mission in France.

He had a keen interest in the Jews, also, and was trying at this time to raise money for a new mission to that people in

---

[5] That is, Anglo-Indian, or Anglo-Burman.

Palestine. The project failed, but Judson was nevertheless able indirectly to win some of the Jewish race to Christ.[6]

He had scarcely returned from his Karen tour in 1833 when the Bennetts left for Rangoon. He hated to have them go. "I never had a tighter fit of low spirits," he wrote, "than for about a week after you had gone. I sometimes went, after dinner, to take a solitary walk in the veranda, and sing, with my *harmonious* voice, 'Heartless and hopeless, life and love all gone.' However, I am rallying again, as the doctors say. But I have not yet got the steam up in the Old Testament machine."

So when the Karens around Rangoon began to listen to the preaching of Christ, and Bennett asked Judson to send him several Karen workers, he was enthusiastic, and sent several from Moulmein. He himself continued the evangelizing of the Karens around Moulmein, through assistants. One of these was "Old Rajah," as he called him, who was evidently overflowing with zeal. "He is full of the matter, and intends to march forthwith upon the north pole, and clear away all the intervening darkness."

It was now twenty years since the missionary vision had come to Judson at Andover. How his world had widened! And what jungle trails he and others had explored! Rangoon —Ava—Amherst—Moulmein—Prome—Arracan—Palestine— France—America and its far west. He was eager to have a part in making Christ known to all the world. But his own place was in Burma. And he kept feverishly at his great task, preaching to the Burmans, directing Karen evangelists, and completing the translation of the Bible. His preaching was never more earnest or effective than now. Justus Vinton, who arrived in 1832, told how impressed he himself was, before he could even understand the language. "My attention was never more closely riveted on any sermon I ever heard. It was impossible to escape the conviction that his whole soul was in his work. Every hearer sat motionless, every eye was fixed immovably upon the preacher, and every countenance seemed to change with every varied expression of sentiment."

---

[6] See p. 228.

And now his great work of translating the Scriptures was nearing its end. On the last day of January following his return from his final jungle tour—January 31, 1834—he laid down his pen, for the translation was finished.

CHAPTER VIII

AT LAST THE BURMAN BIBLE

At last the Burman Bible was completed. It had been the task of twenty years. And revisions and improvements were yet to be made. But the Burmans had their Bible. It was the supreme achievement of Judson's career. Reference has more than once been made to this great work of translating the Scriptures, but it was of such significance that we shall do well to pause and take a comprehensive view, looking back to the early beginnings and forward to the final revision.

Three years and a half after he arrived in Rangoon Judson went to work on the Gospel of Matthew. As a basis for his work he had Chater's translation of this book and Felix Carey's revision. The Portuguese Roman Catholics had also left a version of parts of the Scripture, and Judson made use of this as well. But all of these were imperfect and unsatisfactory, and Judson's translation was independent and practically original. He finished Matthew on the twentieth of May, 1817, and two days later began to compile a Burmese dictionary. The next two years he spent on the dictionary, and after that he was so busy in his zayat that he scarcely did any translating for another year. But on the twentieth of April, 1820, he was able to record the completion of the Epistle to the Ephesians. Then he began on The Acts. Then came the Gospel and Epistles of John. His visit to Ava with Dr. Price interrupted his progress, but after his return to Rangoon he gave himself almost exclusively to translating while he waited for Ann's return from America. At last, on July 12, 1823, one day short of exactly ten years since he had first set foot in Burma, he could enter in his "Autobiographical Record," "Completed the translation of the New Testament in Burmese."

The vicissitudes of the precious New Testament manuscript during the imprisonment in Ava and Aungbinle have been described. Soon after his return from Crawfurd's embassy he commenced the translation of the Old Testament. But it was not till he had hidden himself away in the garret in Rangoon, following his visit to Prome, that he could go to work in earnest on the Old Testament. By February of 1831 he had finished the Psalms, the Song of Solomon, and Daniel. Then came Isaiah and Genesis, with a part of Exodus. Then another interruption for two years. Finally he settled down to the task of completing the Old Testament, and in Chummerah of the Karen country and in his cottage at Moulmein he toiled day after day, first on the major prophets, then the minor prophets, finally the remaining books. At last the great work was done. The great achievement toward which he had been striving for more than twenty years was accomplished. On January 31, 1834, he finished the task. The Burmans had the Bible in their own tongue. Hear his own words: "Thanks be to God, I can now say I have attained. I have knelt down before him, with the last leaf in my hand, and imploring his forgiveness for all the sins which have polluted my labors in this department, and his aid in future efforts to remove the errors and imperfections which necessarily cleave to the work, I have commended it to his mercy and grace; I have dedicated it to his glory. May he make his own inspired word, now complete in the Burman tongue, the grand instrument of filling all Burma with songs of praise to our great God and Saviour Jesus Christ. Amen."

It was achievement enough for a life time. But Judson was not content. He must make the translation more nearly perfect, if that could be done. Many questions had been left unsettled, questions as to meaning, questions as to the best Burmese word or phrase. So while he was translating the Old Testament he gave himself with equal intensity to the revision of the New. At first he had some help from Wade. But after a few months he was compelled to toil at it alone, with such advice as he could get from others. On November 14, 1829, he completed the revised New Testament.

"Our final translation," he called it. But he was not yet content. He had a "lust for finishing," as he said—for making a thing perfect. Soon he was examining his translation of the

Book of Hebrews, in the light of a recent commentary by his old friend and teacher Professor Stuart. But most of his time for translating had to be given to the Old Testament, and it was not till 1836 that he could turn with vigor to the perfecting of his New Testament version. On January thirty-first of the following year he finished the second revision. But two months later he was at it again. "I thought I had finished the revision of the New Testament above a month ago," he writes; "but there is no end of revising, while a thing is in the press." So he continued to revise and correct and improve.

It was the same with the Old Testament. As soon as his first translation was finished he began on a revision. He was half through with this when he received from America a complete set of Rosenmüller's work on the Old Testament, and he went over the whole ground once more.

An amusing illustration of the need for this careful revising appeared shortly after he married Sarah Boardman. A faithful old Christian came to him very much troubled, and told him of his fear that his teacher was to be among the lost.

"You know," he said, "the Bible says that God will deliver his children from the snare of the widow. But he has not delivered you; you have been snared by the widow."

They turned to the Psalm (91:3), and found that it read just as the old man had said. The feminine form of the word "hunter" had been used, which in Burmese is the word for "widow"! Judson lost no time in revising that passage.

On September 26, 1835, the Old Testament revision was completed. Still he was not content. A new quarto edition of the whole Bible was planned—why not see if what had been done could be done better? It *must* be better if possible. It must be perfect, so far as human ability and knowledge could make it. So there was more revising, more study of the Hebrew text, more examining of the latest exegetical books of the best scholars. At last, on the twenty-fourth of October, 1840, the great work was ended, the last revision was complete. The two chief objectives of his life—the gathering of a church of a hundred members and the turning of the Bible into Burmese—were now achieved. Improvements and corrections in his translation he continued to note, but the literary work of the years that remained was to be the making of a dictionary. "It is one main duty of the remnant of my life to study and labor to perfect the Burmese translation of the Bible"—so he had stated his life aim. He had held to it faithfully. And now his work on the Bible was done.

Equally important with the translating of the precious Book was the printing of it. As soon as Hough arrived with the press in 1816 he got out a small edition of Matthew. No further printing had been done until Bennett came in 1830. Luke and Ephesians had then appeared, and finally on December 19, 1832, the whole New Testament in Burmese was off the press and ready for the Burman people. Parts of the Old Testament then began to be printed, and on December 29, 1835, the great day came when Judson was able to record that the whole Bible, in four octavo volumes, was printed in the language of the Burman people. The revised New Testament followed in 1837, and the final revised quarto in 1840.

A Bible in every village in Burma—that was Judson's aim. "To deposit the Bible at the principal place of resort in every village is the least we can do for Burma." Five million people could read—what an opportunity! The Bible could go where a missionary could not. That tells why in one year (1836) he printed forty thousand copies of the New Testament, though the whole number of converts from the beginning to that time was less than twelve hundred.

The results in some measure justified his plans. Many Burmans were awakened to an interest in the Christian faith—some were definitely won to the faith—through reading the Gospel of Matthew, or one of the tracts, before they ever heard a sermon or even met a Christian. In his later years he modified his opinion as to the value of Bible circulation apart from preaching, convinced that the Burmans were not crying out for the word of God as he had thought. But that did not diminish in any degree his conviction of the need of the people for the Scriptures in their native tongue, or of the importance of an accurate translation. As much as he believed in the preeminence of the proclamation of the gospel by word of mouth, he felt in his later years that there was a tendency, in the emphasis on preaching, to cast somewhat into the shade the written communication of the truth through the Scriptures and tracts. And he believed that while preaching would bring more immediate results, the permanent success of missionary work would rest upon the Bible, in the language of the people. "Those missions which give the highest place to the divine word will be most owned of God and blessed. . . . The preached gospel and the written word are the two arms which are to pull down the kingdom of darkness and build up the Redeemer's." Judson lived among a people who could read, who had an abundant literature, and who set great store by the sacred books of their religion. So he gave them the best possible gift—the Bible.

Some idea of the thoroughness with which Judson did his work can be gathered from the fact that much of the time he translated only twenty-five or thirty verses a day, though giving all his time to it. He pointed out that there were two ways of translating: one original, the other second-hand. "The first must be adopted by a missionary whose lot falls in a section of the globe where there is no translation of the Scriptures in any cognate language, or in any language known to the learned men of the country. In that case he must spend some years in reading a great many books, and in acquiring a competent stock of the language; that, like as the spider spins her web from her own bowels, he may be able to extract the translation from his own brain. The other mode may be advantageously adopted by a missionary who has in his hand the Bible already translated into some language known by learned natives of the country. In that case he has only to get a smattering of their vernacular, enough to superintend their operations, and then parcel out the work, and it is done by steam." He made it clear that he did not intend to speak disparagingly of what he termed "second-hand" translations. In fact such translations might be superior to an original one. He was only showing that his own had to be original, not based on any other in the Burmese or any cognate language. This took time. Ziegenbalg's in Tamil, Carey's in Sanskrit and Bengali, Morrison's in Chinese—these were original and were the basis for others in similar dialects or tongues. Judson's Burmese translation was in this group. It was slow work, but thorough.

Judson was qualified in the highest degree for the exacting task which he set himself. In the first place he had a keen literary enthusiasm. Probably he gained it from his father. As a boy he devoured good books—theology from his father's library, novels of Richardson and Fielding from neighbors, with plays of Ben Jonson, and the classics in school. At Brown the Philermenian Society developed his literary interest through its library, its essays, its poems, its orations and debates, while the regular curriculum gave him rhetoric, logic, Latin and Greek. The grammar and arithmetic which he prepared and published during his first year out of college, are sufficient proof of his liking for books and his intense interest in creative writing. In his journal and letters he frequently quoted gems of poetry. Many of these were original with him. But now and then he quoted other poets, like Pope, Burns, Goldsmith, Cowper and Milton, in such a natural way as showed perfect familiarity with them. Buddhist literature attracted him, too, and its poetry and beauty fascinated him. This literary instinct was basic for his Bible translating. Without such interest he never would have been able to hold himself to his task of putting the whole Bible into Burmese, and more than once revising his translation so thoroughly. And without his wide literary knowledge he would not have put into his translation the high qualities that have made it live through the years.

A second qualification was his scholarship. Of this he had given ample proof during his days at Brown. His mastery of Latin and Hebrew was revealed (to his practical advantage) during his exciting voyage to England. So apparent were his attainments in scholarship that on his arrival in Calcutta from America a position in Fort William College was proposed. He had the scholar's insistence on exact accuracy, the scholar's wide-ranging search for facts and materials. On shipboard he spent his hours in such scholarly work as translating the Greek New Testament and digging into the meaning and significance of baptism, instead of idling or playing games; he could give himself steadily to a difficult intellectual task. In his breadth of interest and knowledge, in his studiousness and ability to concentrate, in his thoroughness and exactness, he was fitted as a scholar for his literary work in Burma.

A third qualification was the unusual training he had enjoyed for this very work of translating the Scriptures; for he was a student under Professor Moses Stuart at Andover, the outstanding scholar in America in New Testament interpretation and textual criticism. Stuart was one of the first to make known German biblical scholarship in this country, and was fearless in his use of all the materials of biblical study on which he could lay his hand. "The father of exegetical studies in America,"[1] he has been called. Judson had only the last few months of his course with him, but Professor Stuart could impress himself upon his students in a very brief time. And, indeed, Judson had remained at Andover for a while after his graduation. Stuart was not only an indefatigable student and an inspiring teacher, but he was keenly interested in missions. It was in his home that the meeting was held that led to the formation of the American Board and the appointment of Judson and his associates. And this missionary interest would intensify his influence upon Judson, as it did upon others of his students who as missionaries became skilled translators, like Elias Riggs and William G. Schauffler. What Judson received from him at Andover was exactly the training he needed. And in Burma he continued to make use of Stuart's growing critical and exegetical studies. Scarcely any words could overestimate the importance of those few months of study with Professor Moses Stuart.

A fourth qualification was his thorough mastery of the Burmese language. How earnestly and untiringly he gave himself to this task we have already seen. The Burmans themselves testified to his remarkable grasp of their language. No missionary in Burma (and scarcely anywhere else) since his time has had the opportunity for so long a period of uninterrupted language study; for six years he did little else. Moreover, few since his day have studied under such favorable conditions. There was no temptation to speak English, for there was hardly another foreigner in the land, and his teachers did not know English. Conditions made it possible for him to come into closest contact and fellowship with the people.

---

[1] Quoted in Enc. Brit., 13th Ed., art. Moses Stuart.

Everything contributed to his opportunity for acquiring the language. And of course his literary interest and scholarly aptitudes came to his aid with tremendous effectiveness. In his student days at Brown he had laid solid foundations for linguistic work; his training at Andover under Professor Stuart had helped; he had a natural liking for foreign languages and unusual facility in acquiring them—all of these aided him immensely. The result was that he became a master of the Burmese, its rich vocabulary, its peculiar idioms, its niceties of phrase, its literary and colloquial forms. He largely gave up the reading of English books so as to become more naturalized in Burmese. Before his return to America he had become much more at home in Burmese than in English.

Finally, he had another qualification that was absolutely essential for interpretation of the Scriptures, a deep and genuine experience in the things of which the Bible speaks. He could not have hoped to turn into the language of the Burmans, with accuracy and effectiveness, what he did not fully understand through his own experience. But he had that experience; and his strong, glowing, Christ-reflecting religious life furnished the vital element in his translation work.

He made his translation direct from the original Greek and Hebrew. Before he left America he laid the foundation at Brown and Andover for a mastery of these ancient tongues, and he kept up his study of them as he proceeded with his Burmese Bible. At the same time he dug deep into the Burmese until he knew that as well as any Burman scholar. To aid him in the arduous task of transferring the thought from the Greek or Hebrew to the Burmese he made use of all the helps on which he could lay his hand. American, English and German authors were called upon for this service.[2] Some wrote in Latin as well as in modern tongues. So that he worked in five or perhaps six languages.

He and Ann had with them on shipboard a good collection of books. In one of her letters, written on the *Caravan,* Ann mentions the extensive commentary by Thomas Scott, which

---

[2] Wayland, II, pp. 129, 160. If Judson used the German authors in the original, he must have learned the language after reaching Burma. Perhaps he used only such works as were translated into English.

had an immense circulation and a very wide influence in that day, also George S. Faber's *Sacred Calendar of Prophecy*. As Judson was at work on a translation of the New Testament during the voyage, he probably had a number of critical and exegetical books, though we do not know their titles. In his early work on the New Testament in Rangoon he made large use of Parkhurst's Greek Lexicon, and Johann Griesbach's well-known critical edition of the New Testament. This great German scholar had inaugurated a new epoch in New Testament criticism, and was then the standard New Testament editor. Judson followed him in his textual readings, "as all the world did then," he explains. Gradually, however, he came to distrust Griesbach, and in preparing his quarto edition he turned to Knapp,[3] whose text he followed pretty closely; so that the final New Testament version in Burmese accorded more nearly with the English Authorized Version than had the earlier versions. Prrobably, too, he made use of Bloomfield's Greek Testament, as he was eager to secure it.

In his Old Testament work Judson at first depended largely upon the critical works of others, like Bishop Robert Lowth's edition of Isaiah, and Samuel Horsley's annotated translations of Isaiah, Hosea and the Psalms. Later he went back directly to the Hebrew text for more independent and original study. Gesenius' works were always at his hand, certainly his Hebrew Lexicon, probably others of his works. Johann Rosenmüller's commentary on the Old Testament gave him large assistance. And he had many books whose titles he does not give.

Most of these works have been superseded, but the significant point is that he used the best and most scholarly aids available; and at the same time he exercised his own independent judgment.

He was constantly eager to secure all the best books bearing on his critical and exegetical studies, and as soon as a new publication was announced he ordered it. This took so long that he suggested to Solomon Peck, then secretary of the mission board, that as soon as new works came out, by American schol-

---

[3] George Christian Knapp, professor of theology at Halle and co-director of Francke's foundations; his edition of the New Testament first appeared in 1797, 5th edition 1840, but Judson may have used the 4th edition.

ars such as Stuart, Edwin Robinson, Calvin Stowe and others, or by leading German authors, they be sent at once without waiting for his order—"sent out to the library," as he put it, for he counted all such books as belonging to the mission, not to himself personally. "I frequently see a sterling work on the cover of the *Herald* or *Magazine,* and am ready to scream, with some variations, 'The book! the book! my kingdom for the book!'" President Wayland tells of Judson's large demand for books as early as Ann's visit to America in 1822, and how he yielded to her requests—as everyone did—and "stripped my library," as he says, "of what I considered some of its choicest treasures, to supply a part of his most urgent necessities." Doubtless Judson secured many similar gifts from others, and he must have gathered a large and certainly valuable library. A complete list of his books would be of the keenest interest. It is very certain that he had every book in English, and probably in German or Latin, that would aid him in making his great work perfect.[4]

All the help he could get from other missionaries he gladly welcomed. In preparing the earlier editions there was scarcely any associate with sufficient knowledge of the language to aid him. Wade and Jones gave him valuable assistance for a while, but Wade was away a good deal, and Jones early removed to Siam, so their aid was limited. In the later editions he gained much from Mason, who was Boardman's successor in Tavoy, Grover Comstock who came in 1835, and E. A. Stevens, to whom he later bequeathed the task of finishing his dictionary. Several hundred suggestions came to him, and most of them he adopted, though often with modifications. Of course he gained much from his Burman associates, and to one of them, Maung En, who was with him from Prome days, he gave special praise—"one of our most judicious and devoted assistants." He knew his work was not perfect, and begged his successors

---

[4] Among the scholars whose works he ordered were Josiah Gibbs of Yale, translator of Gesenius; John Butterworth of England, author of a concordance; Benjamin Blayney of Oxford, whose edition of Jeremiah he wanted; Edwin Robinson of Andover, on whose Greek and Hebrew lexicons he depended greatly; Charles Hodge of Princeton, author of the well-known commentary on the Book of Romans; Friedrich Tholuck of Berlin and Halle, for whose commentary on the Gospel of John he asked; and many others.

not to spare his errors, but at the same time not to correct a supposed error without consulting the authors he had consulted, so as to understand his position, and also comparing parallel and similar passages.

Judson tried with the utmost faithfulness to translate the Bible as it was in the original Greek and Hebrew so as to give the exact sense in the Burmese. That meant spending hours studying the original, together with versions in other languages, and delving into the critical works of many scholars, before he decided on the exact meaning. Then the correct word or phrase had to be chosen, a task peculiarly difficult in the matter of ideas and teachings distinctively Christian, for which there were no parallels in Buddhist thought. He spent more time and labor on his revisions than on his first translations. He felt that much of the translation work of missionaries had been "dreadfully misdirected," and great sums of money thrown away, by rushing through a translation without being willing to take time to be thorough and exact. "I consider it," he said, "the work of a man's whole life to procure a really good translation of even the New Testament in an untried language." Here was his "lust for finishing."

This desire to be faithful in giving to the Burmans just what God had revealed to men in His holy Book led him to translate the words that appear in English versions as "baptize" and "baptism." He saw no valid reason why he should withhold from the Burmans the meaning of these words, which could be readily translated. So he used a Burmese word meaning "immersing rite." As to the words in the English version his attitude was apparently quite different. The British and Foreign Bible Society and the American Bible Society [5] had decided that they could encourage only such versions as could be used by all the denominations cooperating with them, which would mean that the Greek words for "baptize" and "baptism" would not be translated, but merely transliterated. This decision had led American Baptists to organize the American and Foreign Bible Society, in order to provide translations by their mis-

---

[5] This society had greatly aided in the publication of the Scriptures in Burmese by generous contributions, for example, $5,000 in 1833. After the decision referred to, in 1836, the Baptist General Convention declined further contributions.

sionaries which should frankly translate these words, like all other words, and also to prepare a similar English translation.

Judson gave enthusiastic approval to the new society. But apparently his approval had reference only to the foreign versions, not the new English version. Emily Judson [6] emphasized that strongly in a letter written shortly after Judson's death.[7] He felt, she said, that the words "baptize" and "baptism" had become acclimated in English, as it were, and heartily disapproved, as a substitute for the King James version, a new English translation substituting "immerse" and "immersion"; such a change would be childish at this date, he said. Emily Judson was emphatic in her insistence that "he never contemplated a new English version for general circulation, and that what he heard of the new movements caused him great pain." But she made it equally clear that "he was very strenuous about his Burmese version, and would no doubt have persevered in his translation if the whole world had been against him." So faithful and conscientious was Judson in giving to the Burmans what he believed to be the word of God.

Emily Judson has left us her husband's deep impression of the importance of what he was doing in translating the Scriptures: "He felt, when making his translation, an almost overpowering sense of the awfulness of his work, and an ever-present conviction that every word was as from the lips of God." One can well understand his modesty, therefore, about the merits of his Burmese Bible. He knew it was not perfect. He was confident that the language of his New Testament was simple, plain and intelligible, and the testimony of the Burmans themselves encouraged him in this belief. But with the Old Testament he was not so well satisfied. He thought that he had done the historical books pretty well, but that in the poetical and prophetical books he had not attained "the beau ideal of translation," and was sure that much more work would be necessary on these books—partly indeed because of the uncertain meaning of difficult passages. The best he could

---

[6] Judson's third wife, whom he married in 1846.
[7] On the other hand, some of Judson's letters might seem to indicate sympathy with the proposed new English version.

say was that he hoped that he had laid a good foundation for his successors to build upon.

How good that foundation was has received ample testimony. Wayland said that it was the opinion of competent judges that "Dr. Judson's translation of the Scriptures is the most perfect work of the kind that has yet appeared in India." And he quoted the judgment of an unnamed "distinguished linguist, proficient in the Burmese language," that "as Luther's Bible is now in the hands of Protestant Germany, so three centuries hence Judson's Bible will be the Bible of the Christian churches of Burma." How it appeared to his colleagues is expressed in a letter written after Judson's death by one of the Burma missionaries: "The translation of the Holy Scriptures into the Burman language is admitted to be the best translation in India; that is, the translation has given more satisfaction to his contemporaries and successors than any translation of the Bible into any other eastern language has done to associate missionaries in any other parts of India. It is free from obscurity to the Burmese mind. It is read and understood perfectly. Its style and diction are as choice and elegant as the language itself, peculiarly honorific, would afford, and conveys, doubtless, the mind of the Spirit as perfectly as can be." [8]

But Judson was quite justified in assuming that he had only laid a foundation. The great development of biblical scholarship since his day, both in textual criticism and in interpretation, has revealed not a few mistakes in Judson's translation. Occasionally, too, he allowed himself to be turned aside from the accurate translation of a word or a passage by his presupposition as to the meaning. And finally, the Burmese language itself has changed. Hence naturally a revision of the Judson Bible has been necessary. [9] Other revisions will be made in the

---

[8] Quoted by Wayland, II, p. 168.

[9] A new translation of the New Testament into Burmese was made by the late U Tun Nyein in 1903, not from the Greek but from the English; this was revised by the British and Foreign Bible Society, and was published by that society with a later translation of the Old Testament. About 1904 a revision of Judson's Bible was begun by a committee of the Baptist mission. The New Testament was completed in 1924, the work being done by Rev. John McGuire, D.D., Rev. W. F. Thomas, D.D., U Tha Din and U Lu Din; the Old Testament was revised by Dr. McGuire and U Tha Din, and was completed in 1933. In 1915 an attempt was made to unite the two committees (Baptist and Bible Society), but the ideals of translation and publication were found so different that the effort was abandoned.

future. And we may hope that "three centuries hence" the Bible of the Burmans will be a translation made by Burmans themselves, rather than that made by Judson or other foreigners. Moreover, to speak of Judson's translation as "the most perfect work of its kind" is extravagant praise, though the claim may have had a measure of truth at the time it was made. Since his day other scholarly translations have appeared, in other languages, and comparisons made by his contemporaries might not be true in the same degree now.

Taking all this into account, however, Judson's translation must be recognized as a great achievement. Basically the Burman Bible is his. Considering the scholarly effort for exactness in the interpretation of the original Greek and Hebrew text, the high quality and naturalness of its Burmese diction, the satisfaction with which it has been accepted by Burmans and foreign missionaries since Judson's day, and its permanent value as a basis for later revisions and for translations into cognate tongues, we may say that the Bible that Adoniram Judson gave to the Burman people must rank not only as one of the most important productions of literary scholarship during the nineteenth century, but as one of the really great historic versions of the Scriptures. Well might Judson say, as he laid aside his pen, "I commend the work, such as it is, to God, to the church in Burma, and to my successors." For it was work well done.

Judson's great literary achievement was the Burman Bible. All his other literary work grew out of this or was supplementary to it. This was true even of his dictionary, to which he was to give so much of his later life. And of course it was particularly true of his Epitome of the Old Testament, his life of Christ, his various tracts and similar publications, and his sermons. They were all based on the Bible, and were intended to explain its truth and to win acceptance for its message.

Judson's first publication was a tract with the title *The Way to Heaven*. This title was later changed to *A View of the Christian Religion*.[10] The *View* was first printed in 1816 in Burmese, and later was translated into Talaing and Siamese.

---

[10] Given in full in Edward Judson's *Life of Adoniram Judson*, p. 568.

Throughout the years it was Judson's mainstay in introducing people to the Christian faith.[11]

This chief tract was in three parts, historical, practical and preceptive, to which was later added a fourth, devotional. Its opening sentence cut under the very foundation of Buddhism, which denies an eternal supreme Being: "There is one Being who exists eternally; who is exempt from sickness, old age and death; who was, and is, and will be, without beginning and without end." Again and again this sentence seized the attention of persons to whom Judson gave the tract. A Buddhist philosopher, attended by his pupils, was passing the Rangoon zayat on his way to a neighboring pagoda, when he had to stop on account of the crowd gathered about Judson. His eye happened to fall on a copy of the tract, and he read the opening sentence: "There is one Being who exists eternally." His attention was suddenly arrested. It was an entirely new idea. He stood for a long time wrapt in thought. Then he passed on. But he could not forget what he had read. He began to study and investigate, with the result that he became a Christian. He was taken by the authorities, tried and condemned to death, but succeeded in making his escape and got away from Rangoon. Judson never saw him again, but every now and then he heard of him through people who came asking for tracts or Bibles, and who told how he was preaching Christ far back in the country, and how they themselves had been won to Christ by him.

The *View* proved immensely useful, and was constantly in circulation. It was written in Burman style, and made use of Buddhist terms, such as describing a Christian disciple as a *thawtapan,* that is, one who has gained a new nature which will attain at last to salvation. And it ended with the date: "In the year of Christ, 1816; in the Burman year, 1178; in the 967th day of the lord of the Saddan elephant, and master of the Sakyah weapon; and in the 33rd year of his reign; in the division Pashoo; on Tuesday, the 12th day of the wane of the moon Wahgoung, after the double beat, this writing, entitled

---

[11] The American Tract Society contributed liberally to the Baptist and other boards for the circulation of approved tracts; in 1833 it gave $4,000 to the Baptist board for this purpose. The Religious Tract Society of London also made generous grants.

'The Way to Heaven,' was finished. May the reader obtain light. Amen."

The Golden Balance was another tract perhaps equally useful—indeed still used in revised form.[12] It was translated also into Talaing by Sarah Judson. The idea of a balance was based on the words of Elijah, "How long halt ye between two opinions?" (I Kings 18:21). And a challenge was presented to the reader to choose between Christianity and Buddhism, between Christ and Buddha.

Other important publications were a *Catechism of Religion,* originally prepared by Ann and translated into Siamese and Talaing; a *Liturgy of the Burman Church* with forms of worship; the *Baptismal Service,* the *Marriage Service,* and the *Funeral Service,* each consisting of extracts from Scripture; the *Teacher's Guide,* a digest of parts of the New Testament relating to the duties of teachers and pastors; and a *Digest of Scripture,* consisting of extracts from the Old and New Testaments. Another was the *Septenary,* or Seven Manuals, a handbook for pastors and other workers in seven chapters, dealing with the ordinances and similar important matters. Judson also revised Wade's tract entitled *The Investigator,* which he valued highly, and Boardman's *Ship of Grace.*

During the eleven-year interval between the completion of the New Testament and that of the Old, Judson used an *Epitome of the Old Testament.* This he prepared in 1823, as soon as the translation of the New Testament was out of the way; and even after the Old Testament was in print the *Epitome* continued to be used for some time. It was in twelve sections, and included a summary of Old Testament history and an abstract of the principal prophecies of the Messiah, as given in the Psalms, Isaiah and other prophets. As it was mostly in the words of the Bible itself it was especially valuable, and the new disciples welcomed it with great eagerness. Like all of Judson's publications, it received careful revision, and came out in several editions.

---

[12] It appears in Wayland, II, p. 449. Mr. Hanna says of this tract, "It has probably more powerfully influenced the thinking of the Burmese people, and caused them to see the insufficiency of Buddhism, than anything else ever written by a foreigner." (Letter to the author.)

Apart from the Bible, Judson's largest publication was perhaps his *Life of Christ,* prepared in 1836, after the revision of the Old Testament was finished. It was a book of two hundred pages, and was first printed in an edition of fifteen thousand. So enthusiastic was its reception that within a year it was back on the press for a second edition, this time forty thousand copies. The *Life of Christ* was translated into Talaing by his wife Sarah.

Besides these biblical or religious books, there were *Catechisms of Astronomy and Geography,* which he prepared for use in schools, the *Catechism of Geography* having a map of the world with Burmese names.

The question of alphabets or characters is one which the first translators in a country often have to face, especially in countries where there is no written language. The Burmans, however, had a great literature long before Judson came, with their own distinctive letters or characters. Judson used these characters. But when he was revising the Bible for his quarto edition, a proposal was made by Charles Trevelyan, an officer of the Indian Government, who was deeply interested in Christian missions, that the native Indian alphabets be given up and the Roman substituted. The noted missionary Alexander Duff supported the proposal, as did other prominent men. Certain of Judson's associates were enthusiastic over the plan, and wanted the new edition of the Bible printed in the Roman character and all the children in the schools taught the new way of writing their language. But Judson opposed it. For a language just being committed to writing he could see advantages in the Roman alphabet, though he thought these were somewhat exaggerated. But for an established language like the Burmese, or even the Karen (now reduced to writing), he felt strongly that the proposal was entirely impracticable. The Roman letters could not be used in their simple form, but would need "all manner of diacritical marks attached hither and thither and yon," to indicate the variations in the vowel sounds. And it would take generations for the Burmans to change from their old system to the new. Judson's counsels prevailed, and nothing was done about the plan in Burma.

Judson was a poor correspondent, in spite of the fact that

he was "unquestionably one of the finest epistolary writers in our language." [18]   He tried to be regular in his letters to Lucius Bolles, secretary of the mission board at home, and later to Solomon Peck his successor.   But sometimes he found it necessary to apologize for his delay: "I am surprised to see that my last date is three months ago."   His journal, however, he had kept up religiously until now.   And during brief periods after this he was to make daily memoranda.   It is to his journal and his letters to the mission board that we owe most of our knowledge of his work.

The journal was not a daily record, often several days intervening between one record and the next.   Judson evidently wrote it up at night, after the events of the day were over, so it is fresh and vivid.   Only the important events were mentioned, and these were recounted without waste of words.   But they were told with animation and interest, and the people who appear on the scene are described in pithy phrases or colorful words that give to each an individuality of his own.   Here are some of his visitors: Maung Tha E, who "descended into his native element, and stormed and raged"; Maung Lon, "a complete sceptic, scarcely believing his own existence"; three men from Nandawgon, whose "one characteristic is a particular love for the Scriptures"; a Siamese—"his mind is just on the poise between Buddhism and Christianity"; the "quiet and modest" Moung Nau; Maung Aung Hmat, who "listened with the air of an awakened man"; Ma Min Hla, "a woman of very superior discernment and mental energy"; Ko Ning Tsoo, "once a Pharisee, but lately disposed to change his character"; the wife of Maung Lon, who "proved to be as sharp as himself, and has been harassing Mrs. Judson with all sorts of questions."

He expressed his feelings in his journal as frankly as though no one would see it but himself or his wife.   Sometimes he is discouraged a bit; often he is eager and enthusiastic.   Frequently when in perplexity or danger he closes the day's record with a prayer that comes right out of his heart: "O Lord Jesus, look upon us in our low estate, and guide us in our dangerous course!"   "O Lord, send now prosperity; yet not my

---

[18] A. C. Kendrick, *Life and Letters of Mrs. Emily C. Judson*, p. 154.

will, but thine, be done." "O Lord, send help. Our waiting eyes are unto thee!" And often there is a burst of praise or thanksgiving as he thinks of the day's work and its results. But there is scarcely a touch of humor. His journal was to be sent to the board in America, and at that period humor in public would have been thought unseemly. Occasionally, if you look between the lines, you can see Judson smile as he writes. But not often in the earlier record. During those first ten years in Rangoon he and Ann walked almost constantly in the shadow of death. Life was serious business, and his journal reflects it. One must read his later journal and his personal letters for anything like playfulness or humor.

The letters that Ann had she destroyed, with all other writings of every kind, the night when she was a prisoner in her home in Ava after Adoniram's arrest. Fortunately some of his letters to his mother and his sister Abigail were saved, in spite of his direction that they be destroyed. And a few letters to friends were preserved by them. But though he wrote home regularly he did not write to many others. In fact, after a time he definitely gave up writing except to a limited few. But there are letters from the period after his marriage to Sarah Boardman, and they tell us more of Judson himself than we can learn in almost any other way.

He composed a number of hymns. But he wrote practically no formal articles for American periodicals. His journal, and some of his letters to his mother and sister, were published in the *Missionary Magazine,* but communications from his pen grew few in later years. He was asked to write, but as he said to Professor Knowles of Newton, his practiced pen was sadly unpracticed in English. For "a missionary who would become familiarly acquainted with a foreign tongue," he said, "must in a great measure sacrifice his own."

Judson lived a lonely life during those years following the death of Ann and little Maria. For some time he dwelt by himself, in the small cottage that he built near the Wades. A bell called him to meals with them, or if he wished, Mrs. Wade sent his meals over to him and he ate alone. After the Wades went to America he boarded with the Bennetts, though still living in his own little cottage. When the Bennetts went to

Rangoon the Cutters took him in. And when they went to
Ava to join Kincaid, the Hancocks provided for him. But he
was not quite alone. Maria had had a dog, Fidelia, and when
her little mistress died Fidee (as Judson affectionately called
the pet) came to live with Maria's father in his cottage. A man
and his dog can be very chummy, and the picture of Fidee
stretched out on the floor beside her master, as the latter studied
and wrote at his desk, tells us more about the human side of
Judson than a whole paragraph of description.

But however much Fidee might be loved for Maria's sake
and Nancy's, she could never take their place. No one could
take Nancy's place. But into Adoniram's loneliness another
was now to come, to make her own place in his life, and to
enrich his life in her own way. On April 10, 1834, Judson
married Sarah Boardman.

CHAPTER IX

HOME AND EVANGEL

THE next eleven years revolve about the new home with Sarah in Moulmein. How one would like to see Adoniram's letters to Sarah, and hers in reply. How one would like to know about their courtship and their developing love. But there are only a few casual references to her in his journal before their marriage, and she left almost no letters. Just four things tell of their interest in each other. One is the name of her second son, born in 1829, Judson Wade Boardman, telling of the high place that Judson had (with Wade) in the respect and affection of herself and her husband. Another is the letter of sympathy which he wrote to her on the death of Boardman in 1831, which she treasured and kept. The third is a watch that Judson gave her, while Boardman was still living, a watch that he had previously given to Ann. The fourth is a letter from her to Judson, written less than two months before their marriage, praising his translation of the New Testament, and signed "Yours affectionately"; evidently they were engaged by that time. Probably they had no long period of courtship. Judson was impulsive and acted quickly when he decided on action. He met Ann for the first time late in June, and in less than two months asked her to be his wife. He was introduced to Emily in December and they were engaged in January. Quite likely he acted as impulsively when he proposed to Sarah. In the close fellowship of the mission, however, all knew one another well, and Sarah and Adoniram had no need of long courtship. And in spite of his impulsiveness, not many made as few mistakes as he. Certainly he made no mistake in choosing his wives.

Sarah Hall was born in Alstead, New Hampshire, in 1803,

so was fifteen years younger than Adoniram.[1] Her parents early moved to Danvers, Massachusetts, then to Salem, where she lived until she went to Burma. Her home was very different from that of Ann. Ann's father was prosperous, and she had every opportunity for culture and education that a girl of her day could have. In Sarah's home means were scanty, and she was the oldest of thirteen children. Just after her twelfth birthday she wrote in her journal, "Tomorrow will be the day which is called Thanksgiving, but I have some fear that it is only in the name." So school facilities, though ample in Salem, were not for her. But she made up for this lack in other ways, partly at least. And at seventeen she was teaching school.

She reveled in the poetry of the Bible, and began early to write poems on biblical and religious themes. When she was seventeen she was baptized as a member of the First Baptist Church of Salem, her pastor being Dr. Lucius Bolles, who was so closely related to Judson and the Baptist missionary enterprise. Shortly afterwards she read the life of Samuel J. Mills, which stimulated a missionary interest she already possessed. The death of James Colman deeply impressed her, and she wrote a poem on the subject. Ann Judson not long after returned to America, and came to Salem. There she spoke at a women's meeting, and after her address Sarah was prevailed upon to read her poem on Colman. Thus Ann and Sarah met.

Sarah Hall's poem came to the eyes of George Dana Boardman, a student in Waterville College, now Colby, who had decided to offer himself in Colman's place. He and Sarah found each other, and in 1825 they sailed for Burma, arriving in 1827, just in time to see Ann's little Maria before she died. In Tavoy they took up the work for the Karens with which Boardman's name is imperishably connected. Her husband died in 1831, but she continued the work he had laid down, carrying on schools and touring in the jungle. It was a rough, hard life, threading the forests and fording the streams, in all sorts of weather. Judson's life had been marked by similar devotion, with sorrow like hers. When the time came that

---

[1] For the story of her life see *Emily Judson's Memoir* and W. N. Wyeth's *Sarah B. Judson, a Memorial*.

he asked her to unite her life with his she found herself ready, and turned from Tavoy to Moulmein.

No portrait of Sarah Judson remains, and so far as we know none was ever made. Judson spoke of "her soft blue eye, her mild aspect, her lovely face and elegant form." His wife Emily described her as "of about middle stature, agreeable in her personal appearance, and winning in manners." She did not have the striking personality or vivacity of Ann, nor her imperial spirit or commanding influence upon others. But she had qualities of her own: gentleness, cheerfulness that at times developed into playfulness, love of home and friends, and a genuine devotion to Christ and his work. At Calcutta she had been regarded by English friends as "the most finished and faultless specimen of an American woman that they had ever known." And in spite of the subduing influence of the hard experiences through which she had passed, she retained her attractiveness, enriched by a warm and deep spiritual nature.

It was a very simple home that Adoniram and Sarah enjoyed in Moulmein, with walls made of bamboo mats and roof of thatch. Along the front were three rooms, with two smaller rooms behind, and a detached kitchen. A wide veranda ran the full length of the house, and faced on the principal street. Not far away was the printing house, while close at hand was the school for Burman and Karen children. The chapel and residences for other missionaries completed the buildings on the mission compound. A chapel for the English-speaking congregation, and Bennett's English school, were in another part of the town.

Judson's house cost only $300, but no home could have been happier. The disturbance and persecution, the danger and tragedy, that had crowded the fourteen years with Ann, had made impossible a quiet home life. But after his marriage to Sarah he spent the years almost entirely at home, completing the Burman Bible, working on the dictionary, preaching in the chapel, and directing the Burman evangelists in their daily work. It was a delightful home, and Judson's genial spirit, his vivacity, his cheerfulness and humor came to the fore once more.

During those eleven years eight children came: one daughter, Abigail Ann, and seven sons, Adoniram Brown, Elnathan, Henry, Luther, Henry Hall, Charles and Edward. Luther was still-born. But the others were the joy of Judson's life. He entered heartily into their fun, joined in their play, romped with the boys, and often would be down on the floor on his hands and knees playing horse for them. There were other children in the mission, and they all had plenty of good times together. On rare occasions one of the neighbors' children might be invited to dinner, and then Adoniram, Jr., and Elnathan would take full advantage of their opportunity, and from their side table would make ample requisition on their indulgent father for what they and their young guests wanted.

Bluebeard and Jack the Giant Killer and other such heroes were familiar figures around the mission compound, for Judson's boys were real boys and Abby was a boy with them. And Judson had not forgotten his own boyhood love for good stories. The stone baptistry at the foot of the glen was a fine place to play after the water had been drawn off. One day it was a den of lions, with Elnathan Judson or James Haswell as Daniel, and Abby Judson, Julia Haswell, Sarah Stevens and David Howard as the roaring lions. Or it might be the Red Sea, with Moses—Brainerd Vinton or Edward Stevens—and the children of Israel crossing it, and marching through the wilderness toward the promised land in the bamboos across the compound. Occasionally they even had a baptismal service, with young Adoniram taking the place of his revered father and one of the smaller children serving as the candidate —summarily interrupted one day when they heard a voice up on the bank and recognized it as that of Papa Judson.

Just as any other fond parent, Judson liked to talk about his children. Young Adoniram "is one of the prettiest, brightest children you ever saw. Abby is growing fast. She runs about, and talks Burman fluently, but no English. She attends family and public worship with us, and has learned to sit still and behave herself. But Fen, or Pwen,[2] as the natives call him, when he is brought into the chapel and sees me in my place, has the impudence to roar out 'Bah!' (as the Burmans call

---

[2] Meaning "Flower"; the reference is to Adoniram, Jr.

'father'), with such a stentorian voice that his nurse is obliged to carry him out again." Abby sends her father some shells from Mergui and he is eager with interest; and he writes her with sympathetic sorrow that "both the kittens are dead, and the old yellow cat has been missing for several days." He wrote often, also, to his wife's son, George Boardman, who had gone to America soon after their marriage, telling him the news and advising about many things.

With Sarah, Judson was as tender and kind as any husband could be. She on the other hand gave him her heartiest cooperation in all his plans and work. And she usually went with him on his morning and evening walks, often climbing to the top of Pagoda Hill back of the city to see the sunrise.

By 1836 Judson had been out in the east longer than any other missionary then living except John Marshman, Robinson and Moore of the Serampore mission. He had never been home, and no one had been out to visit him or the mission. In the spring of that year, however, Rev. Howard Malcom of Boston arrived, a member of the board, sent out to study the work and advise the missionaries—the first of the long line of official visitors to the mission field, secretaries, board members and others. He was well chosen. He was pastor of Federal Street Church in Boston, later to become president of Georgetown College and then of Bucknell University. He was a seasoned traveler, able to adapt himself happily to circumstances, and was perhaps in a better position to understand the conditions of missionary life and work than any of the other leaders at home. In general he was sympathetic, broad-minded and friendly (though inclined to credit idle tales too readily), a recognized Christian leader, with years of experience on the mission board to give him intimate knowledge of the work.

His visit was a notable event. At the conference of the missionaries in Moulmein he preached, and Judson listened to the first sermon in English that he had heard in many years. In Judson's zayat he worshiped with the Burman congregation, and sat on the mat-covered floor with the others as Judson preached. With Justus Vinton he went to locate a mission station for the work among the Karens that Judson had begun five years before. With Sarah Judson he went on a tour of observation up the Dagyaing River, and on another up the Salween with Judson himself. It is an interesting picture of Judson that he has given us—"the venerable founder of the mission," as he calls him. "His age is but forty-seven; his eye is not dim; not a gray hair shows itself among his full auburn locks; his moderate-sized person seems full of vigor; he walks almost every evening a mile or two at a quick pace, lives with entire temperance and regularity, and enjoys in general steadfast health."

For four years and more Judson preached regularly, apparently remaining seated while he preached, following the custom of Buddhist teachers. Of course that had been his practice in the zayat; and it was his custom in his Moulmein chapel, at least in 1838, when Mrs. Stevens heard him preach soon after her arrival.[3] But later he changed this practice. Some who remembered him after his return from furlough, have described him as he preached, standing erect in his long black gown, often dramatic but always dignified in bearing.

He was now in charge of the Moulmein Burman Church. This was the work he loved best, and he kept at it all the time when he was so busy with Bible translating. At sunrise each morning he met with a carefully selected group of Burman evangelists, for prayer and discussion of the work they were to do in various parts of the city. The early morning hours he spent at his desk, translating or reading Burmese. Then came several hours in a zayat, usually with a Burman associate, eagerly telling the Good News to visitors. In the afternoon he was again at his desk, writing or revising or proof-reading. In the evening he conducted worship in the chapel, met any inquirers who wanted to see him, and conferred with Burman leaders. For he made full use of the nationals as associates and leaders. That was his method from Rangoon days. It was followed in his jungle touring. In Prome and now in Moulmein he used it systematically. Burma must be won through Burmans, of this he was sure. Leadership by the nationals was a central feature of his missionary policy.

---

[3] *American Baptist Magazine,* April, 1831, p. 84.

The chapel soon grew so crowded that a new and larger one had to be built. Baptisms were frequent. A noteworthy convert was Moo-chil, Ann's faithful servant of Ava days. He had come with her from Bengal when she returned from America, had gone with her to Ava, and after her death had continued in the employ of one or another of the missionaries. He had deeply loved Ann, and frequently shed tears as he talked of the tragic days at Ava and Amherst. Another baptism was that of the first Taungthu convert. Judson had baptized the first Burman Christian, the first Talaing, and now the first Taungthu; and he had won the first Karen, Ko Tha Byu, though Boardman had baptized him.

Here is illustrated the breadth of Judson's interest. First of all, to be sure, he was a missionary to the Burmans. They were the dominating race of Burma, and as such he gave them most of his atteniton. But his interest in the Karens was almost as deep. He was eager for the training of Karen leaders, and had organized the first training school for Karens of the jungle. He urged Wade to carry on the school, with both Karen and Burman students; he served as one of the visitors for the school after it had been removed to Tavoy with Karen students in the majority; and when later he opposed Joseph Binney's project for a central Karen seminary and urged him to become a preacher to the Burmans, it was chiefly because so little was being done for the Burmans.[4] He was enthusiastic about all the peoples of that polyglot land —Burmans, Karens, Talaings, Taungthus, Lahwahs,[5] Shans, Chins. He had become interested in the Siamese in Burma, had encouraged Ann to learn their language, and had warmly approved the transfer of Jones to Siam. It was he who suggested to Nathan Brown that he go to Assam. "My heart leaps for joy," he wrote, "and swells with gratitude and praise to God, when I think of brother Jones at Bangkok, in the southern extremity of the continent, and brother Brown at

---

[4] Mrs. J. G. Binney, *Twenty-six Years in Burma*, p. 190. Referring to Judson's urgent statement of his reasons she adds, "They were . . . especially enforced by the consideration that there was no man then in all Moulmein who was giving himself wholly or indeed very much to the Burmans."

[5] A large jungle tribe northeast of Moulmein.

Sadiya, in Assam, on the frontiers of China, immensely distant points, and of all the intervening stations, Ava, Rangoon, Kyaukpu, Moulmein and Tavoy, and the churches and schools which are springing up in every station, and throughout the Karen wilderness."

Towards the close of 1838, after Judson had passed his fiftieth birthday, he began to be subject to coughing. An inflammation of the throat and lungs appeared. He could not continue his preaching, and he almost entirely lost the use of his voice. It was the beginning of the pulmonary disease that ultimately ended his life. Doctors advised him to try a sea voyage. So in February of the next year he took a trip to Calcutta. He loved the sea, and this voyage on the *Snipe* was full of interest. Other passengers were aboard, but "no religious person." Nevertheless, he conformed to all the habits of the others, "except that I do not take beer or wine," he noted. He longed for Sarah and the children, and his letters reveal his love, with the little touches that mean so much in the intimacy of affection.

"My dear Love," (thus he begins his letters) "you know I love you more than all the world beside . . . It seems an age since I left Moulmein . . . I have found your beautiful braid of hair; and I hunted for some further note or token, but in vain . . . No wife ever deserved her husband's gratitude and love more than you . . . It seems an age since we exchanged the parting kiss . . . How joyfully do I hope to see your dear face, and take you to my longing arms, and find again 'that home is home.' "

In Calcutta he was on familiar ground. More than a quarter of a century had passed since that night when he and Ann and Rice had stolen away in the darkness from the city and the persecuting Company. The remembrance must have come back to him vividly. How eagerly he would visit those scenes once more, the house where he had lived with Mr. Rolt, the streets along which the little procession of fugitives had crept, the dock through whose gates they had been admitted to the ship which they had hoped would carry them away from the heavy hand of the government. How different the situation now! Honors and rewards had come from that same government, and he and other missionaries could carry on their work unhindered anywhere in the Company's domains.

He had a delightful time with the many missionaries in Calcutta and Serampore. But none of those he had known in 1812, or in 1820 when he visited the city with Ann, were among the number except Dr. Joshua Marshman's widow. He went up to Serampore and stayed with her over a weekend, and one can imagine how they talked of those early days, of her husband, of Ward, who had baptized Judson and Ann, and of the great William Carey, who had died but three years before. "The glory has departed from Serampore," he wrote to Sarah. But fine new men were there, Marshman's son John C., John Mack, and especially Dr. William Yates, outstanding scholar and Carey's successor in Bible translation. There were others also whom he appreciated, in all the missions. Archdeacon Dealtry of the Church of England took him down the river to call on the Bishop of Calcutta, Dr. Wilson, who did him the honor of entertaining him at breakfast and showed him the buildings of Bishop's College. And he joined in worship in the college chapel. Dr. Wilson always held Judson in the highest esteem, and eleven years later, after Judson's death, he sent a message of sympathy to his wife Emily, and called upon her in Moulmein to do honor to her husband's memory.

In India Judson had many friends outside his own denominational circle, Church of England, Congregational and others. Always his relations with other Protestants were warm and friendly. It will be recalled how deeply he regretted that his change of church relationship seemed to make impossible the joint mission he and his Congregational colleagues had planned; and in spite of the feeling occasioned by his withdrawal from the American Board he always had "the warmest filial affection" for that organization. More than a quarter of a century after his appointment he could say that he had read every number of the *Missionary Herald* of that board from its very first issue. He kept up correspondence with few persons, but one of these was Rufus Anderson, the long-time secretary of the American Board.

Judson's natural enjoyment of social intercourse had full

play in Calcutta. In Moulmein he had withdrawn from society because he felt that the demands of his work made seclusion a duty. Here there were no such demands and he could enjoy himself freely, with the result that he spent many delightful hours with his India friends. One evening a large missionary party gathered at the home where he was staying, and he and Dr. Yates had a long talk about the standard text of the Bible, meanwhile enjoying snatches of a discussion on schools, and another on the chronology of the Scriptures, overheard from other groups. He spent a full evening with Yates comparing the principles each had adopted in his translation work. He had breakfast at one home and tea at another. A day or two before he left the city all the missionaries gathered for an evening of fellowship in his honor. And he reciprocated by calling in succession on all of them. That was his last day in Calcutta, and in the evening, after four weeks in India, he set out in a small boat down the river, and the next morning, Sunday, overtook the *Snipe* at Fultah—the very place where on that other Sunday, twenty-seven years before, he and Ann and Luther Rice, sitting at supper in the inn, had been handed the pass that dramatically provided their way of escape to the Isle of France. Two weeks later Judson was again with his family in Moulmein.

But his health had not materially improved. He found he could not preach. Fortunately he could carry on conversation. So he settled down once more to give himself with new zeal to personal evangelism and translation work.

"Master Henry came into notice the last day of the year (1839); but there was no earthquake, nor anything." So Judson announced the birth of his son Henry. Six weeks later he took a needed two weeks' trip to Rangoon. On shipboard he spent the time reading the life of Napoleon—"a history of infernals—rich source of meditation." In Rangoon he visited friends, met the disciples, went out to the old deserted compound—now only a wilderness—and made an attempt to distribute tracts. But scarcely a thousand of these had been given out when Ko En, Judson's helper, was summoned to the court house, and was not released until two influential English friends of Judson interceded in his behalf. No further efforts were made to distribute tracts; the opposition of the government was all too evident. So he spent the time in fellowship with his English acquaintances, thoroughly enjoying, here as in Calcutta, the freedom for social intercourse that absence from the place of regular duties afforded him. On February twentieth he was back in Moulmein, ready for work once more.

Judson's preaching and the personal work of his Burman associates brought a steady increase in the number of members. But he was concerned about some whose interest seemed to be growing cold. He watched closely over them all, and if he learned that anyone was in danger of falling away he set himself with the utmost zeal to save that one. His tremendous earnestness and his power of dramatic appeal are illustrated by the story told by a Burman Christian woman, who was tempted to do something that threatened her spiritual life. Judson heard of her intention and sent for her. For some time he argued with her, but to no avail. Suddenly he snatched up a ruler from the table, and drew a crooked line on the floor.

"Look here!" he exclaimed. "Here is where you have been walking. You have made a rather crooked path, but you have kept to it and have grown in grace. Now after fifteen years here is where you stand"—and he brought the ruler down with emphasis at a certain point—"and you know what is before you, some struggles, some sorrows, but finally eternal life and a crown of glory. But to the left branches another road, with a pretty bubble floating along in the air. You want to go off and catch the bubble and then come back; but you never will. Woman, think! Dare you leave this strait and narrow path, drawn by the Saviour's finger, and go away for one moment into that of the enemy? Will you? *Will you?* WILL YOU?"

By this time the woman was sobbing and Judson knew the battle was won; and he knelt down and prayed that God would preserve her in her determination.

"I have made a good many crooked tracks since," added the woman as she told the story, "but whenever I am tempted I see the teacher as he looked that day, bending over in his chair, the ruler placed on the floor to represent me, his finger pointing along the path of eternal life, his eye looking so strangely over his shoulder, and that terrible 'Will you?' com-

ing from his lips as though it were the voice of God; and I
pray, for I am frightened."

While he gave himself with patient love to saving any
who were going astray, Judson did not hesitate to urge the
disciplining of those whose life was not in accord with the
high standard to which he held, excluding the guilty one from
communion. If such a member did not listen to pastor,
deacons and church he was excluded a second time, or a third.
If still unrepentant after three communion seasons, that is, a
year, he was excluded from the church.

Added to his care for the church was his care for all the
mission family. He loved them all. One of his associates said
that "he had a peculiarly fascinating way of endearing himself
to everybody whose hearts were open to his kindness." And
in his later years his wife Emily said that "he was always
planning little surprises for his family and neighbors." He
was outspoken, and emphatic in both speech and action, so
that sometimes there was a natural reaction against what he
said or did. But this was only momentary. And he himself
generally added an acknowledgment of his own shortcom-
ings. His plans and policies were usually followed by other
missionaries, but not because he was domineering or dicta-
torial. His colleagues were impressed by his devotion to high
personal and missionary ideals; they saw that he stood by himself in his knowledge of people and language, and they recognized the precedence that his sacrifice and suffering rightly
gave him. His achievement and his spirit were such that he
was inevitably—and usually with gladness—accorded the first
place, and had the right to the deciding vote when occasion
arose.

It must be noted, too, that he always recognized the
authority of the board at home, never disobeying its instructions, and never appealing from its decisions to the churches.
He was absolutely loyal, to the Christians in Burma, to his
fellow missionaries, and to the mission board. Indeed he constantly sought the advice of his fellow missionaries and of
friends and teachers in America, and often felt that he "would
give anything for one hour's free conversation with the members of the board."

Toward the close of the year 1839 the board for the second time formally invited him to return to America on furlough in the interest of his health. The following April the invitation was repeated. But his health was now improved, and he could not feel that it was either necessary or right to go. Besides, he had been in Burma so long, and had become so completely naturalized in the life of the Burman people, that he was more at home there than he could possibly be anywhere else. His home was there, his work was there, the consuming interest of his life was there. So he thanked the board and stayed on in Moulmein.

Sarah had worked at Tavoy mostly among the Karens. When she came to Moulmein as Mrs. Judson she took up vigorously the study of Burmese and became expert in that language. According to Judson, scarcely a foreigner in Burma could speak or write Burmese as well as she could towards the close of her life. She "professed to take more pleasure and derive more profit from the perusal of that translation than from the English, and to enjoy preaching in the native chapel more than in any other." This knowledge of Burmese she used to good effect in supplementing the limited supply of Christian literature. Her translation of *Pilgrim's Progress* is still in use. Her poetic ability she used effectively in writing hymns, and added twenty to the hymn book. Four volumes of *Scripture Questions,* for use in Sunday schools, came from her pen. And in addition a number of tracts, with a series of what Judson described as "Sunday cards," on which was a verse of Scripture, accompanied by a stanza or two of a hymn. At Adoniram's suggestion she took up the study of Talaing, or Mon, and set herself to translate the New Testament and Judson's *Life of Christ.*

As the Judson house was close to the road, people would often stop and come in. One day Sarah was sitting at her study table, working at her translating, with the children playing on the veranda just outside her door, when she happened to look up and saw a man leaning over the railing watching her intently.

"What do you want?" she asked him pleasantly.

"I was watching you write," he replied.

"Won't you come in?" asked Sarah, as she laid down her pen.

The man promptly came in and sat down. He proved to be a Shan, and before that day had never heard the story of Christ. They talked of what she was writing, and he listened with surprise and delight as Sarah told him of her great Friend. Before he left he promised to pray that God would give him a new heart, that he might believe in the Saviour. Thus to a fourth race the glad message was given.

Judson's early attempt at the making of a dictionary has been mentioned. He had continued at the task till about 1819. Then the manuscript, still incomplete, had apparently been taken to Calcutta by Hough, and in 1826 this or Wade's revision had been printed in Serampore. Judson and others used it for the next fifteen years, but it was imperfect, and was almost as much a handicap as a help, especially to new missionaries. A new and revised dictionary was greatly needed. Doubtless he and other missionaries had spoken of the need in correspondence with the board. At any rate, the board repeatedly urged him to undertake a new dictionary. His fellow missionaries joined in the request. His heart, however, was in preaching. When in October of 1840 the final revision of the Bible was out of the way, "Now for the real work of a missionary!" he thought. And he went at preaching to the Burmans and caring for the church in Moulmein with all the eagerness of a boy, hoping to give the remainder of his life to this joyful task.

But he was to be disappointed. Tuberculosis attacked him, and he lost his voice, as we have seen. At last he yielded to the urgings of the board and his colleagues, and began to "dabble at the dictionary," as he put it. "It is such a chaotic affair," he wrote to Grover Comstock of Arracan, "and seems to me so unmissionary, that I am constantly hoping that something will turn up to relieve me from the work."

Something did turn up that very month: Sarah and the children became seriously ill, so ill that he had to leave his dictionary and take his family to Calcutta, and then on a long voyage that carried them to the Isle of France and occupied the rest of the year.

All four children had come down with the whooping cough, and before they recovered three had been attacked by dysentery, which brought two of them almost to the point of death. Sarah was expecting a fifth child, and in March of 1841 Luther was born; but to his parents' sorrow was dead ere he began to live. On top of all this Sarah's old enemy, dysentery, attacked her, as it had the children, and Adoniram nearly lost her. So on the insistence of doctors, missionaries and other friends, Judson took his wife and family and in June of that year 1841 embarked for Calcutta. Of course they went on a sailing vessel, and their cabin was crowded. The four children were stowed away in a series of berths built for the trip one above another on one side of the stateroom, Sarah had a berth on the other side, and just room enough was left between for Judson to set up a cot at night.

It was a tempestuous voyage. The "wild southwest monsoon," as Emily Judson later described the prevailing wind of the season, gave them a rough trip. They went off their course and struck a shoal, and for twenty minutes—it seemed two hours—they thought all would perish. It was night and all was dread darkness, but even in her weakness Sarah's practical nature asserted itself, for she crawled from her berth and hastily filled a small trunk with such articles as might be needed if they had to take to the boats. Fortunately they got off without damage, and reached Calcutta with no further adventures.

But not with better health. They went up the river to Serampore for a more favorable location, and secured a good house looking out on the Hugli River. It was an attractive scene, with boats constantly passing up or down, while beyond the view stretched away over a wide plain, broken here and there by palms and groups of low native houses. Not far away, too, was the fine college building, with Carey's home and his wonderful garden. But sometimes it was so hot they could hardly breathe, and then it would turn cold and the winds would come whistling in at the windows, chilling them all and setting back their recovery.

The doctors advised a further sea voyage. Just at that juncture an old Moulmein acquaintance, Captain Hamlin of the ship *Ramsay*, an earnest Christian man, came to call on them. He was about to sail for the Isle of France and thence to Moulmein; and when he discovered their situation he generously offered to take them on the long trip at no greater cost than the usual fare direct to Moulmein.[6] It would be a long voyage, and this was a dangerous season on the ocean. But all except baby Henry were growing worse, and they quickly decided. Only a few days remained, and there were purchases and other arrangements to which only Sarah could attend, so she and the older children, Abby and Adoniram, went down to Calcutta, leaving Henry and Elnathan with their father.

But Adoniram and Abby grew worse, so sick that the doctor said their only chance was to get to sea. One can imagine Sarah's anxiety as she watched over her little ones, counting and counting again the days they must still wait before the *Ramsay* would sail. Then unexpectedly she received an urgent message from her husband that Henry was seriously ill. "I must go back at once" was her quick decision —only to find that the next tide was not till six that night. Her friends urged her to wait till morning and not to risk the night trip on the river; but she could not delay. At sunset she put the children to bed inside the cabin of the little boat and took up her dreary watch outside.

It was a long, desolate night. To add to her anxiety the tide turned before they reached Serampore and the men could not row against it. Slowly, foot by foot, they had to pole the craft up the stream. And just as slowly passed the long night hours. It was two in the morning when her boat reached Serampore. Henry was still living. But when the day dawned it was only too evident that the little one was dying, and that night, July thirtieth, he slipped away. The next evening friends gathered, Dr. Mack offered prayer, and they laid the little body to rest in the mission cemetery, where lie Carey, Marshman and Ward. And Serampore was added

---

[6] At the end of the voyage Capt. Hamlin declined to take anything at all. A fair charge would have been Rs. 2,000, nearly $1,000.

to Rangoon and Amherst as sacred places in the memory of Judson.

The *Ramsay* was delayed in sailing; it was the twenty-second of August before they left the shores of India, and October first when they reached the Isle of France. The voyage was one of the stormiest Judson had ever experienced. For days a regular succession of frightful squalls struck them. One day two topmasts, a topgallantmast and the jibboom were carried away, with all their sails, coming down with a tremendous crash. Meanwhile the ship rolled and pitched at a dreadful rate. But they managed to refit at sea and arrived safely at the Isle of France, to which Judson had come with Ann twenty-eight years before. A month there and they set sail again, with the health of all greatly improved, and reached Moulmein the tenth of December, after an absence of nearly six months.

Shortly after their return to Moulmein they moved into another and more comfortable house. Judson hoped his mother and sister might come out to Burma, and built a small cottage for them adjoining his own house. Later, after returning from his American furlough, he renewed his efforts with his sister. But they never left home. They shared his life, however, by sending frequent gifts of money, Abigail continuing to do so after their mother died. His growing family obliged him "to look after the rupees a little more carefully," as he put it, and he accepted the gifts with gratitude.

Three other children came to the Judson home after the return from the Isle of France, Henry Hall (recalling the other Henry they had lost in Serampore), Charles and Edward. Before Edward's birth in December, 1844, Sarah fell ill with dysentery again, and after he came she began to decline at an alarming rate. At the invitation of the civil commissioner and his family, she and Abby spent several weeks at Mergui and Tavoy. Many hours she passed looking out over the blue water, through the groves of flowery cassia trees with their waving panicles of yellow blossoms, and the tall casuarinas with their silken branchlets. And her friends did all that could be done for her. But she only grew paler and thinner, and when she came back to Moulmein it was evident to all that only a return to America could possibly save her life.

Sarah was indeed desperately ill; so ill that Judson and his friends frankly agreed that it would be "nothing but savage inhumanity" to let her go alone. So he made ready to accompany her. The three older children, Abby Ann, Adoniram and Elnathan, they decided to take with them to America for their health and education. The three younger, Henry Hall, Charles and Edward, must be left in Burma. Henry was less than three, Charles was sixteen months, and Edward only four months. What suffering it cost their mother to leave them only a mother can know. But Sarah could not possibly take care of them during the long, hard voyage, and they were too young to be cared for by their father. So there seemed nothing to do but leave them with missionary friends, trusting God to protect them. Henry was committed to the kindness of Mrs. Haswell in Amherst, and Judson made a hurried trip down there with him—characteristically taking time to remember that Mrs. Haswell's daughters had not been vaccinated, and carrying along his lancet and vaccine. Charles was left with the Osgoods in Moulmein. The baby, Edward, was to be cared for by Mrs. Stevens in Moulmein. Years afterward Sarah Stevens, then the wife of Rev. D. A. W. Smith, told with what self-sacrifice her mother, with children of her own, one of them at her breast, mothered the "wee, puny little baby" that Judson brought to her home. She was sure that the only way to save his life was to put him in her own baby's place; so she took a chance with her baby, and Edward was saved for his long life and his great ministry. Three weeks after Sarah returned from her trip down the coast she and Adoniram, with the three children, sailed on the *Paragon*, bound for London.

Judson had been working on his dictionary since his return from the Isle of France, having at last undertaken the task which he had "resolved and re-resolved" never to touch. At first he had planned a single work, Burman-English. But as he studied the question it had appeared desirable to have it in two parts, English-Burman and Burman-English. The English-Burman section he undertook first, and he had kept at it as steadily as possible, assisted by two very able Christian Burmans, one formerly a government secretary in Rangoon, the other a nephew of the former premier in Ava.

But now of course the work on the dictionary had to be interrupted. And Judson's notes were in such a state that no one else could use them until the work had been carried further along. To stop now would mean the loss of all the time and labor put into it. So he took his two assistants with him on the *Paragon*, planning to devote some time every day to his manuscript. In fact he purposed to use the months in America on this work, as he believed his voice would not permit him to do any speaking, except in a small room. Moreover, he had deliberately renounced his native tongue, in order to become an eloquent preacher in Burmese. For thirty-two years he had scarcely made one speech in English. So he begged the mission board—to use his own words—"to allow me a quiet corner, where I can pursue my work with my assistants, undisturbed and unknown." Little did he anticipate the great public welcome that awaited him.

The first month of the voyage was very rough and all were seasick. Even Judson himself, seasoned voyager as he was, suffered with the others. So that with the seasickness, the unsteady roll of the ship, and his care for Sarah, Judson accomplished little on the dictionary. But the second month was better, and Sarah began to improve, so much so that Judson felt confident that she was on the way to recovery.

As they neared the Isle of France the ship sprang a leak and the captain decided to put in for repairs—the third time that Judson had been at Port Louis. As they approached the island Sarah appeared so convalescent that it seemed quite safe for Judson to leave her, and they agreed that it was his duty to return to Moulmein, while she went on to England and America.

It was not easy to separate. Would she, after all, get well, and live to return once more to Burma? And he, subject to a threatening disease and back in a tropical climate, would he without his wife's loving care be able to ward off the illness until she came back? And the children—ah! what of them? Would they all meet again? She and he bravely faced it all and made their decision. But what it meant to her and to Adoniram she told in verses which she penciled on a scrap of paper as they came into the harbor—the last she ever wrote:

"We part on this green islet, Love,
   Thou for the eastern main,
I for the setting sun, Love—
   Oh when to meet again?

"My heart is sad for thee, Love,
   For lone thy way will be;
And oft thy tears will fall, Love,
   For thy children and for me.

.   .   .   .   .

"Yet my spirit clings to thee, Love,
   Thy soul remains with me,
And oft we'll hold communion sweet,
   O'er the dark and distant sea.

.   .   .   .   .

"Then gird thine armor on, Love,
   Nor faint thou by the way,
Till Boodh shall fall, and Burmah's sons
   Shall own Messiah's sway." [7]

A vessel was already about to sail for Moulmein, and he sent off his assistants on her, planning to go himself on another that was to sail for Calcutta in a fortnight or so. After the first vessel had sailed Sarah and the children were offered passage on the bark *Sophia Walker* direct to Boston, so they decided that she should transfer from the *Paragon* to the *Sophia Walker,* while Judson returned to Moulmein.

Suddenly all was changed. Sarah had a serious relapse, and sank lower than ever before. It was evident that Adoniram could not leave her. So that just at the time when he expected to bid her farewell with high hopes for her recovery he carried her with heavy heart aboard the bark, and together on July twenty-fifth they sailed "for the setting sun."

For a while Sarah seemed to grow better, especially as they rounded the Cape of Good Hope—harbinger of good hope to Judson. But then came a series of relapses, and before they reached St. Helena Judson had given up hope. In the early

---

[7] The full poem is given in Emily Judson's *Memoir,* p. 235.

morning of September first, as they lay quietly in port, she slipped away.

Brief services were held on the bark, at the cemetery the Church of England rector read the service, and Sarah's worn body was laid away under a spreading banyan tree, by the side of the grave of Mrs. Chater, wife of the first evangelical missionary to Burma. After the funeral the Christian people of St. Helena took Judson to their homes and hearts, and their comforting words and prayers gave him "unexpected relief and consolation."

Judson's words are a sufficient tribute to his wife: "The worthy successor of Ann." [8]

But the bark was to sail that evening. His friends accompanied him to the shore and he sorrowfully went aboard. The anchor was weighed and they stood out to sea. In the morning no sign of the island was to be seen.

Six weeks later, on the fifteenth of October, Judson arrived in Boston.

---

[8] See his whole tribute to Sarah, in Wayland, II, pp. 204f.

CHAPTER X

THE HERO WELCOMED HOME

IF ADONIRAM JUDSON thought he could slip into the home land unnoticed, and retire to a "quiet corner, undisturbed and unknown," he quickly found that he was mistaken. The Boston *Traveller* reported his arrival in a brief six-line item. The news that the great pioneer had come spread like wildfire. Throughout the city and community people were deeply stirred and word of the famous missionary's arrival was quickly passed on far and wide.

The enthusiasm aroused by his coming can scarcely be imagined. More than thirty-three years had gone since he had left American shores. Few whom he had known were still living. So far as he was aware, all of that first American missionary band of 1812 had died except himself. Hardly any of the people who now so eagerly welcomed his coming had ever seen him. But they knew his name. They had heard his story. The thrilling tale of his imprisonment had been told again and again. Some remembered Ann's visit more than twenty years earlier. Many recalled Sarah Hall Boardman and her departure for Burma, and knew of her life as the wife of Judson. Now he was home! They must see him. They must hear him.

Judson landed on Wednesday and a welcome meeting was arranged for Friday.[1] In spite of the short time for spreading the announcement the large Bowdoin Square Church was crowded to the doors. Even the aisles were filled. A Psalm and a prayer, then Daniel Sharp arose, pastor of Charles Street Church since the year of Judson's sailing, one of the leaders who had organized the Society for Propagating the Gospel in India and Other Foreign Parts, and now president of the

---

[1] Fletcher, p. 355, and Wayland, II, p. 216, give detailed accounts.

mission board. Through the years he and Judson had often written to each other, and now at last they looked into each other's faces. In behalf of all his brethren and friends he welcomed their great leader to his native land, to their churches, to their hearts. And as the representative of all the great throng who were present he gave him a hearty hand grasp— "the hand of an honest, unchanging and cordial good will."

The air was charged with intense expectancy. Everyone leaned forward eagerly as Judson arose and came to the front of the platform. William Hague, pastor of Federal Street Church, stepped over to Judson's side. Briefly he explained that the weakened voice of their beloved brother would not permit him to be heard by many in the great congregation, and that he himself had been asked to act as an interpreter, so that all might know what their honored guest was saying.

"Through the mercy of God I am permitted to stand before you here this evening, a pensioner of your bounty." Thus Judson began. "It is one of the severest trials of my life not to be able to lift up my voice and give free utterance to my feelings."

But this, he said, he could not do, and he could only beg their prayers for his brethren in Burma and for the feeble churches there, and urge them to pray "that the good work of God's grace may go on until the world shall be filled with His glory." He was able to say no more. But Dr. Hague continued, speaking eloquently as he contrasted conditions when Judson left his native land with the situation now on his return.

But who is that who is quietly but urgently crowding his way from the farthest corner of the church up the aisle toward the platform? People turn from the speaker to watch him, struck with the eagerness and emotion that show in his face. He reaches the front of the room but does not stop. Dr. Hague is still speaking, but he goes straight up on the platform and hurries over to Judson. Judson turns and sees him, draws back for an instant in sudden surprise, then leaps to his feet, and as a thrill of emotion sweeps over the vast congregation he and the stranger grasp each other by the hand and embrace with a gladness that causes tears to start from many an eye.

Who could it be? Dr. Hague stops speaking, Judson quickly introduces his newly-discovered friend to Dr. Sharp, and the latter presents him to the audience. It is Samuel Nott! The only one still living, besides Judson, of all that group of five pioneers who sailed for India so long ago. Compelled to return on account of ill health, he is now pastor of the Congregational Church in Wareham, Massachusetts. Word has reached him of the arrival of Judson in Boston. His old friend! The man by whose side he stood as they faced the American Board and insisted on action! The associate whose sincerity he championed when others questioned his motives! He has not seen him since that night in Calcutta when they separated in their flight from the persecuting Company. He takes the first conveyance to Boston, and arrives just in time to hear that a welcome meeting is in progress. And now at last, after all the years and the many vicissitudes, he and Judson are reunited.

Words are inadequate to describe the scene. Stirred with deep feeling Nott addresses the great throng:

"More than thirty years ago I gave my brother the right hand of fellowship, and when he became a Baptist it was not withdrawn. It is a very trifling question," he says, "whether Adoniram Judson or Samuel J. Mills was the originator of foreign missions. Samuel Nott, Jr., certainly was not. They were all mere boys, but with God's blessing on their efforts they have begun a work that is now spreading over the world."

Then it is discovered that Hiram Bingham is in the audience—pioneer of the American Board in Hawaii. He too has heard that Judson has come, and he has joined the welcoming throng at the church. He is called to the platform, and the congregation is thrilled again as he greets Judson, and tells how the missionary movement initiated by Judson and his associates has spread westward as well as eastward, and has brought triumphant success in the Hawaiian Islands.

Finally the great meeting is over. Never has such an occasion taken place before, and never will it occur again. It will stand with that other great meeting in Salem when Judson and the others of the immortal five were ordained. It is one more in the series of dramatic events that crowd the life of Adoniram Judson.

How we would like to follow Judson and Nott as they leave the church. Who can doubt that they found a time when they could be alone, and talk of Rice and Hall and Newell, and Nancy and Harriet and Roxana,[2] and of the great events in which they had all had a part? And did not Judson seek out the great secretary of the American Board, Rufus Anderson, or perhaps was sought out by him, to renew their friendship, and to talk of Ann, whom Rufus Anderson had known so well?[3] We do not know. But on the following Monday he was officially welcomed by his own board, and he and they talked intimately of his experiences and of the work that meant so much to them all.

Judson felt out of place in America. He had been away so long that everything was strange. So he had the greatest difficulty in adjusting himself to American ways. He had never traveled on a railroad. One day soon after he reached the home land he boarded a train, took a seat, and a newsboy came along.

"Paper, sir?"

"Yes, thank you."

And Judson, taking the paper, settled himself to read. The boy stood a few minutes in perplexity and growing impatience, waiting for his customer to pay for the paper he had sold him. But Judson paid no attention. Sitting by his side was a woman passenger, and noting the situation, she finally said, "The boy is waiting for his money."

Judson woke to the situation with a start. "Why," he replied as he handed the boy a coin, "I have been so long distributing papers gratuitously in Burma that I had no idea the boy was expecting any pay."

He soon gained experience, however, for he began right away to travel about the country, and kept it up most of the nine months he was in the United States. Promptly after his

[2] She was still living. Nott died in 1869 and Roxana in 1876.
[3] He attended Bradford Academy while Ann was there. He and Ann played together, and she "used to chase him about the Academy grounds with a stick," as he afterward told.

meeting with the board he went to Salem, probably to visit the parents of his beloved Sarah. Lucius Bolles, Sarah's pastor, who at Judson's suggestion had founded the Salem Bible Translation and Foreign Mission Society, and who had been foreign mission secretary so long, and always Judson's warm friend, had died just the previous year. Samuel Worcester and almost all the others who had taken part in the memorable ordination service in Tabernacle Church more than thirty-three years before, had also gone on. But the scene was still vivid in Judson's mind and memory, and he visited once more the ancient edifice, to live over again that great day, to sit on the old settee, and to recall the faces of those who had been pioneers with him in the great enterprise to which they had given their lives.

Then he traveled by the old familiar stage-coach route to Bradford, the home of his dear Nancy. Here were scenes that belonged to him because they belonged to her. Here they had met. Here they had been married. And here the American Board had been formed. Few other places meant to him what Bradford meant. From Bradford he went to Plymouth—to his home! How he had longed for a sight of that spot. Only his sister was living. But she had a great welcome for him. And as he sat at a favorite window and looked out over the harbor toward the lighthouse he exclaimed, "This is the most natural scene I have looked upon in America!" [4]

Another pilgrimage he was eager to make was to his old alma mater, Brown University. Early in November he went to Providence at the invitation of President Francis Wayland, and on Sunday worshiped once again in the historic First Baptist Church, where at Commencement thirty-eight years before he had delivered his valedictory and received his degree. A great mass meeting was held in the church on Sunday evening, and all denominations joined in the welcome. Long before the hour of beginning the large church was crowded to overflowing. "Not a pew in any part of the house, not a

---

[4] The old house is still standing at 17 Pleasant St. When Judson left for Burma again his sister closed his room, and it remained untouched and dust-filled as long as she lived.

place in all the aisles, not the remotest corner, above or below, remained unoccupied." So a Providence paper reported. Dr. James N. Granger, pastor of the church, presided, and President Wayland gave an address, sketching the life and work of their distinguished visitor, and welcoming him once more to the community he had known long since. Judson's voice was so weak that he could not speak loud enough to be heard, so Professor Caswell of the University stood by his side and interpreted. Frankly Judson confessed that though he was stirred by what he saw on all sides in his native country, "the conversion of one immortal soul on those heathen shores awakened in him deeper emotion than all the beauty of this glorious land." And he told them that the greatest favor he could ask was that he might be allowed to return as soon as possible to his home on the banks of the Salween.

The next day was spent looking around the campus and buildings of the old college. The whole student body assembled in the chapel in Manning Hall to greet him, keenly interested at seeing and hearing their famous alumnus, and he addressed them informally. The Philermenian Society held a special meeting to welcome him. The records of the session in 1804 when he joined were read, and he spoke of his continued interest in the society and his wishes for the intellectual and spiritual welfare of the members. As it happened, one of his fellow members, Thomas Williams of the class of 1809, was present, and told of their early friendship and of Judson's life and character in college days.

Then he met the Society for Missionary Inquiry. On the table before him was a copy of his own Burman Bible. As he rose to speak the record book was placed in his hands, and for a moment or two he looked over the list of members, not a few of whom had followed him to the mission field. Then he addressed the society in impressive tones:

"My dear young brethren, there is one and only one right path for every man—for each one of you—to follow, in order to insure the full approbation of God, and the greatest success in your efforts to do good and glorify him."

He told how he had sought that path for himself, and emphasized the necessity of having an unwavering conviction of

their duty and of God's will if they were to succeed as missionaries. Then he closed the meeting with a brief, earnest prayer.
And one who was present wrote, "I doubt not all felt, as the
man of God turned to depart, what it was to live and labor for
Jesus Christ, as they never felt it before."

Baptists of the south had gradually been drawing away
from those in the north. The principal centers of Baptist population were in the south, while the headquarters were far away
in Boston. Moreover, slavery had been agitating the churches,
and the board's attitude on this was directly opposed to that
of most of the southern leaders. The matter came to a head
in 1845 when the churches of the southern states withdrew
from the Triennial Convention, and in May formed the
Southern Baptist Convention. To meet the situation a special
session of the Triennial Convention was held in New York on
November 19, and it was an occasion never to be forgotten.
Disaster seemed imminent, and the delegates assembled with
troubled hearts. But wise and hopeful counsels prevailed, and
out of what threatened loss came new and larger things, north
and south. The name of the Triennial Convention was
changed to the American Baptist Missionary Union, and plans
were adopted for extinguishing the debt of $40,000, and for
pressing forward in all the mission fields.

Judson was present at this historic meeting, as were two of
his Burma colleagues, Kincaid and Abbott. Unquestionably
the presence of these missionaries had large influence in bring-
ing matters through successfully and harmoniously. Judson's
arrival in America was hailed with joy, and his presence at
the New York meeting and his wise counsels were of inestimable aid and encouragement.

The meeting convened in the Tabernacle Church—a name
thus strikingly connected with two historic missionary
occasions. Dr. Spencer H. Cone, former president of the Triennial Convention, in an impressive address referred to the
day in 1815 when, shut up in Baltimore by a British army, he
had heard Luther Rice tell the story of the change of Judson
and himself to Baptist views and picture the need of the eastern
lands for Christ. He contrasted those early days with these
to which they had come under the leadership of Judson, and

presented resolutions of gratitude to God for his blessings on their senior missionary. They were unanimously adopted. Then stepping over to Judson he took him by the hand, and turning to the president said, "I present to you Jesus Christ's man."

The president now arose, Francis Wayland, whose sermon on "The Moral Dignity of the Missionary Enterprise" while pastor of the First Baptist Church of Boston had brought him to the forefront among preachers and missionary leaders, and whose position as president of Brown University, with his nationally recognized ability as an educator, thinker, orator, and wise adviser had made him one of the outstanding Christian leaders in America. He addressed their honored guest:

"Thirty-three years since, you and a few other servants of the most high God, relying simply upon His promises, left your native land to carry the message of Christ to the heathen. You were the first offering of the American churches to the Gentiles. You went forth amid the sneers of the thoughtless, and with only the cold and reluctant consent of many of your brethren. The general voice declared your undertaking fanatical, and those who cowered under its rebuke drew back from you in alarm. On the voyage your views respecting Christian ordinances became changed, and this change gave rise to the Convention now in session before you."

Then he traced Judson's labors and achievements through the years, told how he had "tracked with bleeding feet the burning sands between Ava and Aungbinle," referred to the angel whom God had provided to minister to his needs, spoke of the ingathering among the Karens, expressed the sympathy of all for him in his recent bereavement, and in behalf of the whole company welcomed him back to the land of his fathers. To this stirring address Judson replied, with thanks for the welcome he had received everywhere, and with the hope that it would "promote his humility and the more faithful discharge of his duty."

No one present at the Convention ever forgot a dramatic scene that took place on the morning of the third day, in which Judson was the central figure. The heavy debt threatened the continuance of the foreign work, and in the course of the debate on the situation it was suggested that some of the mission stations be given up. Arracan was mentioned. That brought Judson to his feet. Disregarding the warning of physicians that he must not speak in public he burst out,

"I must say a few words. I must protest against the abandonment of the Arracan mission!"

Then his voice sank to a whisper, and Dr. Cone had to repeat his words to the audience as he showed why Arracan should not be given up—"If the Convention think my services can be dispensed with in finishing my dictionary, I will go immediately to Arracan; or if God should spare my life"— Dr. Cone broke down at the thought suggested by the words, and sobs from the audience showed how deeply everyone was stirred—"if God should spare my life to finish my dictionary, I will go there afterward and labor there and die, and be buried there."

The Convention was thrilled. An appeal by Kincaid stirred the feeling yet more. And immediately it was voted not to abandon any station but to reinforce and strengthen the mission. Arracan was saved.

During the Convention meeting, Judson was at dinner one day when someone referred to the scars made by the cords with which Spotted Face had bound him that day when he was seized and thrown into prison. The interest of everyone was so evidently sincere that for once he did not avoid the subject, but drew up his sleeves and said in a matter of fact way, "There are the marks." It was one of the rare occasions when he referred to himself or his sufferings.

From New York Judson went to Hamilton to address the students and faculty of the college—now Colgate University. Thence to Philadelphia and Washington, speaking a number of times, always through an interpreter as his voice continued weak. Then on to Richmond, where on the eighth of February a meeting was held in his honor which was quite as significant as the session of the Convention in New York. He had been the representative of southern churches as well as northern, and though southern Baptists now had a separate Convention he was their own great missionary pioneer and they were eager to see him and give him their welcome. Their greetings

was presented by Dr. J. B. Jeter, president of the Foreign
Mission Board of the new Southern Baptist Convention, who
eloquently sketched the history of the thirty-four years—
almost to a day—since Judson's ordination and sailing in 1812,
and referred with regret to the fact that henceforth he and
they of the south would labor in connection with different
boards. He told how long and fervently they had wished to
see him. "This privilege," he said, "we now enjoy. Welcome,
thrice welcome are you, my brother, to our city, our churches,
our bosoms . . . We honor you as the father of American missions . . . And now I give you my hand in token of our
affection to you, and of your cordial reception among us."

To this hearty welcome Judson made a significant reply,
congratulating the southern churches on the formation of their
own Convention, saying that "such an organization should
have been formed several years ago," partly because of the
extent of the country. And he pointed out the motive that
should dominate Christians everywhere in their missionary
efforts, a supreme desire to please God.

He had hoped to go farther south. The churches of South
Carolina had especially invited him to visit them, and doubtless he was eager to see his old college room-mate, Willard
Preston, now pastor of the strong Independent Presbyterian
Church in Savannah. But increasing throat and lung trouble,
coupled with the need of making preparations for his departure once more for Burma, warned him that he must decline,
and he turned north again.

Naturally everyone was interested in his adventures and
prison experiences and all were eager to hear him tell about
them. To the disappointment of many he scarcely mentioned
them. In fact he told very little about his missionary work.
In most of his addresses he spoke of the Saviour, of what He
has done for us, and of our debt to Him. Doubtless he would
have strengthened his appeal if he had used more illustrations
from his missionary experiences; but he did not believe so.
In one place after he had spoken many persons expressed their
disappointment.

"Why, what did they want?" he asked, when told of their

feeling; "I presented the most interesting subject in the world to the best of my ability."

"But they wanted a story," said his friend.

"Well, I am sure I gave them a story," replied Judson, "the most thrilling one that can be conceived of."

"But they wanted something new of a man who has just come from the antipodes."

"Then I am glad to have it to say," and Judson was emphatic, "I am glad to have it to say that a man coming from the antipodes had nothing better to tell than the wondrous story of Jesus' dying love. My business is to preach the gospel of Christ, and when I speak at all I dare not trifle with my commission. When I looked upon those people today, and remembered where I should next meet them, how could I stand up and furnish food to vain curiosity—tickle their fancy with amusing stories, however decently strung together on a thread of religion? How could I hereafter meet the fearful charge, 'I gave you one opportunity to tell them of me—you spent it in describing your own adventures.'" Such was his single-mindedness and his tremendous earnestness.

But not all were disappointed in his message, by any means. When he spoke at Plymouth one of his hearers was Daniel W. Faunce, later an eminent Baptist minister and father of President Faunce of Brown. He was a boy, but he never forgot the impression Judson made on him:

"The old church was crowded, and I was able to find a seat only in a corner of the gallery. Shall I confess my disappointment at first when a slim, worn man with a weary voice arose in the pulpit and gave out the text, 'These are they that follow the Lamb.'

"Trained in a religious household, where missionary names, and especially those of Judson and Rice, were familiar words, somehow in my boyish fancy I had thought of him as a great orator, with a loud voice and commanding tones, who would sweep down all before him with a resistless eloquence. Hence my disappointment. But as he went on, in simple language, to unfold his thought, and repeated over and over again his one theme, pleasing Jesus, somehow I forgot all about the eloquence. There stole over me, a boy convert of only a few months' standing, a great tenderness. Was this venerated man influenced in all he had done by the simple thought of pleasing Jesus? Well then, might not I, boy as I was, strive to please Jesus also? My eyes began to fill and my heart was in my throat. Was there anything I could do to please Jesus? A hundred times since, the single simple thought of that sermon has come to me, and the memory of that summer afternoon in the corner of the gallery, and the scene and the words have been an inspiration. And if that is eloquence which gets its thought written imperishably upon the heart of an auditor, then the simple, almost childlike words of that hour were truly eloquent." [5]

The duty of pleasing Jesus—no wonder the theme impressed young Faunce as Judson presented it. For it was the dominant note of his life. As early as December 30, 1810, while he was still at Andover, he had written to Ann, "I have some hope that I shall be enabled to keep this in mind in whatever I do—is it pleasing to God? To assist my memory I have used the expedient of inscribing it on several articles which frequently meet my sight." And before long it was written in his heart. Again and again he would repeat the words—"to please God," "to please the Lord Jesus."

Thousands of others, young and old, were affected as deeply and as permanently as was that Plymouth lad. Just to look upon the heroic pioneer was enough to bring thoughts and resolves that stirred thousands to new consecration—stirred a whole denomination and many denominations to new devotion to the great cause—turned their thoughts heavenward and their purposes eastward. Many felt that inspiration who never saw him—as did Henry Jessup, noted Presbyterian missionary to Syria, who later said that when he reached heaven the first one whose hand he would want to grasp, after the Apostle Paul, would be Adoniram Judson.

Judson revealed himself only partly, however, in his public appearances. When he was making an address he must have seemed in the highest degree solemn and serious. Indeed he was. But when he was released from duty and responsibility

---

[5] Edward Judson, p. 460.

he became the joyous, youthful, vivacious, cultured friend, at home in social circles, as brilliant and fascinating as before he left American shores for his eastern home. He limited his social relations to small groups of those who were sympathetic and could understand him and his purposes, so that the general public, even the religious public, did not see the genial side of his nature. This was reserved for intimate friends, and these enjoyed and appreciated him to the full. To estimate a biography we must know the biographer. Wayland, his chief biographer,[6] was massive, severe, and saw the great figure of Judson in its grand proportions. We are indebted to him for an interpretation of Judson's moral character, his Christian purpose and his missionary principles such as no one else in America could have given. On the other hand Wayland paid little attention to the human side of Judson, his social qualities, his cultural interest, his informal friendliness, his attractive pleasantries.

But Professor A. C. Kendrick, Emily Judson's biographer, saw Judson from quite a different angle. He met him in home circles where he relaxed and was most at ease and most natural, and he has preserved for us a picture of the smiling, humorous, cultured and friendly Judson, poetic in imagination, warm and tender in his love, while earnest and aspiring in his Christian devotion and purpose—the Judson we saw as a youth and have glimpsed from time to time in Burma. Kendrick saw in him "an inextinguishable warmth of heart, a delicacy of taste, and a breadth of culture"; he noted "the exuberance of his joyful spirit"; he admired his offering to the missionary cause: "what a weatlh of endowments and susceptibilities—what exquisite tenderness—what exuberant vivacity and humor—what capabilities and aspirations after every form of worldly excellence"; he spoke of his "general character" and his "intensely, unconquerably youthful" spirit; he told how

---

[6] Wayland had an almost extravagant admiration for Judson. Sarah Boardman's son George was a student at Brown during his presidency, and one day some of the boys dared him to wear into the president's class one of Judson's high collars, that came up to his eyes. Wayland spied it at once and said sternly, "What sort of collar is that you have on, sir?" "It is my stepfather's, Dr. Judson's, sir," replied Boardman. Like a flash Wayland retorted, as deep emotion filled his countenance, "I apologize. Wear it every day of your life, sir!" (*Memories of Brown*, p. 94).

Judson, "with renovated health and buoyant spirits, casting off all reserve, gave loose rein to his matchless powers of captivation, and made himself the life and soul of many delighted circles"; in swift strokes he pictured Judson as he himself knew him—"his were no ordinary fascinations, a character of the rarest quality, in which the hero of practical life and the hero of romance blended their seemingly incongruous elements; in which, by a rare felicity of temperament, the energetic will of the man of action and the almost ascetic devotion of the saint were blended with the playfulness of the child, the tenderness of the woman, the enthusiasm of the poet, and the clear vision of the sage." [7]

William Hague, too, who was with him a great deal, said that he showed "a fine susceptibility of deriving enjoyment from everything around him," and pointed out that his grand qualities were joined with social and domestic characteristics not seen by those who viewed him only at a distance. And John Marshman, in India, who knew him well, said that his face was always lighted with a smile. [8]

Many have in their minds a different picture of Judson. They see him borne down by depression and foreboding in the threatening months of Ava and Aungbinle, or straining to reach the light through the sorrow and mental tension of the dark days that followed the Ava tragedy, or appealing solemnly by pen or voice for the great cause that dominated his thoughts. He was all of this; but he was more. He was what Kendrick and Hague saw—what we have seen in the letters that remain from the early days with Ann—what he was in the delightful home life with Sarah and Emily—what he was as John Marshman saw him. He had depths like the sea he loved so well, and under a clouded sky seemed oppressively dark and somber; but under brighter skies his nature sparkled like the sun-kissed ocean. In the missionary years he was not essentially different from what he was in the youthful years, only mellowed, and deepened, and richly ennobled. Kendrick lets us see him in

[7] Kendrick, *Life and Letters of Emily C. Judson,* chaps. X, XI, XII.
[8] Wayland, II, p. 359.

this brighter aspect, in one of the most fascinating chapters of his life, his marriage to Emily Chubbuck.

He met her at the home of a mutual friend, Rev. A. D. Gillette, pastor of the Eleventh Street Baptist Church of Philadelphia,[9] who had gone to Boston to persuade Judson if possible to visit his city. The effort was successful, and on their return to Philadelphia Mr. Gillette took Judson to the home of Mr. W. S. Robarts, who with his wife was thereafter in the circle of his warm friends. The next morning, Christmas Day, he called at the Gillette home, and was promptly introduced to the young authoress Emily Chubbuck, who was visiting the Gillettes, and whose recent book, *Trippings in Author Land,* he had seen on the journey from Boston. At once Judson with his usual impetuosity asked her how she could conscientiously use such noble talents as she evidently possessed in writing books of so little spiritual value as *Trippings.* For answer she told him something of her story.

She had lived in Eaton and Hamilton and other villages in central New York since her birth on August 22, 1817. Her father had never prospered and the family had endured privation and poverty. Once they lived in a two-room shack with a little loft reached by a ladder. Sometimes they did not know what they would have to eat the next day. Often in the winter Emily and her sister and mother went out into the fields and dug in the snow for stray pieces of wood to keep them all from freezing. She worked in a woolen factory, and went to school only at such odd times as she could be spared. A rare spirit of affection and understanding, with deep piety and real culture, pervaded the family circle and Emily's parents did their best to help her toward the realization of her hopes. At fifteen she was teaching school, at seventeen she was baptized by William Dean, later missionary to China. Her opportunity came when through the kindness of friends she became a student and teacher in Utica Female Seminary. Almost by chance she secured the publication of a sketch that won approval, and before she realized it she was famous as an author, known as "Fanny Forester." It was because of the need of helping her

---

[9] Kendrick gives the interesting account, chap. X.

parents, she explained to Judson, that she was writing the kind of books she was, which though light were of unquestionable moral standard, as she pointed out.

As Judson listened to what she recounted of her story, his sympathies were won and he admitted that she was quite right. Then he told her that he had desired to have someone write a memoir of his late wife Sarah, and suggested that she do it. For the next few days they were much together discussing the work which Emily agreed to undertake. They were drawn to each other in a way that neither had expected. And when in less than a month he asked her to share his life she was ready with her "Yes." Judson's formal proposal was made in a note as beautiful and revealing as it is unique:

"January 20, 1846.

"I hand you, dearest one, a charmed watch. It always comes back to me, and brings its wearer with it. I gave it to Ann when a hemisphere divided us, and it brought her safely and surely to my arms. I gave it to Sarah during her husband's lifetime (not then aware of the secret), and the charm, though slow in its operation, was true at last.

"Were it not for the sweet sympathies you have kindly extended to me, and the blessed understanding that 'love has taught us to guess at,' I should not venture to pray you to accept my present with such a note. Should you cease to 'guess' and toss back the article, saying, 'Your watch has lost its charm; it comes back to you, but brings not its wearer with it'—O first dash it to pieces, that it may be an emblem of what will remain of the heart of

"Your devoted

A. JUDSON."

The news of the engagement stirred up a tempest of public discussion. It was nobody's business but their own, but the public was taken by surprise and promptly made it their business. The admirers of "Fanny Forester" pointed out what a ridiculous sacrifice she was making in exchanging her attractive literary position for the home of a missionary. She had indeed gained a high literary standing. Bancroft and Longfellow and Prescott and Bryant, with some of the leading literary critics of the day, notably Nathaniel P. Willis, recognized her as one of the foremost writers of descriptive sketches and fiction, while her poems were increasing in power and popularity. More brilliant prospects were ahead. So she was criticized for yielding to the dark sorceries of this missionary from heathendom, and giving up her bright future for an infatuation with a fanatical dreamer.

On the other hand the Christian public was equally critical of Judson for taking as the successor of the sainted Ann Hasseltine and Sarah Boardman just a popular writer—as they thought of her. They looked on him as if he were living in a different world from that of ordinary people. Love and home life were lost sight of entirely in the halo of piety in which they framed him. They did not really know him, nor did they know the depth and loveliness of Emily Chubbuck's character. So they made free with their criticism.

To so sensitive a soul as Emily Chubbuck the public criticism of herself and her lover was most distressing. As for Judson, "I have been so cried down," he said, "at different periods of my life—especially when I became a Baptist and lost all, all except Ann—that I am a little hardened." But everyone did not criticize them adversely. "President W.," undoubtedly President Wayland, whose opinion Judson told Emily was "worth that of ten thousand," wrote to him:

"I know not where you are, but hear that you are tripping in author land under the guidance of a fair Forester. I am pleased to hear of your engagement, as far as I know of it. Miss C. is everywhere spoken of as a pious, sensible, cultivated and engaging person. I write at a venture, to say that our house is at your service whenever you will come and occupy it. Should you bring anyone with you both will be equally welcome."

And Emily's close friend Anna Maria Anable often used to tell of the magnetism and fascination of Judson, and said that there was not a woman living but could understand why Emily said "Yes."

Judson had made Emily's acquaintance through her attractiveness as a writer, but what really drew him to her was her own attractiveness—what she herself really was. Kendrick has

described her: "So much humor and so much genius—so play-
ful and so brilliant—so exactly like himself [Judson], all running over with buoyant and irrepressible enthusiasm." Her
letters to Judson reveal her uncommon warmth of affection:
"I thank God constantly for the sweet way he has chidden my
follies, and pointed out a better path for me to walk in . . .
He has sent you, dearest, to love and care for, to guide and
strengthen me . . . The place is not what constitutes my
home—it is your presence . . . God will lead us both, but my
hand will be in yours . . . Take the hand I place upon your
lips, and lead your 'unuseful' one through life up to heaven—
thine through life, thine in death, thine when we shall both
awake in our blessed Saviour's image."

Judson came to Hamilton in March and spent two weeks
in Emily's home. From Hamilton he and Emily went to Sche-
nectady for a brief visit with her friend and former teacher,
Mrs. Nott, and with the latter's husband, President Eliphalet
Nott of Union College, uncle of Samuel Nott. Then Judson
went east, speaking at Colby College and a number of other
places, visiting his Plymouth home, sending Adoniram and
Elnathan to Worcester to the home of Dr. and Mrs. Newton,
and arranging for George Boardman to enter Brown. Early
in May he returned to Hamilton, and he and Emily had a few
days together there and at Eaton, Emily's early home. In Hamilton he had the great privilege of meeting again his old Andover teacher, Dr. Leonard Woods, who had preached the ordination sermon at Salem. Dr. Woods was visiting in Hamilton,
and on Sunday morning preached in the village church. He
and Judson sat together on the platform; and after the sermon
Judson arose, and in a humility and tenderness that deeply
moved his hearers referred to the time thirty-eight years before,
when as "a poor blind skeptic," he had taken his seat at the
feet of the preacher and had learned from him the way of life.

From Hamilton he went to Brooklyn for the final meeting
of the Triennial Convention: "Out all day at Brooklyn; such
crowds, and shaking of hands, and exclamations of congratu-
lation, and frequent inquiries from old acquaintances whether
Miss C. was present and could be seen. In the evening it came

my turn to address the assembly, which I did in a small speech —a dead one—but brother Stow [10] galvanized it.

Emily was anxious to bring out a complete edition of her stories and sketches, and Judson undertook the business of securing a publisher and transferring the copyright of *Trippings in Author Land*. He personally bought the plates, and the new edition was published in two volumes as *Alderbrook,* named for the alder-fringed stream in the pleasant Eaton valley of her girlhood. Judson also advanced money to pay off the debt on her parents' home, which she had bought, and financed further purchases at a cost of $350. He also engaged to provide for the needs of Emily's father and mother as long as necessary. To be able to do so much it is certain that he must have come into a private income which he had not previously had, though probably a very moderate one. "My pecuniary arrangements are such that we shall have an ample sufficiency for all our purposes," he wrote to Emily.

On the first of June Judson arrived in Hamilton again, and the next day, Tuesday, they were married by Dr. Nathaniel Kendrick, whom Emily had known years before as pastor of the Eaton church. As a girl she had confided to him her desire to become a foreign missionary, a thought that had been implanted in her through reading the memoir of Ann Judson. Dr. Kendrick had advised her to await the openings of Providence. And Providence had opened the way most marvelously, making her the successor of Ann herself.

Again Judson was eagerly pressing forward toward Burma, still the pioneer as in the days of 1812.

---

[10] Baron Stow, then pastor of Baldwin Place Church, Boston.

CHAPTER XI

ONCE MORE THE PIONEER

THEY expected to sail on the first of July, and a large farewell meeting was held in the Baldwin Place Church the preceding afternoon. But the sailing was delayed, and Judson took the opportunity to go once more to Worcester for a last visit with his boys. Then, two days before they sailed, he took Abby Ann to Bradford to leave her with Abigail Hasseltine, sister of Nancy and preceptress of Bradford Academy. Emily had proposed that Abby return with them to Burma; but that did not seem wise. However, she was happy in having one of her old Utica school friends, Lydia Lillybridge, go with her and Adoniram as a new recruit for the mission. And other new missionaries were sailing with them, Mr. and Mrs. Norman Harris and Mr. and Mrs. John S. Beecher. The Executive Committee of the mission board met and presented to Judson a special address of veneration and farewell. And on Sunday evening, July fifth, a united missionary service was held, with an address by Judson, read by one of the pastors.

The sailing took place on Saturday, July eleventh, when the Judsons and their new associates embarked on the ship *Faneuil Hall*, Captain Hallet. They had been hospitably entertained in Boston in the home of Mr. and Mrs. Gardner Colby, and these and a host of other friends assembled at the wharf to bid them godspeed. The Gillettes had come from Philadelphia. So had Anna Maria Anable. Boston on a July day can be oppressively hot. It was that kind of a day when the *Faneuil Hall* sailed, and noon at that. But this did not keep the great throng away. A small platform had been erected on the wharf, and just before the sailing a farewell service was held. Mr. Gillette offered prayer for Judson and Emily and the others, and a hymn written for the occasion was sung by the throng:

"Fare ye well, O friends beloved!
    Speed ye on your mission high;
Give to lands of gloomy error
    Living truths that never die.
        Tell, O tell them,
    Their redemption draweth nigh.

. . . . .

"Fare ye well! till toils are ended,
    And on earth we cease to dwell;
Till around the throne we gather,
    Rapt in bliss no tongue can tell;
        Friends in Jesus!
    Precious kindred—fare ye well!" [1]

The ship cast off, Judson and Emily waved to their friends
as the vessel slipped away down the harbor, the city gradually
faded from view, and Judson had seen his native land for the
last time.

It was an uneventful voyage. They passed St. Helena, not
near enough to see the island but close enough to think of it
and of the one whom Judson had left there but a year before.
Emily, with the rare delicacy and appreciation that distinguished her, expressed her thought in verse:

"Blow softly, gales! a tender sigh
    Is flung upon your wing;
Lose not the treasure as ye fly,
Bear it where love and beauty lie,
    Silent and withering.

. . . . .

"Bloom, ocean isle! lone ocean isle!
    Thou keep'st a jewel rare;
Let rugged rock and deep defile
Above the slumbering stranger smile,
    And deck her couch with care." [2]

Judson never enjoyed a voyage more than this one. The
Faneuil Hall was a good sailer, accommodations were excellent,

---

[1] The whole hymn, in six stanzas, is given by Fletcher, p. 400.
[2] The whole poem, seven stanzas, appears in Emily Judson's *Memoir of Sarah B. Judson*, p. 249.

table fare was ample and good, and Captain Hallet quite endeared himself to all by his many kindnesses and his genuine Christian interest. Worship was held every evening, and on Sundays a Bible class, with public worship for the crew. Judson was all eagerness to get at his work once more, and spent a considerable part of the voyage revising what he had done on his English-Burman dictionary.

On the twenty-seventh of November, one hundred and forty days from Boston, they dropped anchor off Amherst. Judson looked again on the familiar scene—the old wooden pagoda half covered by the water, its white and gold companion on the bluff above, the brown-roofed cottages among the trees, the purple hills beyond. And already he had borrowed the captain's telescope, and had spent some quiet moments looking at the little inclosure under the hopea tree, where slept Ann and Maria.

Very different was the greeting they received from that which had met Judson at Rangoon thirty-three years before! Emily wrote about it to her sister Catharine: "We were scarcely anchored this morning when a boat of six or seven men came bounding toward us, who by the fluttering of gay silks and the display of snowy jackets and turbans were judged to be something above mere boatmen. As they drew sufficiently near to be distinguished by their features, one of our number who had been for some time silently watching them from the side of the vessel leaned far over for a moment gazing at them intently, and then sent forth a glad, wild hail. In a moment the glancing of oars ceased, a half dozen men sprang to their meet, to the imminent peril of the old nut-shell in which they floated, and a wilder, longer, and if possible more joyous cry showed that the voice of the salutation was recognized. Christian beckoned me to his side. 'They are our Amherst friends,' he said; 'the dear, faithful fellows!' . . . In a few minutes the men had brought the boat alongside and were scrambling up the sides of the vessel. How the black eyes danced beneath their grave brows, and the rough lips curled with smiles behind the bristling beards! Then came a quick grasping of hands, and half-choked words of salutation, in a strange deep guttural which he only to whom they were addressed could understand; while I, like the full-grown baby that I am, re-treated to the nearest shadow, actually sobbing . . . Then a venerable man, who as I afterward learned is a deacon in the church, came forward, and bending his turbaned head respect-fully, commenced an animated address, waving his hand occa-sionally to the troop behind him, who bowed as in assent."

Judson was deeply moved by the greeting, and Emily was quite overcome. Soon they were all on shore, to receive other greetings from the Christians of Amherst, and to visit the hal-lowed spot that meant so much to both Adoniram and Emily.

Three days later, on Monday, November thirtieth, they went up to Moulmein in a small boat—"very much like a long watering trough, whittled to a point at each end," in which they were "all nestled like a parcel of caged fowls." So Emily wrote. How wonderful the scenery after the long voyage—the wealth of green along the shore, the white rice birds, and the brilliant flowers, amber and lemon and vermilion, some in clusters, others in long wreaths. Even Moulmein was not un-attractive, in spite of the low shacks and warehouses in the foreground, in front of the mission buildings and other Euro-pean homes. For the hills beyond, covered with green, made a background that threw a beauty over the scene. At any rate it was home.

Judson received a lively welcome from his two boys, Henry, now four years old, and Edward, now two. Charlie, alas! had died four weeks before his mother; the news reached his father in America late in November. So there was a vacant place in the circle of those whom Judson was so eager to greet. Sarah's place, too, was taken by another. But Emily and Adoniram were warmly welcomed by the missionaries, Emily quickly won a fond place in the hearts of Henry and Edward, and Judson was happy, in spite of memories of those gone from earth and thoughts of those far away.

All departments of the work had made advance since his departure for America—the Burman church, the schools, the Karen work in the jungle, and the printing of the Talaing New Testament and the Burmese textbooks. But he was look-ing toward the real Burma. Moulmein had an ample supply of missionaries, while there was not a single one in Rangoon or all Burma;[8] in Rangoon he could have more help on his dictionary than in Moulmein, with learned men and Burman books; and if a way opened into the heart of the country, especially to Ava, he would be in a better situation to take advantage of it. He was happy in Moulmein—so happy that he wrote to his sister, "It seems to me harder to leave Moulmein for Rangoon than to leave Boston for Moulmein." His home was only a very simple thatch-roofed house, made of plain teak boards unvarnished, with only the simplest of furnishings; yet it was home, Emily was there, the children were there, and friends were near. But duty seemed to call to Rangoon. So he took a brief reconnoitering trip to the city he knew so well.

The governor received him kindly, but all he could get was an offer of land for an English church, and permission to settle as minister to the foreigners in town. No open missionary work was possible. "Buddhism is in full feather throughout the empire," he wrote to Emily. "The prospects of a missionary were never darker." He saw opportunities for private work, however, and if he were on the ground he would be ready for a better chance if one appeared. So he rented a house for his family, and returned to Rangoon.

The letters that he wrote to Emily during the trip are revealing. Off Amherst he wrote:

"The hopea tree is just visible from the shore. I seem to have lived in several worlds; but you are the earthly sun that illuminates my present. My thoughts and affections revolve around you."

And again on his way back to Moulmein:

"Here we lie, with Amherst in sight from our cabin window. Amherst, whither I brought Ann, and returned to find her grave; Amherst, whither I brought Sarah, on returning from my matrimonial tour to Tavoy, and whence I took her away in the *Paragon,* to return no more; Amherst, the terminus of my long voyage in the *Faneuil Hall* with Emily. The place seems to be the center of many radii of my past existence, though not a place where any of us have lived for any length of time. Ann never saw Moulmein;

---

[8] Wade, Kincaid and others had spent brief periods there, trying to get a foothold, but with little success owing to opposition of the government.

Sarah never saw Rangoon. If we should remove to the latter place, it would seem to me like beginning my life anew. May it be under more propitious auspices, and may the latter part of life make some atonement for the errors of the former. May we be luminaries to Burma, and may our setting sun descend in a flood of light! Who shall paint the glories of the eternity before us? Eye hath not seen, nor ear heard."

This letter brings out the frank attitude of Judson toward his previous wives. He never hesitated to refer to Ann in the presence of Sarah, nor to Ann and Sarah in talking to Emily. The perfect understanding between Sarah and Emily and himself made that possible. He had a boundless love for each of his wives, and on the other hand Ann and Sarah and Emily each loved him with a full devotion. Ann's effervescent nature, deeply joyous, richly loving, fascinatingly attractive, drew him to her with a perfect union of spirit that had little need for words. Sarah was quiet, devoted to her work and her home, lacking the inspiring qualities of Ann, but by her exquisite womanhood winning from Judson a love that matched her own. Emily, with less of missionary zeal and perhaps of Christian consecration, poured out her love like a torrent, with a bright happiness and a marvelous devotedness that was equalled only by Judson's full, joyous love in return. It was Ann's high privilege to dare the unknown for his sake and Christ's, to share the pioneering of the early years, and to save Judson for his great achievements by the gift of her own life. After the dark years of loneliness, Sarah gave him the comfort and delight of a home, and drew forth once more that bright, youthful spirit that was so largely the real Judson. To Emily it was due in rich measure that the ending of his day of life was so happy and peaceful, and that so vivid and human a picture of him has been given to us, a picture that no one but Emily could have painted.

The home Judson had rented in Rangoon was just the upper story of a large brick house on a street occupied by foreigners, all Moslems. It had not a foot of land around it, and the place looked "as gloomy as a prison." Rangoon was a poor city compared with Moulmein, and Judson shrank from the thought of Emily's trying to make a home there.

"When I turn away from all the filth and wretchedness around me, and think of you, it seems like looking from hell to heaven. How can I take you from all the comforts of Moulmein, and shut you up in this den?"

But Emily, like her husband, was eager to give the great message to those who had not heard it. So on the fifteenth of February (1847) they left Moulmein, and on the twentieth reached Rangoon, where after a few days as guests of Captain Crisp, son of a friend of Judson in the early Rangoon years, they set up their own home in "Bat Castle"—for so Emily named their house. Her description of it to her sister Catharine is too picturesque to be missed:

"Think of me in an immense brick house with rooms as large as the entire 'loggery' [4] (our center room is twice as large, and has no window), and only one small window apiece. When I speak of windows do not think I make any allusion to glass—of course not. The windows (holes) are closed by means of heavy board or plank shutters, tinned over on the outside as a preventive of fire . . . Imagine us on the second floor of this immense den, with nine rooms at our command, the smallest of which (bathing room and a kind of pantry) are I think as large as your dining room, and the rest very much larger. Part of the floors are of brick and part of boards; but old 'Green Turban' whitewashed them all, with the walls, before we came, because the Doctor told him, when he was over here, that he must 'make the house shine for Madam.' He did make it shine with a vengeance, between whitewashing and greasing. They oil furniture in this country, as Americans do mahogany; but all his doors and other woodwork were fairly dripping, and we have not got rid of the smell yet; nor with all our rubbing is it quite safe to hold too long on the door.

"The partitions are all of brick, and very thick, and the door sills are built up, so that I go over them at three or four steps, Henry mounts and falls off, and Edward gets on all fours, and accomplishes the pass with more safety. The floor overhead is quite low, and the beams, which are frequent, afford shelter to

[4] The name she gave to her father's home in Hamilton.

thousands and thousands of bats, that disturb us in the daytime only by a little cricket-like noise, but in the night—O if you could only hear them carouse! The mosquito curtains are our only safeguard; and getting up is horrible. The other night I awoke faint, with a feeling of suffocation, and without waiting to think jumped out on the floor. You would have thought 'Old Nick' himself had come after you, for of course you believe these firm friends of the ladies of the broomstick incipient imps. If there is nothing wickeder about them than about the little sparrows that come in immense throngs to the same beams, pray what do they do all through the hours of darkness, and why do they circle and whizz about a poor mortal's head, flap their villainous wings in one's face, and then whisk away as if snickering at the annoyance? We have had men at work nearly a week trying to thin them out, and have killed a great many hundreds, but I suppose their little demoniac souls come back, each with an attendant, for I am sure there are twice as many as at first. Everything, walls, tables, chairs, etc., are stained by them. Besides the bats we are blessed with our full share of cockroaches, spiders, lizards, rats, ants, mosquitoes and bedbugs. With the last the woodwork is all alive, and the ants troop over the house in great droves, though there are scattering ones besides."

Emily's name for the house was certainly appropriate. Judson wrote to Binney at Moulmein: "We have had a grand bat hunt yesterday and today—bagged two hundred and fifty, and calculate to make up a round thousand before we have done. . . . The sound of their wings is as the sound of many waters, yea, as the sound of your boasted Yankee Niagara; so that sleep departs from our eyes and slumber from our eyelids."

And another trial met them. Scarcely had they settled in "Bat Castle" when word came from Moulmein that the Stevens house had been set on fire in the night by an incendiary and had burned to the ground with all its contents, including presents and other valuables that the Judsons had brought from America. But with characteristic unselfishness they minimized their own loss, and Judson wrote at once to Stevens to express his sympathy with him and his family, who had lost everything and had barely escaped with their lives.

Judson promptly settled himself to work in Rangoon. Only a handful of Christians could be found—hardly any traces at all of the Christianity of the early days. Nominally there were twenty members in the church gathered by Pastor Tha E, yet many were scattered and not a few had lost their interest. But on the first Sunday in March Judson collected those who could be discovered and they observed the Lord's Supper together in his house—ten Burmans, one Karen, Emily and himself. Worship was held every Sunday, but secretly for fear of the government. By the middle of March, however, he could report four hopeful inquirers, and on the last Sunday of the month he baptized one of them, in the very pond where twenty-eight years before he had baptized Maung Nau. Visitors came from time to time, and he missed no opportunity of telling them the gospel story. His work on the dictionary occupied many hours of the day, but he found time for companionship with Emily and frolics with the boys. "Wife and I occupy remote ends of the house, and we have to visit one another, and that takes time. And I have to hold a meeting with the rising generation every evening, and that takes time. Henry can say 'Twinkle, twinkle,' all himself, and Edward can repeat it after his father! Giants of genius! Paragons of erudition!"

Judson's chief interest, in Rangoon as everywhere else, was evangelism. He made no effort to distribute tracts—in fact he had brought none from Moulmein, remembering his experience during his last visit seven years before. But he eagerly talked with everyone he could reach.

All had to be done with the utmost secrecy. The greatest care was used by the disciples to avoid suspicion, and on Sundays they never came or went in a company. They would appear at various hours during the morning, one or two at a time. Some would bring packages or dishes of fruit, some came dressed as coolies, others as though making an ordinary call. When all had assembled the outer door was barred and quiet worship began. But the numbers rose to twenty, thirty, then still higher, and they were afraid the police would notice it and report them. They had no fear of the governor, for he was mild and friendly; and sometimes Judson would smile at the precautions they were taking. But the *ye wun,* or vice-governor, was a cruel despot—"the most ferocious, blood-thirsty monster I have ever known in Burma," wrote Judson. Screams of his victims came from his house almost night and day, and he had not hesitated to put even foreigners to the torture.

Their retired location, on the street of the Moslems, was an advantage, and so far as Judson knew their meetings had not been discovered. But suddenly events drew to a cli-max. One Friday evening late in May they received secret information from "friends at court" that the *ye wun* had been told of the numbers of people coming and going, and had or-dered that the house be watched, and that any who were turn-ing to "Jesus Christ's religion" should be seized.

No time was to be lost. Several Karens who were staying with them were spirited away in the night toward their jungle home. Two Burman assistants were sent out to warn all the other disciples to stay away. Hurriedly they went from home to home, and from village to village, carrying a word of cheer from Judson, warning the disciples to stay hidden out of sight, and advising them how to worship secretly. The Christians proved loyal; and on that dark Sunday, with torture and death threatening them all, little groups gathered here and there in secret places, and joined hearts and voices in quiet but earnest prayer for their teacher and for one another.

The danger was very real; but in spite of it one Christian, with his father-in-law, insisted on coming to see Judson, that the old man might present the request of his son, a fine young fellow of twenty, for baptism.

But as Judson that Sunday night thought over the turn of events, the situation seemed so disappointing—indeed so hope-less—that he gave way for a time to despondency, and paced the room, back and forth, in silence. Emily tried to cheer him, without success. Suddenly she said, "Would you like to know the first couplet I learned to repeat?"

Judson did not answer and she went on, "I learned it before I could read, and then I used to write it everywhere, sometimes at the top of the page when I was preparing a story on whose success more depended than its readers ever dreamed."

"What was it?" asked Judson; and Emily replied:

"Beware of desperate steps; the darkest day,
Live till tomorrow, will have passed away."

"Why," declared Judson, at once all animation again, "those two lines have been my motto too! I used to repeat them over and over in prison. I have them now, written on a slip of paper for a bookmark." And he added, "Well, one thing you didn't do: you never wrote 'Pray without ceasing' on the cover of your wafer box."

"No," replied Emily, "but I wrote it on my looking-glass!"

No wonder they were drawn to each other—"we are so alike in everything," as Judson put it.

The drastic action of the *ye wun* began a series of annoyances and insults that prevented any effective work. Christians and inquirers came for private conversation, but no worship service could be held. In spite of that, on the very first Sunday in June another young man was baptized, in a place hidden by bushes on the further side of the pond, with only two or three trusted disciples witnessing the ordinance.

The next morning the young man's father was arrested, and one of the disciples hurried to inform Judson. "Now the end has come!" he thought. But providentially the man was taken to the governor's office, not that of the *ye wun*.

"Why have you brought this man?" demanded the governor's assistant.

"Here is your written order," answered the accuser.

"What! I have given no order. It is a mistake. Go about your business."

Then the man who had been arrested spoke up: "I thought it was strange that you should arrest me on a charge of heresy, as it is well known that I worship the true God."

"God?" rejoined the officer, "worship any god you like."

"Or the devil," put in a woman sitting by his side; "pay your taxes and what more do we want?"

Judson learned afterward that the officer had really signed the order, but that when he reported it to the governor the latter promptly canceled it.

In the midst of all these trials and dangers Judson and Emily were perfectly happy with each other. On June second, their first wedding anniversary, Emily wrote to her sister, "Just one year ago today I stood before good old Dr. Kendrick and said the irrevocable 'love, honor and obey.' It has been far the happiest year of my life; and what is in my eyes still more important, my husband says it has been among the happiest of his. We have been in circumstances to be almost constantly together; and I never met with any man who could talk so well, day after day, on every subject, religious, literary, scientific, political, and—and nice baby-talk."

But they could not get satisfactory food. The only bread to be had was black and sour, and what passed as milk was a mixture—buffalo milk, water, "and something else which we cannot make out." The rainy season came on, with the Buddhist Lent, when neither flesh nor fowl was to be had, and the few fish they could buy were half decayed. There was practically nothing to eat but boiled rice and fruit.

"You must get something that mamma can eat," said Judson to the cook one day.

"What shall I get?" asked the cook.

"Anything," replied Judson.

"Anything?"

"Anything."

The result was—but read it as Emily described it to her sister Catharine:

"Well, we did have a capital dinner, though we tried in vain to find out by the bones what it was. Cook said he didn't know, but he grinned a horrible grin which made my stomach heave a little, notwithstanding the deliciousness of the meal. In the evening we called Mr. Bazaar-man. 'What did we have for dinner today?' 'Were they good?' 'Excellent.' A tremendous explosion of laughter, in which the cook from his dish room joined as loud as he dared. 'What were they?' 'Rats!' "

More serious was the epidemic that threatened them. Almost everybody around them was ill, and many were dying. They themselves were sick. Emily had not sat up an hour at a time for six weeks, and Judson himself came down with what proved to be dysentery of the worst form. Meanwhile Edward was taken with erysipelas and Henry by "Rangoon fever."

Even the children's nurse was sick. There was no physician in Rangoon, and all they could do was to consult their medical books and use such medicines as seemed to fit their several cases. For a while it looked as though Judson and Edward would surely die. But by God's good providence all came through safely.

One wonders why they did not turn to a Roman Catholic priest for aid, as they did in the early days. Perhaps the priests in Rangoon at this time were not skilled in medicine. And relations between them and the Protestant missionaries were not as friendly as in the earlier period. In religious work, to be sure, Judson had no direct relations with either Roman Catholic priests or Armenians. It would not have been possible to work with Roman Catholic missionaries, if he had wished to do so. But as a matter of fact the Roman missionaries in Burma proper worked solely among foreigners and people of mixed blood, not among the native Burmans; so their ways and his did not often cross. The same was largely true in Moulmein.

Most of these days in Rangoon Judson was able to work steadily on his English-Burman dictionary. But he could not keep Ava out of his mind. No hope of success could be seen anywhere in Burma unless the government would grant toleration. Perhaps if he went up to the capital [5] again he could secure that longed-for boon. The governor had given him permission to go, and the fierce opposition of the vice-governor made an appear to higher authority seem absolutely necessary —"not an individual ventures to come near me," wrote Judson. The board also had given their approval.

But just when this hopeful project began to take shape the whole thing was crushed by a letter from Moulmein—"like a sudden tornado on a sunny day," as Emily said. The Moulmein missionaries informed him that appropriations from home had been cut down, and that retrenchment was necessary. All they could allow for his expenses in Rangoon would be seventeen and a half rupees a month. And it was actually costing him eighty-six a month! Here was a pretty pass. He

---

[5] Actually the capital was now once more Amarapura, or New Ava.

could not succeed in Rangoon without at least a visit to Ava, yet there was no money for an Ava trip, and not even enough to let him stay in Rangoon. Only one choice was left—he must "fall back upon Moulmein."

"I thought they loved me," he said mournfully to Emily, "and they would scarcely have known it if I had died."

But he soon recovered from his disappointment. "God has done this thing," he said, "and done it, as He always does, for good. It is not His will that we should go up to Ava now."

They could not have gone to Ava just then anyway. Judson and the boys were still suffering from their various illnesses; and the care of her family, the lack of food, and the threatening relations with the government, had brought Emily down so that she was "as thin as the shad that went up the Niagara," as Judson described her to Mrs. Stevens. So they stayed on in Rangoon, doing what they could—Judson working on his dictionary and talking with occasional visitors, and Emily finishing her memoir of Sarah Boardman Judson.

One day—perhaps often—they went out to the old mission compound. Of course the house, the old home of Adoniram and Ann, was entirely gone. A tangle of betel now covered the whole place, and the climbing creepers were so thick that one could scarcely get around among them. So changed was the place that Judson could not even find the spot where the house had been.

"It must have been somewhere here," he said to Emily, as he indicated a place; "that mound was the site of an old pagoda, and I leveled it as you see."

The old well would identify it if he could find it, and he mentioned it to a Burman who was following them in curiosity —"It was close by my house, and was bricked up."

"Your house!" exclaimed the man with astonishment.

"Why, yes," said Judson; "I used to live here."

The Burman looked around on the tall betel vines with a smile of incredulity and shrugged his shoulders. But Judson continued his search. And sure enough! there was the well, covered with moss and lichens, yet proof positive that close at hand was the spot where the old home had been.

They visited the grave of little Roger, too. A brick monument had been built over it, and this was a little out of repair. But there it was, with a tall azalea growing out of its base and almost covering it. Judson called to mind the scenes of thirty years before, and the lovely one who had shared those days of suffering and sorrow; and Emily's tears started in sympathy for her husband, and for Ann, now become so real and human, as she herself stood in that place where Adoniram and that other had lived so happily and suffered so keenly.[6]

During the summer Judson's friend the governor was removed, and likewise the vice-governor. Judson stayed a few weeks to learn what the attitude of the new governor might be, but found nothing to encourage him. So they closed "Bat Castle," embarked for Moulmein, and as they sailed down the river Judson looked back for the last time on the city to which he had given so much of his heart and his life. On the fifth of September they were all in Moulmein once more.

Surveying the situation, Judson found that twenty-four of the twenty-nine missionaries were in Moulmein, eleven working for the Karens, nine for the Burmans, two for the Talaings, and two in the press. Of the others, four were in Tavoy and one in Arracan. This crowding into one station was never in accord with Judson's ideas of mission policy, and he had more than once protested against it. Now again he wrote to the board, pointing out that half the number would be sufficient, and indeed that the smaller number would work more efficiently. He admitted that he found it "very pleasant to enjoy such a large and agreeable society," but from a sense of duty felt that he ought to urge the board to "send out no more missionaries to these parts, until they can devise some way of making men go where they are sent, and stay there." Nevertheless, (and this was his habitual attitude) "if they [the board] take a different view of the subject from mine, I shall cheerfully acquiesce."

On the twenty-fourth of December (1847) a daughter was born, Emily Frances, and two months later they moved into their old home from the house they had been occupying some

---

[6] The old mission compound was never used again, and no effort was made to preserve it. Even its location is now unknown.

distance away from the chapel. Judson was soon busy as pastor of the church, with its one hundred and fifty members, preaching once on Sundays, with Stevens assisting in the preaching and in other ways.

Look into Judson's chapel on a Sunday morning. It is crowded with worshipers, men on one side, women on the other. On the low platform, by the side of the table that takes the place of a pulpit, stands Judson, wearing his long black gown. All give close attention as he preaches, for he is as forceful and eloquent as ever, often dramatic, sometimes humorous, always direct and impressive. As he closes the sermon the congregation rise to sing, perhaps one of his own hymns, like

"Kye-zu daw go thi-gyin so."
(Sing hymns of praise to grave divine).

or

"Shwe Pyi kaungin san logyin le."
(I long to reach the golden shore).

More than half a century later, one of his hearers remembered those services, and recalled his bright piercing eyes, and how he seemed to be looking into their very hearts.[7]

Sometimes Judson spoke to the children of the Sunday school. Once a month he took his turn at leading a meeting for the twenty children in the missionary families. He loved children. He frolicked with his own children, and wrote to little Elsina Bennett and others.[8] He still enjoyed being with boys and girls. Often he would bring humor into the talks he gave them, and he was always ready with a conundrum or a puzzle, which he liked now as much as when he was a boy himself. But he was not fond of having babies cry in meeting, and if one began he would ask the mother to take the child out. As a pastor he was ideal, and wanted the members of his church to come to him at any hour of the day or night when they needed him; more than once he rose from his bed to visit some one who was ill.

---

[7] Ma Lon Ma, who was baptized by Judson when a little girl.
[8] When Elsina and her sister Mary went to America Judson had a painting of them made and sent out to their mother in Burma.

He preached the same gospel that he had known back in America. He had been brought up in the strict New England Calvinism of Hopkins, and believed in a sovereign God, who has provided in His Son Jesus Christ the only way of salvation from sin. All who accept Him through faith will be freed from future punishment and enjoy the eternal felicity of heaven. As he once put it, "God's own eternal Son, the Lord Jesus Christ, came down from heaven to rescue us from the delusion of this world, the power of sin, and the doom of the impenitent."

The creed that he prepared for use in the churches [9] was very conservative in its doctrines. But God's love took an increasingly prominent place in his thought and his message as the years passed. "He may cast us in a burning fiery furnace, or precipitate us to the lowest depth of the sea, but His care, His tenderness, His love, are still the same." "Grace" was his favorite word, and he often spoke of "the good work of God's grace"; or said of an assistant, "He has grace and will go safe at last"; or spoke of "that divine Being who is ever with thee and ever waiting to be gracious." His appeal was a simple one: "Give your heart to the Friend and Lover of men, who hung and died on the cross to redeem us from eternal woe, and you shall find such peace and sweetness as you have never conceived of."

He still kept up his exercise, and took his daily walk up the hill before sunrise and in the early evening. Emily had been promptly introduced to those walks, which often proved to be a real frolic. Frequently the morning stars would be shining when she and Adoniram started, accompanied by other missionaries and perhaps some of the children. Up the hill beyond the city they would go, to see the sun rise. It was quite a climb, just the exercise that Judson loved. On the summit they would rest a while until the sun rose out of the eastern hills and jungles; then all the party would gather at the head of a path leading down the hill to watch the race between Adoniram and Emily. It was the regular program. Judson would wait while Emily carefully picked her way down the

---

[9] In Wayland, II, p. 468.

rough and rocky path. Then when she was half way down he would start after her, rushing pell-mell with all the excitement of a schoolboy. Emily ran, too; but the real fun was to see Judson go skipping from rock to rock and from ledge to ledge as he tried to catch Emily, everyone wondering whether *this* time he would not fall! When he was out walking alone he was more sedate, though he would swing along at a fast pace, often with his hat in his hand and his head bare, his long hair tossed back and his face uplifted as if deep in thought.

"We are a deliciously happy family," wrote Judson to his daughter Abby. Letters went frequently to her and the boys, and he was keenly interested in all they were doing. Especially was he eager to hear of their conversion. "I never pray without praying for your conversion," he wrote. And he reminded Abby of her mother, and how she would rejoice at her daughter's conversion. "O my dear daughter, my motherless daughter, meet me at the throne of grace."

Emily made good progress in Burmese, and was able to finish the *Scripture Questions* that Sarah had begun. She conducted a Bible class also, and a prayer meeting for the Burman women. Many a good time she and Adoniram had together. "We don't need a comic almanac to make us laugh sometimes, though we are away in heathendom" (so she wrote to the friend Mr. Gillette); "we have only to recall scores of funny things, some of which you know and some you do not know. You know we are neither of us sad people." So life went on in Moulmein.

It was with satisfaction that Judson looked back to the completion of the Bible translation into Burmese. And now he was eager to finish his dictionary, and kept hard at it. "Mr. J. is digging at his tedious dictionary tonight as usual," wrote Emily. As he advanced in the work he wanted more and more to make that visit to Ava, where he hoped to consult with learned Burmans and have access to literary works not available in Moulmein. Fortunately a Burmese scholar came to Moulmein, and Judson was able to enlist his services, obviating the necessity of going to Ava—"so far as the dictionary is concerned." But he still longed to preach the gospel there.

By the end of the year 1848 the first part of the dictionary was completed, the English-Burman section. A small edition was printed, and was off the press by the end of the next year. Meanwhile he was busy on the Burman-English section. The English-Burman part made a volume of six hundred pages quarto, and represented a prodigious piece of work. The second part was expected to be nearly as large. But he never finished the task; it was left for his dear friend E. A. Stevens to do what he had hoped to do. Yet what he did was complete in itself. Of course the dictionary does not have the same significance that the Burmese Bible had. But it was labor well spent. No one in all Burma, Burman or foreigner, had anything like the combined knowledge of Burmese and English that Judson had. For the sake of his missionary associates and all who would come after him it was of high importance that his knowledge be conserved. All Christian work in Burma since his day is indebted to him for his dictionary. And his contribution was of great value as well to the Burmans themselves. All literary effort in Burmese, or based upon the Burmese, as well as the spoken use of the vernacular by foreigners, had need of just such a work as this to which Judson gave the closing years of his life. Whether reckoned as a piece of literary achievement or looked at from the point of view of missionary work, the dictionary takes high rank in quality and value. Naturally it was not complete. Languages grow, and no dictionary is ever complete. Even the English-Burman part has needed constant additions, and the Burman-English section had to be finished by another. Revisions have been made by the Indian Civil Service and by Dr. F. H. Eveleth of the Burma mission. But Judson's work is still the basis of the revised dictionary and it bears his name. It will always remain the foundation and core of the dictionary of the Burmese language.

But now the clouds were beginning to gather. The evening was drawing on. The pioneering days were over.

CHAPTER XII

THE GOLDEN EVENING

OFTEN I stand in my home at the sunset hour and look off across the bay and out through the Golden Gate toward the great limitless ocean. The setting sun throws a shining path along the water, and as the golden evening brightens in the west I sometimes see a ship sail out along the pathway of light into the shining sea beyond. Here and there dark clouds cast their shadows across the glistening water, but farther out all is light. Gradually the ship slips away out of sight and the golden glory fades, to leave only an after-glow as a reminder of the wonderful picture. Here where I stand the world has darkened, but I remember that out beyond the horizon it is light, and that the voyagers who have gone have sailed away into a world of glory.

That is a picture of the short closing months of Judson's life. The afternoon was beautiful as the day declined toward the west. Then shadows fell across the channel of his life, weakness and suffering, and withdrawal from the work that he loved. If one were to think only of his physical body, of the splendid manhood that had been his through the long years, one might look on the days of growing weakness as a decline, and his last months as an anti-climax. Yet his body was not the real Judson. That indeed was decaying, but his spirit was never more alive. It was a golden evening for him, and he was happy in the love of family and friends, glad for the growing nearness of heaven and Christ, enriched with a deepening experience of God's love. It was an evening brightening more and more toward the eternal glory. It was the climax of his life.

He could look back on achievements greater than he had hoped or anticipated. And though he could not know it, he had made contributions to missionary policy that would last into the far future. Such were his emphasis on the fundamental and central place of evangelism, and the ultimate testing of all other methods by this; the importance of the Scriptures in the vernacular, with the most perfect translation that could be made; the training and use of indigenous leaders, as essential for the evangelizing of the people of the land; the central place of the church, controlled by the Christian nationals themselves; the combination of a well-developed central station with the constant pushing out of missionaries into strategic places elsewhere; and finally, interdenominational fellowship and cooperation. These would continue, though his active work might cease.

Emily's health began to show alarming symptoms. She tried a trip down the coast to Tavoy, but it did her no good; she returned worse than ever. Then she recovered sufficiently to go out riding in a chaise which the Houghs (now in charge of a government school in Moulmein) kindly sent each morning. But her condition continued very serious.

Her illness made her feel a closer kinship with her friends in far away America, and her old literary charm came back as she described her Moulmein home to Anna Maria Anable:

"I wish you were sitting by me now, here before my large open window, in a room, I will venture to say, as comfortable and as clean, if not quite so handsomely furnished, as yours. The dark glossy leaves of the Cape jasmine, just below the balustrade, are sparkling with rain drops, and its magnificent white blossoms fill the house with their rich perfume. The trees too are all dripping with rain; and gorgeous birds, though not with the rich voices of our robin and bobolink, are singing in the branches; while the odd-looking native huts, that peep from the green beyond, add to the picturesqueness of the scene, just as a gnarled tree, or a particularly ugly stump, beautifies an American landscape. The bell has just done ringing, and the gaily-dressed natives—the women with bunches of flowers in their black hair, and the men in snowy turbans—go streaming by to the chapel; and—wait a minute!—there, I have had my kiss, and the teacher, as usual of an evening, has gone to spend an hour with his flock."

Through the summer and fall of 1849 Judson kept steadily at his dictionary—the Burman-English part. Emily wrote to her sister: "'The goodman' works like a galley slave; and really it quite distresses me sometimes, but he seems to get fat on it, so I try not to worry. He walks—or rather runs—like a boy over the hills, a mile or two every morning; then down to his books, scratch-scratch, puzzle-puzzle, and when he gets deep in the mire, out on the veranda with your humble servant by his side, walking and talking till the point is elucidated, and then down again—and so on until ten o'clock in the evening. It is this walking which is keeping him out of the grave."

During this last year 1849 it seemed as if again and again the light from the glory beyond the sunset broke through the clouds. Often he talked with Emily of the eternity that seemed so near. More than ever he found enjoyment in prayer, and remembered especially his children far away in America. He spoke a good deal about brotherly love, often quoting "As I have loved you, that ye also love one another." He referred frequently to the growth of the missionary movement, and exclaimed, "What wonders God has wrought!" Then he would talk of the future, always with unwavering faith in the success of Christian missions, and with a triumphant attitude as though he could already see the desired consummation. His fellow missionaries noted that his preaching was more deeply spiritual in tone; Christ appeared to be his theme as never before. "Rejoice evermore!" seemed the keynote of his thought.

One night, toward the last of September, one of the children was taken ill, and Judson arose to help Emily. The exposure to the chill damp air brought on a severe cold, followed by a fever that he could not throw off. In November this grew serious, and weakened him so much that he could not hold his pen; so that he had to lay aside his work on the dictionary. The disease settled on his lungs, and the congestive fever set in from which he never recovered.

In January he appeared somewhat better, and he and Emily took a short steamer trip down the coast to Mergui. That helped a little, but he soon failed again. Then they went to Amherst, and spent a month by the seaside, where on one hand he could see the hopea tree, and on the other could look off across the waters of the bay.

But he grew weaker daily and there was no doctor at hand. He could scarcely walk, and often took hold of the furniture for support when he thought no one was looking—for he was unwilling to admit that he was not so well. Often he suffered excruciating pain and could not restrain the groans. Then sometimes he would be quite comfortable, and would talk freely. At those times his mind went back to days and experiences long past, and he told Emily stories of his boyhood at home, his college life at Brown, his imprisonment experiences in France, and his early missionary years in Burma. Then he would turn to prayer, and to his favorite subject, the love of Christ. But talking, even a brief prayer, exhausted him utterly, and often he could speak only a few sentences at a time.

His buoyant and hopeful spirits made him speak lightly of his disease. But more and more he gave himself to devotion and prayer. One day he was lying on his couch in quiet meditation, when suddenly he exclaimed with animation,

"I have gained the victory at last! I love every one of Christ's redeemed, as I believe he would have me love them. I would gladly prefer the meanest of his creatures who bears his name, before myself." And he quoted with emphasis, "In honor preferring one another."

On his return from Amherst they moved from their old house (long condemned as unhealthful) to a newer one, and the change brought a considerable improvement, so that their hopes revived. But the gain was only temporary. Soon it became clear to the doctors and to all his friends that his condition was desperate, and that only a sea voyage held any hope for his recovery. He protested, and it cost him a severe struggle before he agreed to go. Emily was about to become a mother, and he would have to leave her alone. The very thought of being absent from each other was almost too painful for him to bear. But when at last he yielded he began to look forward to the trip with some pleasure; for he loved the sea. And he thought he would recover. He gained strength for one more letter to Solomon Peck; it was his last letter, and was dated February 21, 1850.

"My dear brother:

"I cannot manage a pen; so please to excuse pencil. I have been prostrated with fever ever since the latter part of last November, and have suffered so much that I have frequently remarked that I was never ill in India before. Through the mercy of God, I think I am convalescent for the last ten days; but the doctor and all my friends are very urgent that I should take a sea voyage of a month or two, and be absent from this a long time. May God direct in the path of duty. My hand is failing; so I will beg to remain

"Yours affectionately,

"A. JUDSON."

Emily, watching anxiously by the bedside of the one she loved, put her thoughts into verse, as she often did:

WATCHING

"Sleep, love, sleep!
The dusty day is done.
Lo! from afar the freshening breezes sweep,
Wide over groves of balm,
Down from the towering palm,
In at the open casement run,
And round thy lowly bed,
Thy bed of pain,
Bathing thy patient head,
Like grateful showers of rain,
They come;
While the white curtains, waving to and fro,
Fan the sick air;
And pityingly the shadows come and go,
With gentle human care,
Compassionate and dumb.

"The dusty day is done,
The night begun;
While prayerful watch I keep,
Sleep, love, sleep!
Is there no magic touch
Of fingers thou dost love so much?
Fain would they scatter poppies o'er thee now;
Or, with its mute caress,

The tremulous lip some soft nepenthe press
Upon thy weary lid and aching brow;
While prayerful watch I keep,
Sleep, love, sleep!

"On the pagoda spire
The bells are swinging,
Their little golden circlet in a flutter
With tales the wooing winds have dared to utter,
Till all are ringing,
As if a choir
Of golden-nested birds in heaven were singing;
And with a lulling sound
The magic floats around,
And drops like balm into the drowsy ear;
Commingling with the hum
Of the Sepoy's distant drum,
And lazy beetle ever droning near.

. . . . .

"And still the curtains swing,
But noiselessly;
The bells a melancholy murmur ring,
As tears were in the sky;
More heavily the shadows fall,
Like the black foldings of a pall,
Where juts the rough beam from the wall;
The candles flare
With fresher gusts of air;
The beetle's drone
Turns to a dirge-like, solitary moan;
Night deepens, and I sit, in cheerless doubt, alone." [1]

While they waited for a ship he and Emily had many a conversation, and always their thoughts turned toward heaven. "Lying here on my bed, when I could not talk, I have had such views of the loving condescension of Christ and the glories of heaven, as I believe are seldom granted to mortal man." He spoke of his desire to complete the dictionary—the "lust for finishing" strong even yet—and felt that a few years

---

[1] The whole poem is in A. C. Kendrick, *The Life and Letters of Mrs. Emily C. Judson*, p. 330.

would not be missed from the eternity of bliss, if he could but finish his task.

"I am not tired of my work," he said, "neither am I tired of the world; yet when Christ calls me home I shall go with the gladness of a boy bounding away from his school." And he added, "Death will never take me by surprise—I feel so strong in Christ. He has not led me so tenderly thus far, to forsake me at the very gate of heaven. I leave myself entirely in the hands of God, to be disposed of according to His holy will." One day his cup of joy was filled to overflowing when Emily read to him a paragraph from a home paper, telling that an account of his efforts at Ava, printed in Germany, had been read by some Turkish Jews and had won them to his Saviour. When he heard it he exclaimed, referring to his early plans for a Jewish mission:

"I never was deeply interested in any object, I never prayed sincerely and earnestly for anything, but it came; at some time —no matter at how distant a day—somehow, in some shape, probably the last I should have devised—it came. And yet I have always had so little faith!"

The shadows were darkening, but the clouds were bordered with the sunset glory.

So when on the third of April the French bark *Aristide Marie* was ready to sail he too was ready. Thomas Ranney was to accompany him, with a Bengali servant. The bark was bound for the Isle of France, that island of memories. In order that Judson might get to sea as quickly as possible the civil commissioner kindly agreed that the bark should be towed out of the river by a government steamer which was sailing that day with troops. But the military commander, evidently jealous of authority, refused to permit it, and it took five days instead of one to reach Amherst and the open sea.

The delay was serious for Judson, but it gave Emily and other missionaries opportunity to visit him on board several times. Emily longed to go with him, and would gladly have taken the chance on her own life if he would have permitted it; but it was impossible. On Monday, the eighth, the bark dropped the pilot and stood out across the Bay of Bengal. And Emily was left alone with her anxieties and her fears. It

would be six weeks before the bark could reach port, and then
another long six weeks before she could have a letter. It
might be four months, or six months. She could only wait.

Sorrow and anxiety filled her mind as she thought of her
husband, but she had glad anticipation for the babe she was
so eager to greet. Two weeks after Judson sailed her child
was born, and she named him Charles for her father. But
alas! the little one died just as he began to live, and her gladness was turned into mourning. She found solace in pouring
out her grief in the verses entitled "Angel Charlie." To
Adoniram she wrote again and again, hoping against hope
that he was still alive to receive her letters. Then her thought
turned longingly toward her old home in Hamilton, and to
the comfort of her mother's arms. Once again in her desola-
tion and sorrow she took refuge in verse. Perhaps in all literature there is nothing more full of pathos.

SWEET MOTHER

"The wild southwest monsoon has risen,
  On broad, gray wings of gloom,
While here from out my dreary prison
I look as from a tomb—alas!
  My heart another tomb.

"Upon the low thatched roof the rain
  With ceaseless patter falls;
My choicest treasures bear its stain,
Mould gathers on the walls—would Heaven
  'Twere only on the walls!

"Sweet Mother, I am here alone,
  In sorrow and in pain;
The sunshine from my heart has flown,
It feels the driving rain—ah me!
  The chill, and mould, and rain.

.   .   .   .   .

"O but to feel thy fond arms twine
  Around me once again!
It almost seems those lips of thine

Might kiss away the pain—might soothe
This dull, cold, heavy pain.

"With weary feet and broken wing,
    With bleeding heart and sore,
Thy dove looks backward sorrowing,
But seeks the ark no more—thy breast
    Seeks never, never more.

"All fearfully, all tearfully,
    Alone and sorrowing,
My dim eyes lifted to the sky—
Fast to thy cross I cling—O Christ!
    To thy dear cross I cling." [2]

At last, in August, the news came. Judson had failed
rapidly. Ranney and Panapah, the Bengali servant, did all
they could to relieve his intense sufferings; and the captain,
the only other person aboard who could use English, was un-
wearying in his kindness. Finally on Friday it was evident
that Judson was dying. The officers left their meal untouched
as they gathered in silence at the door, seeming to sense the
greatness of the one who was passing from them. The pain of
previous days had gone. "Take care of mistress," he whispered
to Panapah. Once or twice he pressed the hand of Ranney.
Then the shadows lifted. The peace of eventide descended.
And at quarter after four, in the afternoon of April 12, 1850,
Judson passed into the glorious presence.

At eight o'clock that night, as they reached latitude thirteen degrees north and longitude ninety-three degrees east,
just northwest of the Andaman Islands, the bark hove to, the
crew assembled, and with only the captain's voice to break the
silence the body of the great pioneer was committed to the
deep. The golden evening had brightened into the light
eternal.

He was leader in the movement that made the dream of
American foreign missions a reality; he was chief in the little

---

[2] The whole poem is given by A. C. Kendrick, *The Life and Letters of Mrs.
Emily C. Judson*, p. 340.

group of stalwarts who first set forth as missionaries from
America to the East; he inspired a great fellowship of churches
to organize for the spreading of the gospel to earth's remotest
bound; he enriched an ancient literature with the best of all
books, the Bible; he gave to the number of earth's great souls
three queenly women who bore his name; he founded a
Church in an eastern land that will endure while time shall
last; he established principles of Christian service that still
mark successful missions everywhere; he challenges and in-
spires stronghearts of every land, and summons all who follow
Christ to live nobly and to do valiantly—to please God, as he
with unfaltering purpose strove to please him.

On a tablet of enduring bronze, before his Malden birthplace, are inscribed these words—fitting tribute in a fitting
place:

REV. ADONIRAM JUDSON

America's First Foreign Missionary
1788   1850

Malden, His Birthplace
The Ocean, His Sepulchre
Converted Burmans and the
Burman Bible, His Monument

His Record Is On High

BIBLIOGRAPHY

BABCOCK, RUFUS. *God Glorified in His Servants;* a discourse commemorative of the life and labors of the Rev. Adoniram Judson. New York, 1851.

Baptist Missionary Magazine. Boston, 1803-1851. (Entitled The Massachusetts Baptist Missionary Magazine 1803-1817, The American Baptist Magazine 1817-1836)

BARDWELL, HORATIO. *Memoir of Rev. Gordon Hall, A.M.* Andover, 1834.

BINNEY, MRS. J. G. *Twenty-six Years in Burmah.* Philadelphia, 1880.

Brief Narrative of the Baptist Mission in India. London, 1810.

BRONSON, WALTER C. *The History of Brown University.* Providence, 1914.

CAREY, S. PEARCE. *William Carey.* Philadelphia, n.d.

CARPENTER, C. H. *Self-Support, Illustrated in the History of the Bassein Karen Mission from 1840 to 1880.* Boston, 1883.

CLEMENT. *Memoir of Adoniram Judson:* being a sketch of his life and missionary labors. New York & Auburn, 1857.

CONANT, MRS. H. C. *The Earnest Man, or The Character and Labors of Adoniram Judson.* Boston, 1856.

COX, F. A. *History of the English Baptist Missionary Society from A.D. 1792 to A.D. 1842.* Boston, 1844.

CUSHMAN, ROBERT W. *Grace and Apostleship: Illustrated in the Life of Judson.* A discourse delivered before the Maryland Union Association, Nov. 5, 1851. Philadelphia, 1854.

CRAWFURD, JOHN. *Journal of an Embassy from the Governor-General of India to of the Court of Ava in the year 1827.* London, 1829.

DOWLING, JOHN, ed. *The Judson Offering.* New York, 1846.

EDDY, DANIEL C. *A Sketch of Adoniram Judson, D.D., the Burman Apostle.* Lowell, 1851.

EDDY, DANIEL C. *The Three Mrs. Judsons and Other Daughters of the Cross.* Boston, 1860.

ELSBREE, OLIVER W. *The Rise of the Missionary Spirit in America 1790-1815.* Williamsport, Pa., 1928.

FLETCHER, E. H. *Burmah's Great Missionary: Records of the Life, Character and Achievements of Adoniram Judson.* New York, 1854.

GAMMELL, WILLIAM. *History of American Baptist Missions.* Boston, 1850.

GOUGER, HENRY. *A Personal Narrative of Two Years' Imprisonment in Burmah.* London, 1862.

GRANT, COLESWORTHY. *Rough Pencillings of a Rough Trip to Rangoon in 1846.* Calcutta, 1853.

HAGUE, WILLIAM. *Life and Character of Adoniram Judson, late missionary to Burmah:* a commemorative discourse. Boston, 1851.

HEWITT, JOHN H. *Williams College and Foreign Missions.* Boston, 1914.

HILL, JAMES L. *The Immortal Seven.* Philadelphia, 1913.

History of American Missions to the Heathen. Worcester, 1840.

HOWARD, R. L. *Baptists in Burma.* Philadelphia, 1931.

HUBBARD, ETHEL D. *Ann of Ava.* Philadelphia & New York, 1913.

HULL, J. M. *Judson the Pioneer.* Philadelphia, 1913.

JUDSON, ADONIRAM, JR. *Letter to Rev. Adoniram Judson, Senior, relative to the "Formal and Solemn Reprimand."* Boston, 1820.

JUDSON, ADONIRAM, JR. *Sermon preached in the Lal Bazar Chapel, Calcutta, on Lord's Day, Sept. 27, 1812.* Boston, 1817.

JUDSON, ANN H. *A Particular Relation of the American Baptist Mission to the Burman Empire.* Washington, 1823.

JUDSON, EDWARD. *The Life of Adoniram Judson.* Philadelphia, 1883.

JUDSON, EMILY C. *Memoir of Sarah B. Judson.* New York, 1852.

JUDSON, EMILY C. *The Kathayan Slave and Other Papers connected with Missionary Life.* Boston, 1853.

KENDRICK, A. C. *The Life and Letters of Mrs. Emily C. Judson.* New York, 1860.

KNOWLES, JAMES D. *Memoir of Mrs. Ann H. Judson.* Boston, 1831.

MALCOM, HOWARD. *Travels in Southeastern Asia. Vol. 1. Burma.* Boston, 1839.

MASON, CAROLINE ATWATER. *Jesus Christ's Men—A Progress 1813-1913.* Philadelphia, 1914.

Memoirs of American Missionaries formerly connected with the Society of Inquiry respecting Missions, in the Andover Theological Seminary. Boston, 1833.

Memorial of the Semi-Centennial Celebration of the Founding of the Theological Seminary at Andover. Andover, 1859.

Memorial of Rev. Samuel Nott. Printed for private circulation. n.d.

Memorial Volume of the First Fifty Years of the American Board of Commissioners for Foreign Missions. Boston, 1861.

MERRIAM, E. F. *A History of American Baptist Missions.* Philadelphia, 1900.

MURDOCK, J. N. *Our Missionary Pioneer.* An address at the 74th anniversary of the American Baptist Missionary Union, May 21, 1888, Washington, D. C. Boston, 1888.

NOTT, MRS. ROXANA PECK. *Autobiography.* Unpublished ms.

NOTT, SAMUEL, JUN. *A Letter addressed to Rev. Enoch Pond of Ware (Mass.) on the Insinuations and Charges contained in his Reply to Mr. Judson's Sermon on Baptism.* Boston, 1819.

PHINNEY, F. D., compiler. *The Judson Centennial Celebration in Burma.* Rangoon, 1914.

PIERSON, H. W., ed. *American Missionary Memorials,* including biographical and historical sketches. New York, 1853.

POLLARD, E. B., and Stevens, D. G. *Luther Rice, Pioneer in Missions and Education.* Philadelphia, 1928.

POND, ENOCH. *A Treatise on the Mode and Subjects of Christian Baptism.* In two parts. Designed as a Reply to the Statements and Reasonings of the Rev. Adoniram Judson, Jun., A.M., as exhibited in his "Sermon preached in the

Lal Bazar Chapel, Calcutta, on Lord's Day, Sept. 27, 1812," and recently republished in this country. Worcester, 1819.

POND, JEAN SARAH. *Bradford—A New England Academy.* Bradford, 1930.

Records of Philermenian Society. Unpublished ms. in Brown University Library.

Records of Society of The Brethren. Unpublished ms. in Andover-Harvard Theological Library.

RICHARDS, T. C. *The Missionary Pathfinder, Samuel J. Mills.* Boston, 1906.

SPRING, GARDINER. *Memoirs of Rev. Samuel J. Mills.* New York, 1820.

STRONG, WILLIAM E. *The Story of the American Board.* Boston, 1910.

TAYLOR, JAMES B. *Memoir of Rev. Luther Rice, one of the first American missionaries to the East.* Baltimore, 1840.

VAIL, ALBERT L. *Baptists Mobilized for Missions.* Philadelphia, 1911

VAIL, ALBERT L. *The Morning Hour of American Baptist Missions.* Philadelphia, 1907.

WAYLAND, FRANCIS. *Memoir of Rev. Dr. Judson.* Two vols. Boston, 1853.

WILLSON, ARABELLA H. *The Lives of Mrs. Ann H. Judson, Mrs. Sarah B. Judson, and Mrs. Emily C. Judson, Missionaries to Burmah.* New York, 1858.

WOODS, LEONARD. *A Sermon delivered at the Tabernacle in Salem, Feb. 6, 1812, on the occasion of the ordination of the Rev. Messrs. Newell, Judson, et al.* Boston, 1812.

WOODS, LEONARD. *Memoirs of Harriet Newell.* Boston, 1814.

WORCESTER, S. M. *Life and Labors of Rev. Samuel Worcester, D.D.* Two vols. Boston, 1852.

WYETH, WALTER N. *Ann H. Judson: A Memorial.* Cincinnati, 1888.

WYETH, WALTER N. *Emily C. Judson: A Memorial.* Philadelphia, 1890.

WYETH, WALTER N. *Sarah B. Judson: A Memorial.* Philadelphia, 1889.

WYETH, WALTER N. *The Wades: A Memorial.* Philadelphia, 1891.

INDEX